London Calling

London Calling

The Middle Classes and the Re-making of Inner London

Tim Butler with Garry Robson

Oxford • New York

First published in 2003 by
Berg
Editorial offices:
1st Floor, Angel Court, 81 St Clements Street, Oxford, OX4 1AW, UK
838 Broadway, Third Floor, New York, NY 10003-4812, USA

Berg is an imprint of Oxford International Publishers Ltd.

Library of Congress Cataloging-in-Publication Data
Butler, Tim, 1949-
    London calling : the middle classes and the re-making of inner London
/ Tim Butler ; with Garry Robson.
        p. cm.
    ISBN 1-85973-623-8 (Cloth) – ISBN 1-85973-628-9 (Paper)
    1. Middle class–England–London–History–20th century. 2. Gentrification–
England–London–History–20th century.   I. Robson, Garry. II. Title.

HT690.G7B88 2003
305.5′5′9421–dc21

                                                                    2003006205

British Library Cataloguing-in-Publication Data
A catalogue record for this book is available from the British Library.

ISBN 1 85973 623 8 (Cloth)
        1 85973 628 9 (Paper)

Typeset by JS Typesetting Ltd, Wellingborough, Northants.
Printed in the United Kingdom by Biddles Ltd, Guildford and King's Lynn.

www.bergpublishers.com

For Philippa

Contents

Figures and Tables

Figures

Tables

Acknowledgements

This book was the outcome of a three-year research project funded by the Economic and Social Research Council (grant number L13025101). There is no doubt that the research would not have taken place without this financial support and that of the Cities: Competitiveness and Cohesion Programme (CCCP!) and its directors, firstly Duncan MacLennan, then Ade Kearns both from the Department of Urban Studies at the University of Glasgow and, for the last half of the programme, Michael Parkinson from the European Institute of Urban Affairs at the Liverpool John Moore's University. I would particularly like to acknowledge Michael's support in encouraging us to write this book, which was crucial. Working in what is now euphemistically known as a 'modern' university (what used to be called a polytechnic), I have been particularly appreciative of the ways in which the programme through its regular meetings has provided an intellectual culture and climate that is sometimes hard to replicate on the Becontree Estate in Dagenham. I would like, in particular, to thank Ian Gordon for his continued support for the research. This book has been informed by the work that he, Nick Buck, Peter Hall, Michael Harloe and Mark Kleinmann have undertaken on London as a whole as part of the Cities Programme. The resulting book *Working Capital: Life and Labour in Contemporary London* was published just as I finished the final draft.

Most of the fieldwork for this research was undertaken by Dr Garry Robson who was also responsible for drafting many of the papers that inform much of the book. Unfortunately, as is still the way with contract research in higher education, he had to seek employment elsewhere when the grant came to an end. Fortunately for Goldsmiths College he was able to find a position at the Centre for Urban and Community Research. Thanks are also due to Marta Boczar who not only arranged the interviews but also coded and entered the data. Whilst Garry's contribution to the data and idea in the book is immense, he should not be held responsible for any of the errors and omissions because he had left London for Poland by the time it came to draft the manuscript. However, whatever the niceties of authorship, the book is very much a joint effort.

Samantha Jackson of Berg is to be thanked not least for coming up with the title, which should ring several bells with the generation who are the subjects of this study. Thanks also to Kathryn Earle for her tolerance towards yet another academic who was unable to deliver his manuscript on time. Unison also use this title for their London newsletter and I hope that some of the data in this study can be used

Acknowledgements

to support the claim for a realistic allowance to compensate key workers who happen to live and work in London.

Perhaps my single greatest intellectual debt is to Mike Savage whose work has heavily influenced my approach, as will be apparent even to those who only read a portion of this book. Mike, in my view, is leading a renaissance in British sociology, which is in its best traditions of theoretically informed empirical work on subjects that matter.

My second acknowledgement is to my colleagues in what used to be the Department of Anthropology and Sociology at the University of East London and particularly to its head Barbara Harrison who has been a good friend to scholarship and research in difficult times. The fact that we were able to achieve one of only three rankings of 'national quality' research amongst 'modern universities' in the 2001 Research Assessment Exercise owes much to Michael Rustin with whom it has been my pleasure to work for the last 30 years. Whatever the pressures, Mike always has time to respond at length to research grant proposals, drafts of papers, published articles and always with to the point comments. Unlike may other senior colleagues, Mike prioritizes the important over the merely urgent. I would also like to thank the departmental research committee for awarding me a semester's sabbatical in 2002 to complete the manuscript. Finally, and far from least, I wish to acknowledge the contribution of Diane Ball and Sylvie Hudson who ensure that the department actually works and does so with much good humour.

The second group whose help I wish to acknowledge is that of my respondents: nearly 500 of the most intelligent and generous people a sociologist could hope to meet. I know some of you may not agree with all of my findings and conclusions but I thank you not only for providing data but for drawing on your own stocks of intellectual capital and reflexivity to add much of the analysis in the later chapters of this book.

Finally, thanks to my partner Valerie Fraser who not only put up with long absences when I started the second job of the day doing fieldwork but also took an interest in a subject a long way from her own of Latin American architecture and art history. I would like to think that some of my banging on about the gentrification of London helped stimulate our daughter Cristina's interest in geography as one of the more interesting GCSE subjects.

Tim Butler
Harwich

Introduction

The research funded by the ESRC that informs this book involved approximately 450 face-to-face interviews, which were undertaken between 1998 and 2000 in five inner London boroughs and three areas of the Docklands urban development zone. The aim of the research project was to look at the consequences of inner London's transformation into an increasingly middle-class city, even if the majority of residents is not middle class.

We were interested to see whether or not this was leading to an increase in social displacement, as the literature would imply, or whether it was leading to an upgrading of social facilities. Previous research that one of us had carried out (Butler 1997) indicated that perhaps there was a new kind of gentrifier, rather different from the 'ordinary' middle class, who might – as it were – look out for their less fortunate neighbours. Even if they didn't share their sun-dried tomatoes with them, we hypothesized that it would perhaps be in their interests to ensure that schooling improved for all. In this way, economic competitiveness and social cohesion might be becoming a virtuous pairing rather than a vicious cycle as has too often been the case. In particular, we wanted to see to what extent the denizens of inner London's gentrification interacted with the majority population in their neighbourhoods. It is a striking factor of inner London's contemporary gentrification that nowhere, even in its leafiest areas, do the middle classes constitute more than a quarter of the population and are unlikely so to do unless and until huge amounts of social housing are recycled into private ownership.

We also wanted to see to what extent there was what might be termed a 'metropolitan habitus', which might demonstrate that inner London's middle class stood significantly apart from its sisters and brothers in the 'provincial' cities, suburbs, country towns and elsewhere in terms of its 'embodied disposition'. Finally, we also considered in what ways this concept of a metropolitan habitus might be structured to take account of the growing sense of nuance and diversity amongst the metropolitan middle classes.

In the book, hopefully, we avoid a tedious form of habitus mapping but, rather, demonstrate that there are important continuities and discontinuities across the metropolis that account for the highly variegated forms of gentrification we find in London. By including Docklands in our study, we point to a major rupture in how we understand the 'field' of gentrification; the inhabitants of Docklands we show are *in* the *City* but almost never *of* the city. Elsewhere, we find, despite the important difference that space makes to the distribution and disposition of inner London's middle classes, that they share a common relationship to each other that is largely exclusive of everyone else. In a city that is massively multi-ethnic, its middle classes, despite long rhetorical flushes in favour of multi-culturalism and diversity, huddle together into essentially white settlements in the inner city. Their children, for the most part, like their parents, have friends just like themselves. Not a great surprise but perhaps a worrying signal to the future.

The book has nine chapters, many of which are based around data from the lengthy face-to-face interviews we undertook with our respondents between 1998 and 2000. We begin the book by setting out our theoretical and conceptual store and then weave into this the lives of our respondents.

Chapter 1 maps out our main approach to contemporary gentrification processes in London. This draws on recent research on both globalization and on global cities. We look here at the attempts in the UK and the US to make cities more liveable and draw some comparisons with Europe. We also discuss the changing nature of the middle class and focus on the diversity of contemporary intermediate social strata. This is related both to globalization and the new functions of global cities. We argue that a range of groups come together in the city and attempt to establish communities amenable to middle-class life in inner urban neighbourhoods. We propose that Bourdieu's analytical framework of the different relations between economic, social and cultural capital enables us to understand the variety of strategies pursued by the urban middle classes in their attempt to establish inner city areas as sites of community and cultural reproduction.

In the second chapter we develop our core argument, which is that gentrification is a coping strategy for the urban middle classes. We examine and develop Richard Sennett's arguments in *The Corrosion of Character* that the new economy and associated working patterns amongst the middle classes are leading to new social arrangements, particularly in urban settings. These settings are in areas which have either been largely hollowed-out by urban decay (leaving them with little sense of neighbourhood identity and low levels of social capital) or have already been re-imaged as desirable seats of urban living. In London, Brixton and Hackney are examples of the former whilst Wandsworth and Islington illustrate the latter. In both cases, building neighbourhoods or buying-into existing urban dreams provide ways of coping with the stress of globalization by engaging with it rather than escaping it. In all these areas the building of middle-class neighbourhoods occurs in areas where the hegemonists are in a numerical minority.

In Chapter 3 we discuss the range of middle-class experience and develop our argument that gentrification is also a process of middle-class formation and filtration. Areas acquire meanings, resonances and identities that are both attractive to particular middle-class individuals and also deeply socializing of them. We identify – following Bourdieu – four key fields: housing, occupation, education and consumption. We draw on Savage's (1992) asset model but develop it further by locating these processes in streams of culture that are heavily influenced by the spatial factors of different locales. In so doing, we also attempt to avoid falling into what Savage (Longhurst and Savage 1996) terms the trap of 'habitus mapping'. We are thus concerned here to develop some map of the middle classes in inner London and we substantiate the conceptual claims with reference to census and observational data. We reject Savage's tripartite division of the middle classes as insufficiently nuanced to explain the process of creating and consuming local space in London. We propose the notion of a metropolitan habitus

In Chapters 4, 5 and 6 we introduce our fieldwork areas and demonstrate the ways in which the different middle-class groups are operating strategically across these fields. We identify the habitus of different areas and their deviations and dissidences. We examine the habitus of different social class backgrounds and employment fields. This is then related to the housing, education and consumption possibilities in each of the areas as ways of realizing the 'potential' forms of habitus that are waiting to be made collective. This is realized through living in the area – strategies and constraints have a crucial role to play here. In these chapters we draw heavily on our research data and we show that, with the exception of Docklands, which is relatively and, often absolutely, deprived in both cultural and social capital, all the remaining areas have positive capital assets across these three categories. What is significant however is the means by which these are differentially deployed. We argue that in some areas social capital is mobilized initially around relationships forged at the local primary school gate, which then sustains networks that outlast the children's subsequent school careers. Elsewhere we characterize gentrification as having added another layer to an uneasy 'tectonic' structure in which the middle classes are, to some extent, in flight from the obligations of social capital. A third contrast is where economic capital is deployed as the primary source of neighbourhood and identity building. Another source of variation is that of relations with the local state. The Docklands study areas, although interestingly different from each other, represent not just a flight from obligation but also a low level of cultural capital and involvement in the city.

The individual household is the key variable in this study; Chapter 6 discusses the 'lived experience' of different household arrangements, which are again linked to the different areas. There are a variety of household structures both within and between areas. In this and the following chapter, we show how the middle classes create carefully crafted strategies to deal with the problems of living and working in the city. The organization of the home relates both to the external world of work and also the other involvements in the city, particularly to culture, leisure and consumption. We examine the importance of relations with friends and the social networks respondents belong to. We show that much of the social capital on which respondents are able to draw goes back a long way and is embedded in friendships and contacts often made at university. There is thus a high coincidence here between sources of social and cultural capital. In this respect, those living in Docklands could be characterized as relatively impoverished, except in the economic capital/employment field – implying almost the wilful neglect of social capital.

Chapter 7 shows how cultural reproduction is a key factor in class formation – hence the focus on children for many households. As we have already indicated, much of the alienation that our respondents have experienced in relation to globalization manifests itself in terms of a feeling of lack of security in which to nurture their children. Many respondents appear to contrast this with their remembered childhood. It is with respect to this 'crunch issue' of education that much of the talk about 'strategies' arises. It is here that the interaction between middle-class households, global formations and local social systems occur (and collide!). The pressure and anxiety that typify London's middle class emerge most clearly in the context of educational choice and the question of whether these can survive London's conditions. Those households with children devote considerable amounts of emotional, physical and psychic energy to ensuring that their children are able to function autonomously in a world in which global culture is seen to determine their every action. The threat is perceived at every level: the failings of the state educational system, the interaction with non middle-class children at school, on the journey to school, and in the increasingly brand-dominated youth monoculture (at least in the eyes of parents unable to read the nuances of cultural differentiation amongst contemporary youth). At the same time, there is a realization that this is the world in which his or her children will have to operate and for which they need appropriate skills. Elaborate strategies are constructed for each child to negotiate his or her way around and through this minefield. One of the significant variations between the various areas is the extent to which they have established 'circuits of schooling' and we explore how this relates to other strategies and also, ultimately, to decisions about whether to stay in London or to leave.

In chapter eight, we return to our respondents' own words to re-examine the areas through their eyes. They are, on the whole, a highly reflexive bunch of people who are very aware of the consequences for, and effects of their interactions on, the areas in which they live. This reflects both in terms of ambivalence about much of their lives but also about the effects not just that they have on the 'other' but also on themselves, particularly through their children. Our conclusions, which we begin to develop in this chapter, are that twenty-first century gentrification seems to mark a break with that established in the last quarter of the previous century. In some respects, it has become a defensive phenomenon – of imposing values and meanings on differentiated neighbourhoods in order to try to recreate a structure for themselves and their children in the face of globalization. At the same time, the neighbourhoods represent their inhabitants' successful engagement with the new global economy. This is manifested in different ways but particularly in the consumption infrastructure of some of the neighbourhoods. We focus on cultural reproduction because that is perhaps the defining characteristic of the middle class. Our study relates how they do it in the city and the ways in which it is nuanced – particularly in the face of such external constraints as globalization and economic uncertainty. They have good reasons to be anxious not just because of economic factors but also cultural ones that impact on young people in ways that run counter to the aspirations of their parents.

-1-

Marking Out the Middle Classes in London

London has been a global centre for at least the last 300 years. As 'globalization' enters everyday language, increasing claims are made for its effects and consequences – the discussion and the debate is beyond the scope of this book. However, and this explains the book's title, London has become a 'honey pot', pulling in people at both ends of the social structure nationally and also internationally. Approximately, 20 per cent of London's recorded population was born outside the United Kingdom and probably many more are not recorded by census or other data sources. Some of these are investment bankers, IT specialists and representatives of the world's media whereas others are refugees and others fleeing the world's horror spots.

London, as it has for centuries, attracts those who no longer fit into their home towns and villages across the nation and, increasingly, the globe: some may, like Dick Whittington, become Lord Mayor; others end up homeless. Many others gravitate to London having completed their university studies in towns and cities that do not offer graduate employment in the service industries at the level to which they aspire. For some, London is an 'escalator' region in which they acquire skills and experience and then seek promotion elsewhere (nationally or internationally); for others however such is the concentration of economic, social and increasingly cultural power in the city (or City) that not only does it remain somewhere to which they devote all their working lives but increasingly it has also become a place in which to live and play. It is not just London's labour market which is calling but also its cultural ambience which makes living elsewhere – in the 'home counties'[1] or the 'provinces' – almost unthinkable.

There is, of course, another group at the opposite end of the social and economic hierarchy for whom the pull of London is equally powerful, as we have indicated. This group is beyond the scope of this book but is probably an inseparable downside to London's gentrification by the subjects of our study (see Buck, Gordon et al. 2002 for a more rounded picture of the social structure of London). As London, and in particular inner London, has become a middle-class city its changed work and leisure habits and their impacts on middle-class life have created whole new occupational categories. These jobs have, for the most part, been undertaken by new groups of largely insecure and ill-paid workers – many of whom are also new Londoners whether from the rest of the United Kingdom or the world beyond.

It seems, at least to many of the middle class living in inner London, that there is London and elsewhere: they are the cosmopolitans living in a metropolitan environment. 'Locals', to whom they largely counterpose themselves, live elsewhere: either hidden away in social housing, or indeed almost anywhere else in the United Kingdom. In this sense, London's gentrification is a creation of the way in which globalization has spread its tentacles into economic and cultural life of the major cities of the world – London, New York, Paris, Sydney, Los Angeles and San Francisco (Sassen 1991). Ironically, it might be argued that the group with which the middle-class cosmopolitans perhaps share most is the 'other' economic migrants to the city many of whom work assiduously to 'service' them at work, home and play in the 24-hour city.

London has always had a tendency towards social and economic polarization: a 'container' for the richest and the poorest in our society. This was what made for sociology at the cusp of the last century – the discovery that a third of the population of the richest city on earth was living in abject poverty and an even higher proportion was unfit for military service. We have similar figures today: inner London is the richest region in the European Union yet just to the east of the City lie the three most deprived boroughs in the country – Newham, Hackney and Tower Hamlets where approximately half the males of working age are classified as 'economically inactive'. One aspect of this polarization is that you probably need a household income of something like £70,000 (US$100,000) a year to contemplate entering the inner London housing market at the very lowest level. Whilst many people with incomes below this level find ways of resolving this, the fact is that inner London is becoming increasingly middle class – and (on the above calculation) is now moving beyond many of their means. Approximately 20 per cent of the population of inner London at the last census are from what are normally understood as the 'middle classes'. The visibility and influence of this group far outstrip its physical presence – even in the most gentrified parts of inner London boroughs, such as Islington, the middle class is rarely in a majority. This has not prevented the middle classes defining such areas in their own image. One widely perceived consequence of this has been the 'hollowing out' of the inner city; the decline of public services has led not only to public, but also private squalor.

This gentrification of inner London has become more differentiated and diversified over the last decade. This is partly a consequence of the growth in the urban middle class and its diversification and partly because of the renaissance in global cities (Wolf and Friedmann 1982). These are push-pull factors: the attractiveness of the city to increasing numbers of middle-class people and the competition for such people by 'leading edge' cities. The consequence has been growing fragmentation as people have attempted to match their economic capabilities to the housing market whilst, at the same time, trying to create imagined or real 'communities of interest' alongside like-minded individuals. It is this latter strategy that we believe now characterizes the middle classes' attempts to come to terms with the constraints, as well as the opportunities, posed by the globalization of the metropolis.

Geographers have tracked the gentrification of London (and other cities – notably New York) since the early 1970s. As areas of inner north London (particularly in Camden and Islington) became successively gentrified, they moved beyond the reach of the younger and poorer middle class (increasingly public sector professionals). Gentrification in the 1980s moved steadily north east into Hackney, Tower Hamlets and Walthamstow. In the last decade it has also begun to affect large areas of south London outside the affluent south-western corner. The patterns of gentrification have however not been completely dominated by the economics of the housing market. Research (for example, Butler 1997) has shown that a complex of values, ideology, social background and occupational choice influence residential location in inner London, as elsewhere (Ley 1996).

In explaining this, the first distinction that needs to be drawn is between an 'urban-seeking' and an 'urban-fleeing' middle class working in London; this is between those wishing to 'live the city' and those who choose to commute in from the 'home counties' and beyond. This basic distinction goes back to the 'rediscovery' of the city by 'pioneers' who started to gentrify parts of inner London in the early 1960s (Glass 1964). More recently however, important distinctions can be drawn amongst those living in the city, for whom different areas take on different meanings and associations that attract potential residents and then act on those who are settled there. We term this process the formation of a 'metropolitan habitus' and we explore this process of differential gentrification in greater detail than has been done previously.

After faltering in the late 1980s and early 1990s, the renewed pace of gentrification in the mid 1990s onwards has been referred to as 'post recession gentrification' by Lees (2000) with reference to both London and New York. She points to the ways in which those who have risen with the financial services economy have colonized whole new areas of the inner city (examples might be Clerkenwell in London and Brooklyn Heights in New York). She identifies four questions that need to be investigated in contemporary accounts of gentrification. These are 'super-gentrification' by a group she terms the 'financifiers' – the super rich thrown up by the financial industries of London and New York. They are now 're-gentrifiying' (a term we prefer) areas that were originally gentrified twenty-five years previously (the prime example of this in London is Islington). Her second concern is with Third World immigration, the third is with 'race' and finally there is the issue of what she terms liveability (Lees 2000: 402). These are crucial issues but we suggest that they are all functions of contemporary globalization, which has broader consequences both for cities and city living (Amin and Thrift 2002). To some extent these are manifested by the recent Rogers Report (Urban Taskforce 1999) which could be seen as a 'gentrifiers charter'. It is also based in part on a misunderstanding of the nature of the contemporary city – for instance, the report almost entirely ignores the issues of ethnicity and 'race' which are an increasingly vital component of cosmopolitan urban space (Amin et al. 2000).

In our view, we are not simply witnessing an 'onward and upward' phenomenon of renewed gentrification. We suggest that the globalization that is driving the London economy is having a dramatic and potentially malign influence on many of those who might be generally seen as its beneficiaries. Many of these people, the international service class, operate in a world that is without boundaries, where traditional rulebooks have been torn up, where space and time have become compressed and distorted. Even if this group is in a minority, it influences the lives of many more whose lives remain more bounded by constraints of time and space. At the same time as they are 'transrupting' traditional boundaries at work, they are often desperate to lay down some parameters in their personal lives. We borrow here from Richard Sennett's book *The Corrosion of Character* (1999), in which he considers the human consequences of the move to flexibility, downsizing and re-engineering not in relation to its 'normal suspects' (those dispossessed by these changes) but those whose almost missionary zeal is driving them. Sennett suggests that many of the most devoted functionaries of the new economy develop some uneasiness about the consequent loss of structure and stability in their personal lives – especially in families where there are children and more than one bread-winner. Often both partners are working in stressful and demanding jobs where long hours and travel are part of the culture. Lack of security distinguishes this new economy from the old one in which they grew up, and for many of them it is this that creates the frisson which drives them on. However, according to Sennett, many have begun to recognize some strengths in the old household forms and employ-ment relations where their parents put up with the present in the expectation that their children would lead a very different future – as indeed they have. In particular they fear for the effects of this on their own children – one respondent described them becoming 'mall rats' – who of course take their parents' privileged status as a given.

Sennett describes the nature of the change that has taken place in work and family over one short generation. Today's successful managers were raised in the post-war decades in families in which fathers worked and mothers nurtured and where the life course was planned through until retirement and there was a high level of certainty about outcomes. Many of these children despised their parents for their lack of entrepreneurial spirit and their commitment to a particular place and occupation. However, despite their own often successful careers, many have begun to reflect not altogether favourably on the contexts in which their children are growing up compared with (no doubt nostalgic) recollections of the ones in which they were raised. This produces considerable anxieties about the downside of their success and mobility.

We believe that this is a widespread concern and affects many middle-class families – whether or not they are working directly within the interstices of the new global economy. On the one hand, they are escaping from the remembered boredom of their parents' ordered lives – dad at work, mum at home often in single-class suburbs. On the other, they are often becoming frantic about the lack of structure in their lives and particularly those of their children. We suggest that the current process of gentrification in London is an attempt to reconcile this present with a somewhat nostalgic view of the past. This is manifested by a desire to build a local community within the global city that maps onto their particular set of values, backgrounds, aspirations and resources. This we believe accounts for the variability of the gentrification process that we have found within inner London. This has focused on a range of gentrification situations – from areas that are now witnessing second (or possibly third) generation (re)gentrification (in Islington), to a stable and unfashionable middle-class enclave (in Lewisham, South London), to a more recent, brash and relatively unstable gentrification in Brixton (also in South London). We also look at the Docklands redevelopment zone, which presents a very different picture.

We argue that in some areas (such as Docklands and Brixton) gentrification represents at times a flight from social obligation and reflects many of the dominant norms of contemporary globalization and, in Brixton's case, a wish to embrace diversity and hedonism. On the other hand, elsewhere there appears to be a very strong desire to build a secure and supportive social environment by actively creating a neighbourhood in one's own image. We draw on Bourdieu's (1984) work on habitus and capital to explore the ways in which this process is enabled. We conceive of different groups deploying their stocks of capital – cultural, economic and social – in different configurations depending not only on their resources but also their aspirations for the kind of community they wish to live in. To some extent, these map on to occupational differences but these are by no means generative, and we argue that perceptions of space and place are crucial in explaining how capital is deployed in building neighbourhoods.

Of particular importance in our analysis here is the issue of social capital. This tends to be analysed almost exclusively in relation to subordinate social groups and is conceived of as the social glue that will enable them to connect with the vertical institutions of civil society and allow the socially excluded to rejoin the mainstream. We recall that social capital is only realized in social relationships and can either be latent or manifest. In some areas it is highly visible in the social networks that make the area so integrative to its inhabitants whereas elsewhere the white gentrifying population can be seen almost to be in flight from the cloying inclusiveness of social capital. In Wandsworth in South London, social capital is present but latent and masked by a culture in which 'eating out' is preferred over 'joining in'. In other words economic capital is favoured as the main means for discourse. In all of our areas, other than Docklands, there is a considerable stock of cultural capital, which is often deployed in relation to choices and strategies about education. We relate this to globalization by demonstrating the almost frenzied continual activity concerning children, similar in some ways to Max Weber's description of the anxiety created by the Protestant Ethic.

This book, as its subtitle claims, is a study of some of the ways in which the middle classes have been remaking inner London in recent decades. It is an expression not just of different socio-economic sub groups of the middle class but of their (differing) aspirations and values – income and occupation are by no means of defining importance. London has always been a magnet for the ambitions of the middle class, but not necessarily for where they want to live – hence the tradition of living in 'commuter sheds' and commuting (Silverstone 1996). This has been changing over recent decades and now inner London is increasingly a middle-class 'play zone', so much so that it is becoming increasingly differentiated. In this book we not only attempt to unravel the meanings of that differentiation but also what it tells us about the formation of this increasingly significant social group, which has, in many ways, become iconic of the transition to an information-based, globally spread but locally conscious network society (Castells 1996). This group is also struggling to maintain a traditional middle-class way of life in the face of an onslaught from a combination of work-related pressures and loss of class-based cultural hegemony. These are hostile to the maintenance of middle-class family values such as those described by Richard Sennett above and reflect a broad concern to maintain some balance in the household between the competing pressures of work, of consumption and of 'family life'. This issue of the 'work-life balance' was particularly acute for households with children.

The research project that provided the data for this book was funded by the ESRC Cities Programme. The focus of the programme was on three concepts: competitiveness, cohesion and governance – in a sense there was a strong policy imperative in the programme to close the relationship between these three concepts in a way that constituted a virtuous circle as opposed to the vicious cycle into which many feel cities have fallen. The loss of economic competitiveness in many cities had led to an increase in social exclusion and the loss of social capital rich working-class networks in a situation in which urban governance was seen as having lost credibility and connectiveness with a worryingly high proportion of its citizens (Fainstein 2001). The counterfactual case of cities that had benefited economically from restructuring was also of little comfort; there was just as much evidence of social exclusion and lack of connectiveness. The causes arose out of the same loss of working-class employment from the restructuring of the 1980s but was reinforced, rather than mitigated, by the shift to a post-industrial, services-driven, informational economy that boomed during the 1980s and again in the 1990s. London, as the prime exemplar of this, was witness to the best of times and the worst of times: inner London, as we have seen, was simultaneously host to the richest area in the European Union whilst containing the nation's top three deprived boroughs.

There has been a long-running debate about the consequences of these changes for the social structure of global cities. In their original thesis about the emergence of 'global cities' Friedmann and Wolf (1982) suggested, *inter alia*, that this process would lead to greater social polarization. This claim has been strongly supported by the work of Sassen (1991) who has argued that this has caused the dicho-tomization of major cities such as New York and Los Angeles between an increas-ingly rich service class and a pauperized 'servicing class'. The latter has been engaged in servicing the former at work, at home and at play. The development of a service economy in a globalized city has created new areas of employment often working at what were previously defined as 'unsocial hours': cleaning offices at 4.00 a.m., working split shifts to get people to and from work in cities that are increasingly 'at work' twenty hours a day, moving documents around, running copy shops, making sandwiches and so forth. At the same time, other new areas of employment have been created in the domestic sphere servicing the needs of 'money rich: time poor' households involving such tasks as domestic cleaning, child care and (allegedly) dog walking.[2] According to this view, these jobs are largely carried out by migrants and others who are, or have become, socially and economically marginalized. Jobs that either did not previously exist or were carried out by unionized labour with enhanced benefits for working anti-social hours are now done by new groups of workers, with no such benefits.

Essentially what is at stake here is the disappearance of the majority secure working class urban population with access to state-provided or employer-subsidized welfare benefits A variation of this approach focuses on the emergence of a so-called 40:30:30 society in which there is a group at the top that is in permanent, secure employment with good social benefits; below this is a group whose employ-ment is much less secure across the life and economic cycle, with a further third who are effectively marginalized from employment and thus social integration (Mollenkopf and Castells 1991; Hutton 1995). Once again, what we see is the disappearance of the 'working class middle' in the urban social structure and the emergence of a secure/insecure polarity.

This stark, and somewhat apocalyptic, view of class structure has been chal-lenged particularly as it relates to London (and Europe more generally). In a series of articles during the 1990s Chris Hamnett (Hamnett 1994a; Hamnett and Cross

1998) has counterpoised to the idea of social polarization the view that London's workforce has become increasingly professionalized; that there has been an upgrading of skills in the workforce. He has also made a similar argument for the Randstaad in the Netherlands (Hamnett 1994b). The two positions are however not entirely contradictory in that Hamnett's data are derived from an employed population in a city in which large numbers of men in some areas are permanently outside the employment nexus. Hamnett's largely convincing explanation for this is that these populations in Europe are, for the most part, sheltered by 'welfare regimes' (Esping Anderson 1990) whereas the absence of such provision in the United States forces a largely immigrant urban workforce into temporary, ill-paid and insecure work. This, he suggests, is the explanation for the apparent lack of social polarization in London and elsewhere in Europe compared to that of major North American cities. Of course, it may well be that many of the so-called economically inactive are engaged in forms of economic activity but are not formally recorded as such. The conclusion may therefore be that, despite the upgrading of the employed population in London, the overall social polarization referred to by Sassen arising from the restructuring of employment is an accurate portrayal of the social structure of the city.

These processes of social and occupational polarization were predated by that of residential gentrification, noted by Ruth Glass in the early 1960s in Islington in north London, in what is one of the most frequently-quoted passages in urban sociology

> One by one, many of the working class quarters of London have been invaded by the middle-class – upper and lower – shabby modest mews and cottages . . . have been taken over when their leases expired, and have become elegant, expensive residences. Larger Victorian houses, downgraded in an earlier or recent period – which were used as lodging houses or were otherwise in multiple occupation – have been upgraded once again . . . Once this process of 'gentrification' starts in a district it goes on rapidly until all or most of the working class occupiers are displaced and the whole social character of the district is changed. (Glass 1964: xviii)

This description of gentrification is almost chilling in its prescience about how London has been transformed in the forty years which have elapsed since Ruth Glass's initial observations. Her focus on working-class displacement and the changing 'social character' have also proved remarkably accurate in relation to what has happened and what have been the main themes in the study of gentrification. This displacement of working-class residents was, we now know, part of a larger picture in which industrial employment was to suffer massively particularly in large metropolitan centres such as London, which was to lose upwards of half a million manufacturing jobs over the period (Buck, Gordon et al. 1986).

In such a situation it is not surprising that much of the academic study of gentrification has been on the displaced working class (Atkinson 2000) but it is also perhaps not surprising that many were not reluctant displacees. However, and this is part of the point of this book, gentrification as a concept may be reaching a 'sell by date' – largely because of its connotations. Nobody is in favour of gentrification and even those local authorities that wish to change their 'social mix' of housing or population refer to it by any other name.

Gentrification has, at the risk of gross generalization, been researched by geographers and this has influenced the way in which it has been conceptualized. The starting point has tended to be the city and the debate has been about the relative influences on this change in housing, social and cultural practices in the city. Very crudely, the main debate was between those who argued that gentrification was the outcome of tendencies in capital and those who argued that it was a function of the changed cultural practices of the 'new middle class'. Inevitably both sides conceded some ground to each other. Neil Smith – the main protagonist for the first position – has accepted the role of class by adopting a 'restructuring' approach that sees changes in the class structure arising out of long-term changes in the social and economic structure of industrial societies (Smith 1979; Smith 1996). In particular, he now accepts that consumption (which he rightly distinguishes from demand) plays an important role in structuring the city. However, his broad assumption is that class (including the middle class) is essentially about a social relationship to the means of production (1996: 95). He is therefore sceptical, to put it mildly, about there being anything *new* about the new middle class. In this sense, gentrification for Neil Smith is essentially about the ways in which the working class is on the receiving end of capitalist restructuring

> During the 1970s, and perhaps again in the wake of the 1980s, it is becoming increasingly clear that the struggle over the use and production of space is heavily inscribed by social class (as the nomenclature of 'gentrification' itself suggests) and race as well as gender. Gentrification is thereby part of the social agenda of a larger restructuring of the economy. Just as economic restructuring at other scales (in the form of plant closures, runaway shops, social service cuts, etc.) is carried out to the detriment of the working class, so too is the spatial aspect of restructuring at the urban scale: gentrification and redevelopment. (Smith 1996: 89)

We agree with much of this analysis of the broad politics of restructuring that has occurred in recent decades and its impacts on the urban working class. A danger however lies in equating gentrification simply with the usurpation of working-class space by the middle class. Gentrification is in most respects a symptom of wider processes, as Smith indicates in the quotation above, but it is too often seen merely as an outcome of class processes in an urban environment. This needs to be revisited in the light of the changing nature of both social (class) and spatial (urban) environments over recent decades. As we note below, the old and cosy assumption about the nature of social networks being based in class-based neighbourhoods, notably working class areas no longer applies.

Social Class and the City

It is not just the city that has changed. So also has our conception of social class, having for decades been one of the most trustworthy social measurement devices in sociology. At one time, most sociologists would disagree over the nature of class but concur that it was the central concept in ordering social relations – this has now become a hotly debated claim. On the one hand there remain a number of theorists who continue to argue that class is a powerful structuring force and a source of *identity* – (for example, Devine (1998) and Marshall, Newby et al. (1988)). Against this what unites the various critiques of the 'class societies of capitalist-industrial society' is 'the idea of the end of class' as Savage (2001: 877) puts it, in the works of Giddens (1990), Beck (1992), Lash and Urry (1994) amongst others. Savage (2001) develops a third way position which argues that 'class identities are ambivalent and weak, but that this is compatible with a form of class analysis'. Goldthorpe circumvents the problem of class identity by using rational action theory, whereas Savage draws on Bourdieu's work – which essentially holds that such is the power of class that people find it difficult to articulate it in class terms.

Savage and his co-authors (2001) investigate this in a study of four areas in and around Manchester. Their conclusion is that people use class to describe the society around them but are very shy, or at best ambivalent, about locating themselves in that class structure; the language of class is one which they use to explore their identity. This is particularly the case with those who could now be located within the middle class, who stress 'ordinariness' as the defining characteristic of their middle classness or their 'normalcy' in the sense that they are of neither of the extremes of working or upper class. 'Whereas Bourdieu would direct attention to the multiple strategies used to display and construct cultural distinction of one type or another, nearly our entire sample chose to play down any cultural distinction they may be able to lay claim to in order to play up their ordinariness' (Savage 2001: 889). In other words, they are resisting any form of social fixing or typing in order to be 'themselves'. However, as Savage notes, they in fact understand their position in terms of a complex juxtaposition between themselves as individuals and social class as a kind of social benchmark.

Savage's approach to class can be seen as a synthesis of Wright's (1985a, 1997) tripartite classification mated to Bourdieu's (1984) conceptualization of cultural capital and the habitus working through particular 'fields'. Savage is attempting to restore to sociology an engagement with the social transformations that have taken place in Britain in recent decades in which geographers and cultural theorists tend to have made the running. His argument, as outlined in the previous paragraph, is that the recent paradox of class has been that people do not recognize its structural importance to their own lives. It is not, he says, a self-conscious basis for social identity. Nevertheless, Savage argues that the basis for the individualization thesis, proposed by 'third way' theorists such as Beck and Giddens, is the product of a rejection of a largely non-existent collective class culture. If this can be shown not to exist then we have individualization goes the argument. Savage, as we have seen, goes for his own third way, which involves him in rejections of elements of both Marxist and Weberian traditions. Like Wright, he argues that it is the growing middle that needs to be explained, which means that he too has to revisit the Marxist notion of exploitation. The outcome of this is to reject the link between class and capitalist accumulation which means discarding the labour theory of value, largely because of the problematic concept of an 'unproductive' white-collar sector. Whilst Savage is undoubtedly correct to focus on the existing process of social transformation, there is a danger in fracturing the link between the continuing dominance of capitalism and the changing social structures it engenders. Maintaining such a link is likely to be messy while large-scale transformations are occurring but, nevertheless, sociology needs to try to grasp the link between what is happening in people's individual lives and what is happening at the level of the system. It is precisely this failure to do so that enables Smith (1996) to revert to an essentially 'capital logic' position outlined above – to assert that what is taking place in the contemporary city is being driven by the workings of the capitalist land market mediated perhaps through the agency of social class. We need to look at both processes together and to understand how the processes of 'system and social integration' are (or are not) coming together.

Savage's main argument is that the working class has lost its defining role in determining British culture although it still has a ghostly presence. Whereas previously identity was measured in relation to manual – usually male – labour and the working class acted as the 'moral identifier' that lay at the heart of British society, this is no longer the case. It is not, as in a previous era, a question of whether this allegiance is now being transferred to the middle class. Class is now a benchmark against which individual people measure their position and progress but it does not define their lives. The potential power of sociology lies in its ability to understand the class nature of a social system that, for the first time, does not apparently impinge itself on most of its citizens. As Savage puts it, it is not so much that the cupboard is bare but that its contents are past their sell-by date (Savage 2000: 20). For Savage, class matters not through the occupational system, as it used to be understood, but through the changing nature of organizations and how they have affected men's *and women's* lives. People no longer simplistically accept the old divisions of 'us and them' around which notions of the working and middle classes were constructed – a system that has survived only in a few occupations, most of which (such as the police) are finding it hard to adapt to multicultural capitalism. Britain may remain a class society but it is not one that most of its citizens see as defining their lives.

Social Class and Gentrification

This insight has a lot to recommend it in understanding the gentrification process in general and that of London in particular over recent years. Partly, this is because there is a complex relationship between the wish for 'ordinariness' and 'distinctiveness' in the gentrification process where people are seeking out different ways of living distinctively in ordinary settings. It is also relevant because the other aspect that has become lost is the triangulation between social class, social networks and spatial location (Blokland and Savage 2001). The study of working-class neighbourhoods, such as coal mining villages or London's East End, tended to focus on the class aspect and the spatial arrangements received relatively little attention. It was assumed that they were 'relatively class-homogeneous, small uncontested places that hosted cohesive communities' and that the identities that could be drawn from living in a certain place were 'quite straightforward' (Blokland and Savage 2001: 223). The same point might be made about single-class suburbs in which many middle-class people were brought up. However the creation of mixed class communities in which people are choosing to live in close spatial (if not social) proximity to other groups gives rise to the need to understand what the ties of space are and how identities are constructed. These identities are likely to be multiple and contested and to vary from place to place. The extent to which they are driven by space and class needs to be investigated.

Area

Industrial capitalism created cities in which there were clear socio-spatial divisions, in which the working class was the majority population and industrial production was its prime function. Whole swathes of cities were working-class areas, a process noted by Engels in his study of Manchester, *The Condition of the Working Class in England* (Engels 1971). In this study Engels maps the development of Manchester as the first industrial city in which the working classes are herded together not only to provide the fodder for its hungry factories but are also effectively hidden from the view of middle-class Manchester through zoning and other restraints. This ensures their profitability both as workers and the huddled tenants of hastily built back-to-back homes in the dampest and most insalubrious areas of the fast-growing city.

For much of the nineteenth and twentieth centuries industrial cities were heavily structured by class and particularly the working class; this influenced the manner in which the relationship between class and space was understood. In North America, this coincided with its period of urban expansion and the primary concern amongst sociologists and geographers was consequently with the growth of the city. This was epitomized in the work of the 'Chicago School' which, under the leadership of Park, Burgess and Mackenzie (1925), studied the growth of a city that, between the 1880s and 1930s, approximately doubled its size every decade. The 'Chicago School' became the pre-eminent urban theory in sociology. It claimed to demonstrate that the process of urban growth was largely ecological, spreading outwards like the ripples of water on a pond after a pebble is thrown into it. This process was social as well as spatial, the city socialised its new inhabitants so that, as they became acculturated and upwardly socially mobile, they also became outwardly mobile – moving up the ladder and into increasingly desirable housing. It was a theory of the 'American dream' but one which was driven by the relentless expansion of US capitalism rather than any inherent dynamic of the city. When that expansion came to a halt in the late 1920s then the zone of transition quickly became a ghetto, and its last inhabitants drawn largely from the black post-bellum south quickly became its ossified underclass – no mobility for them. Thus were the structures of Chicago and most North American cities fixed, which quickly led to a process of suburbanization and abandonment of the urban core to all but the poorest blacks (notably in rustbelt towns like Detroit and Cleveland). This process was hastened by the urban riots of the mid 1960s in most major US cities. In other words, the spatial structure of most North American cities was ordered by both class and 'race', although it has been argued that the racial dynamic was driven by class – the argument being that the blacks were simply the poorest and it was this that accounted for their position at the bottom of the urban hierarchy (Wilson 1980). Most North American cities have been characterized as having a 'donut'-shaped structure following the large scale white flight of the 1970s. There are, of course, exceptions – on the east and west coasts – but the main socio-spatial structures of North American cities are organized into a hierarchy of racialized disadvantage. It is therefore unsurprising that the gentrification of North American cities is often so brutal – leading Neil Smith (1996) to label the gentri-fication of New York a process of 'revanchism' in which the middle classes 'retake' parts of the inner city.

In Europe the process of urban development in the nineteenth and twentieth centuries has been rather different because most cities predated industrialization, which consequently had to occur in the context of an often highly developed urban system.

Most European cities already had an urban core often dating from the fourteenth century from which the rest of the city radiated and on to which the industrial city was grafted since the nineteenth century. Many European cities followed the remodelling of central Paris in the 1870s by Baron Haussman who drove a grid plan of long straight avenues through its old centre. This was partly to establish the sense of a grand imperial city and partly to inhibit the ability of workers and others to throw up barricades as they had done during the Paris Commune. In the 'Haussmanized' city there were clear lines of sight to fire cannon down these streets and for mounted cavalry to charge – with relative impunity – those manning barricades. The centres of many European cities were remodelled in the same manner: Brussels, Stockholm, Berlin, Barcelona, Madrid and Vienna (Burtenshaw, Bateman et al. 1991). Albert Speer undertook a similar remodelling of Berlin to meet Adolf Hitler's pretensions for Berlin as the centre of a new Empire. In Britain the centres of London and other major cities (such as Manchester) were remodelled in a not dissimilar way, but unlike the rest of Europe, the promoter was not usually the state but private capital motivated – as Burtenshaw argues – by a mixture of utilitarian values and a desire to break up the working-class 'rookeries' of central London. The results were not dissimilar to Paris: large malls and the development of the 'West End' with its large shopping streets (Oxford Street and Regent Street). The centres of all European cities, including London, remained residential for the upper and upper middle classes, only Britain followed the north American example of extensive middle-class suburbanization. In many European cities, the suburbs often became working-class concentrations.

These broad socio-spatial formations were consolidated during the years of post-war reconstruction, which are generally associated with a period of mass production and mass consumption. This is often referred to as the age of Fordism in which the state, capital and labour broadly worked together. In Britain, this was the age of mass state-provided social housing *and* the expansion of owner occupation. The latter took place largely on the periphery of large cities and was associated with what John Rex (Rex and Moore 1967) has referred to as the game of urban leapfrog whereby the middle classes left the inner city for the space and class homogeneity of the surrounding suburbs. 'Council' (social) housing was built in, as well as around, the big cities and this was a major difference compared with much of Europe.

In London, much of the social housing in the inner city took the form of comprehensive redevelopment and high-rise tower blocks, which involved demolishing swathes of working-class terrace housing (Dunleavy 1981). At the same time, the state encouraged the working classes to leave London, through its New Towns policy,[3] by building towns like Basildon, Harlow, Stevenage and others in a circle mainly around the north/north east of London (Young and Willmott 1962). Only slowly, and in a limited number of areas, as noted by Ruth

Glass, did the Victorian terraced housing stay in private ownership to be rehabilitated by middle-class owner occupiers. Unlike the United States, the pattern of ownership in the inner city remained a mosaic of public and private housing and, with the transition from private-rented to social housing and the rise of owner occupation through gentrification, the geography of relative advantage became even more complex.

After nearly forty years of gentrification, the pattern remains one that Professor Ann Power terms 'speckled'[4] – dappling the map of inner London north and, increasingly, south of the river Thames. These areas are often only a few streets, in a few wards in each borough and, unlike the private or social housing estates of the Fordist era, they are usually socially mixed in which the middle class is the minority population. Nevertheless, the middle class is culturally and economically the defining group able to dominate the area wherever it lives.

Notes

1. 'Home counties' refers to those counties surrounding London forming its commuter hinterland: Kent, Surrey, Sussex, Berkshire, Buckinghamshire, Hertfordshire and Essex.
2. I have always been rather sceptical about this and have never come across it in any of the research projects I have conducted in London over the last twenty years, although people tell me it happens. I have however witnessed it in Buenos Aires and more recently in Boston. On a recent visit to the city, I was walking near the Common early in the morning when I came across a minibus picking up a dog to join the other ten, each of which was firmly attached to a seat. Just as the children were picked up for childcare so were the dogs.
3. This was framed by the 1947 Town and Country Planning Act, which in turn reflected the Abercrombie report, drawn up in wartime to plan the rebuilding of London in the post-war period. It made sharp distinction between the city and its surrounding country side which was protected by a Green Belt on which no building was to be permitted.
4. In conversation with the author and Laurie Taylor on BBC Radio 4 'Thinking Allowed' 21 November 2001

–2–

Gentrification of the Global City: A Middle-class Coping Strategy?

Introduction

In this chapter, we focus on the middle class in the city. In so doing, we depart from two tendencies in class analysis: firstly, the assumption that classes are determined in one way or another, by 'structural' factors such as occupation or industrial sector and, secondly that, in contrast to the working class, the middle class has had it – more or less – its own way. In other words, we are arguing, in contrast to the usual assumptions, that whereas members of the middle class may be relatively auto-nomous about some aspects of how they live their lives – such as where they live and what career they choose – in other respects they are experiencing an increasing loss of control over their lives. In the introduction, we made reference to Richard Sennett's (1999) argument in *The Corrosion of Character* about the ways in which many of today's middle class are sensing a loss of control over their lives. The claim, as we have already indicated, is complex because of the inter-connectedness of work and family, which has – it would appear – been transformed in a single generation. So the very values that continue to drive many of today's middle class in their work lives – insecurity, flexibility – prove also to be the greatest worry in their family lives.

> Rico hates the emphasis on teamwork and open discussion which marks an enlightened, flexible workplace once those values are transposed to the intimate realm. Practiced [sic] at home, teamwork is destructive, marking an absence of authority and of firm guidance in raising children. He and Jeannette [his wife], he says, have seen too many parents who have talked every family issue to death for fear of saying 'No!', parents who listen too well, who understand beautifully rather than lay down the law; they have seen as a result too many disoriented kids. (Sennett 1999: 25–6)

His respondent, Rico, the son of a janitor that Sennett interviewed extensively in a previous study (Sennett and Cobb 1972), has been upwardly mobile. He has worked his way through a number of jobs in the 'new economy' until he runs his own consultancy, which is apparently successful although he clearly struggles both to retain employees who are constantly being hired away and to keep up with the technology in a fast-moving field. His wife – Jeannette – has a parallel career in financial services and they have moved for both their careers. The real problem that Rico identifies is that there is 'no long term', so that 'behaviour which earns success or even survival at work thus gives Rico little to offer in the way of a parental role model' (Sennett 1999: 26). He felt that he was unable to make up homilies from his own work, as his father had done to him, for the moral and spiritual guidance of his own children.

> In fact, for this modern couple, the problem is just the reverse: how can they protect family relations from succumbing to the short term behaviour, the meeting mind-set, and above all the weakness of loyalty and commitment which mark the modern workplace? In place of the chameleon values of the new economy, the family – as Rico sees it – should emphasize instead formal obligation, trustworthiness, commitment, and purpose. They are all long-term virtues. (Sennett 1999: 26)

Sennett summarizes Rico's dilemma in the following terms: 'Short-term capitalism threatens to corrode his character, particularly those qualities of character which bind human beings to one another and furnishes each with a sense of sustainable self' (Sennett 1999: 27).

This, in a nutshell, is the focus of this book. We are not making the argument that all those living in inner London have work lives like those of Rico and Jeannette – far from it; many – if not most – have been both occupationally and residentially comparatively stable over years. Many live on their own, even more do not have children; nevertheless we would argue that the basic insecurity of an increasingly flexible world dominates their lives directly or indirectly. The 'new capitalism' has infected the work/home lives of the new middle classes simply by removing the notion of a long term. At a stroke, this removes one of the better notions of middle-class life – that of 'deferred gratification' and the values that the middle class used to be able to attach to that and reinforce by parental authority and reference to their own work lives.

Our approach to the 'middle class in the city' has therefore been heavily influenced by Sennett's work on 'the personal consequences of work in the new capitalism'. On the basis of the fieldwork, which we undertook in inner London in the last two years of the twentieth century, we have been attempting to understand how the middle classes have been coming to terms with the city. In particular we see London's gentrification, in part at least, as the manifestation of a series of 'coping strategies' by its middle classes. This is not to suggest that the middle classes who have been moving into London over the last decade are doing so reluctantly because, for the most part, they cannot really envisage living elsewhere. At the same time, it has presented them with a range of 'challenges' that are very different from the ones they experienced in their own, often middle-class and non-metropolitan, childhoods.

In this book we investigate the ways in which they have developed these coping strategies, which, we suggest, have involved them in conscious attempts to create neighbourhoods that will meet their needs in bridging these often contradictory aspects of their lives. The nature of the middle classes as they have developed in Britain over recent decades is much highly nuanced – as we outlined in the introduction (Savage, Barlow et al. 1992; Butler and Savage 1995; Savage 2000). We return to this in greater detail in the next chapter but, crudely, our approach is to argue that class is increasingly a matter of choice for those in the middle classes. To an extent this is an outcome of decisions reached (or, more likely, which evolve) at university or before about identity, values and personal orientation, which become a major influence on their choices of subject of study and career (Bagguley 1995). One of the ways in which this is represented is in deciding where and how to live – although this will also change as their lifestyles evolve. In a large, global city like London the diversity of the housing market, particularly in a period of great changes such as have marked the closing decades of the twentieth century, means that the process of middle-class settlement will be complex. The making of an urban middle class will be heavily influenced by such concerns. For their part, the middle classes have a range of different assets that they are able to deploy; some of these will be constrained (such as lack of relative economic capability) whereas others are more a matter of choice and conscious decision, such as the wish to create active middle-class networks. It is, in our view, likely that these will be deployed in different ways, which will give particular areas their own distinctive ambiences, and that this can be seen as part of the process of class formation in contemporary London. In this sense, the habitus acquires specific spatial characteristics that, in turn, influence those living in its ambit. In trying to untangle the nature of the urban middle classes in London, the structure of consciousness is likely to prove important and 'place' is likely to prove of enduring influence.

Locating the Research

Since Ruth Glass first noted its appearance there in the 1960s, the gentrification of London has swept jerkily but remorselessly across almost all of inner London. This has been mapped, albeit unevenly, by social scientists – mainly geographers – who have tracked its progress (Hamnett and Williams 1980; Smith and Williams 1986; Munt 1987; Hamnett 1989; Hall and Ogden 1992; Bridge 1994; Carpenter and Lees 1995; Lyons 1996; May 1996; Butler 1997). With the exception of Lyons and Munt's work on Battersea, and Bridge's on west London, most of the work has been focused on north London. South London, east of the London borough of Wandsworth, has not been seen as gentrified territory. This has given us a somewhat one-sided view of London's gentrification based, as it was, largely on one

borough and one stereotype of the gentrifier – the media obsessed trendy epitomized for many years by the Marc Boxer cartoon 'Life and Times in N1' in *The
Times* (Carpenter and Lees 1995: 298).

What has emerged from recent research is that there are quite distinctive
processes of gentrification taking place in inner London (Lyons 1996; Butler
1997). All are concerned with establishing neighbourhoods in which it can be
argued that the reference points of globalization are central but manifest themselves in different ways. In this section we sketch how this has played out in the
areas in which we carried out fieldwork. All represent different responses to the
encroaching globalization of urban space and the reconstitution of social divisions
in London.

We selected six areas in which to undertake our fieldwork, which were intended
to encompass the diversity of the middle classes in London. There were two
important criteria for selection, the first concerned with typologies of gentrification
and the second with how we approached the definition of the middle class. The
second is clearly crucial and complex and we only outline our approach here. It is
further developed in Chapter 3. In relation to typologies of gentrification, we drew
on the key distinction made by Warde (1991) between gentrification by 'collective
social action' and by 'capital'. Most of what has taken place in London can be
described as the former: individual households or occasionally small developers
doing-up old, usually Victorian, houses. Once the pioneers have done their stuff,
then the areas take off into self-sustained growth often trading on the reputation of
the early pioneers – five of our areas represented different stages of this process.
In London, gentrification by capital has been largely confined to Docklands,[1]
where we did fieldwork in three sub areas, the Isle of Dogs, Surrey Quays and the
Royal Docks, in which large and medium-sized firms took advantage of the
possibilities offered by devalued land to make large profits. In the literature on
gentrification, the former process is seen as driven largely by the supply of gentrifiers who, as a result of changes in the socio-economic structure, seek out
gentrified properties in the inner city (Ley 1996). In the case of the latter, this
process is seen as driven by the workings of the land market, and the supply of
gentrified property, which has been theorized by Neil Smith (1979, 1996) in terms
of an emerging 'rent gap'.

Our intention was to 'capture' not only aspects of the 'history' of gentrification
(from the transformation of parts of Islington in the early 1960s to the present) but
also to identify areas that had apparently been colonized by different sections of the
middle classes. Following earlier work (Butler and Savage 1995; Butler 1997), we
decided to follow Savage and his fellow authors (1992 especially Chapter 6) in
which they have identified a three-way split in the formation of the contemporary
middle classes. These are not based simply on differences between 'employment
situs' (for example, those in professional as opposed to managerial occupations)

following Goldthorpe but also incorporate lifestyle and affective differences. Their categorization is based around Bourdieu's work contextualized in an analysis of market research data on consumption patterns for the United Kingdom:

> The TGI [Target Group Index] survey indicates three salient types of middle-class lifestyle which we have labelled the *ascetic*, the *post-modern*, and *undistinctive*. All appear to have a distinct social base within the middle classes: the first among the public sector welfare professionals, the second among the private sector professionals and specialists, and the third among managers and government bureaucrats. But these processes interweave with those of gender, age and location: a young, male, London-based advertising executive is prone to have a post-modern lifestyle, as indeed the 'yuppie' stereotype would suggest. (Savage et al. 1992: 127–8)

We are working in the spirit of this attempt to typify the main groups emerging from the fragmentation of the middle class.

Gentrification research has tended to suggest that there has been a unilinear process of displacement, in other words that as areas become more middle class the working class is displaced. This is probably stated most clearly in Smith's (1996) work and careful work by Atkinson (2000; 2001) who has provided evidence of this for London. Whilst not wishing to dispute the general trend nor to restate the argument that some of the (white) displacees were upwardly socially mobile, it is important to recognize that the relationship between 'incomers' and 'locals' varies considerably between different areas. Partly this is because of the nature of the areas and partly because of the different approaches taken by the incoming middle class to 'locals', who are not a homogenous group – some, for example, share a history of oppression by the local white working class and may not entirely mourn either their passing or downward socio-economic trajectory. The incoming middle class often has a contradictory approach to the locality – on the one hand, wishing to colonize it and make it in their image, but on the other, to express in varying degrees a level of illegitimacy and deference to the long-established 'locals' whose area it is. The exceptions to this appear to be of two kinds; firstly, where the local working class has been comprehensively pushed aside either by carpet redevelopment as in Docklands or by the widespread marketization of social housing as in Wandsworth, and; secondly where the middle-class 'pioneers' have been sufficiently well-established in what has long been seen as a 'hostile' environment (the language harks back yet again to the moving American frontier). A good example of this arises in Brixton amongst middle-class people who lived through the so-called riots in 1981 and their aftermath. In both cases, there is a sense that they have either earned or paid for their rights to be there. In other cases, there is a subtle ambivalence in the relationship between incomer and local that however, has little affect on the need of the former to impose their cultural dominance over the area despite – in every case – their lack of numerical superiority. This is essentially the power of class at work – over consumption, over access to schooling, over lobbying for environmental improvements, over planning consents, in nearly every case relying on a privileged access to information and an ability to link their needs into local and national policy imperatives. To this of course has to be added a good dose of moral superiority! However, as we shall see, the domination is not always seen as legitimate and, being reflexive individuals, they are fully aware of the contradictions of their situation and how this often sits uneasily with their intellectual, ideological or professional orientations towards issues of social justice. Nevertheless such is the power of social class and self-interest that, in varying degrees, the respondents we have spoken to across London have acted in different ways to ensure their hegemony over the localities in which they have settled. In part at least, it has been a necessary condition that this has occurred in a relatively mixed and unstable environment: such are the corollaries of living in 'post-Fordist' times and, as we have seen, working in the flexible economy. It is therefore in this sense that we approach gentrification as a 'coping' strategy practised by many middle-class people in London.

Coping Strategies: What is Being Coped With?

We have introduced the notion of gentrification as a middle-class 'coping strategy' in the spirit of Sennett's (1999) book *The Corrosion of Character*, which generally anchors this in the context of working in the flexible economy. One consequence of this, apart from those already discussed, is the trend for professional work at the 'cutting edge' to be focused on global cities in which the advanced service industries are concentrated. In addition, the professions (old and new) have become increasingly feminized and middle-class professional households tend to be dual income (Bondi 1991; Warde 1991; Butler and Hamnett 1994). These are all good reasons for not having one, or worse both, partners commuting anything up to four hours a day; it does not fit into household routines, especially when there are children, and it is not good for work in a city which, in many occupations, considers itself open for business twenty hours a day. In a previous study, I turned up on a Sunday morning to interview a lawyer and was told by his apologetic partner that he had had to 'pop' into the office because a client needed a lease drawn up on a Boeing 747 the other side of the world – given the costs of keeping an aircraft on the ground, this couldn't wait until Monday morning. From south Hackney this was a short cycle ride; from Bromley it would have been an hour or more. With young children to be looked after, childcare networks are often much easier to arrange in a big city and, for many, the physical and emotional distance would be unbearable if it took two hours to get home to a sick child. Au pairs are not very happy living in Leatherhead or Colchester, compared to Canonbury or

Muswell Hill. Finally, and certainly not least, today's middle class does not wish to live in the safe suburbs in which it was mostly brought up; after university it wants the excitement and difference of living in socially mixed areas with a cultural infrastructure. It does not wish to worry about missing the last train home – for a further discussion of the gentrification imperative see Butler (1997) but for an intelligent counterview on the relation of the suburbs to the centre see Bondi (1999).

Having taken the decision not to flee to the suburbs, living in the inner city presents the middle classes with a number of problems – particularly if there are children. The main issue that needs to be confronted is education and the fact that London's schools perform badly – particularly at secondary level. The necessary strategies to cope with this demand a huge investment of time, emotional energy and resources and will form a major theme to this book – for an overview see Ball, Bowe et al. (1995); Reay and Ball (1998); Butler and Robson (2003b).

What Are the Mechanics of this Coping Mechanism

Our analysis reveals that, amongst those groups – none of whom can be thought of as being in any sense excluded – engaged in 'remaking' the various inner urban neighbourhoods that we studied, issues of social capital are significant (Butler and Robson 2001). However each of the case study areas is characterized by different modes and levels of social capital. These are important in understanding the ongoing social processes through which formerly deprived or 'undesirable' areas are transformed and made congenial for middle-class life.

Current enthusiasm for social capital, however, may be in danger of reifying and oversimplifying a concept with important heuristic potential. The latter can, however, be maximized once it is understood that social capital is *not* a novel sociological concept (Portes 1988: 21), and if it is theoretically reintegrated into an analysis of its relations with the other key forms of *economic* and *cultural* capital. Our purpose here is to examine the dynamics of these forms of capital in the middle-class transformation of five inner London localities. In Bourdieu's (1986) model *economic capital* refers to monetary income and other financial resources and assets, finding its institutional expression in property rights. *Cultural capital* exists in various forms, expressing the embodied dispositions and resources of the *habitus*. This form of capital has two analytically distinguishable strains, *incorporated,* in the form of education and knowledge, and *symbolic,* being the capacity to define and legitimise cultural, moral and aesthetic values, standards and styles. *Social capital* refers to the sum of actual and potential resources that can be mobilized through membership in social networks of actors and organizations. Critically, this involves 'transforming contingent relations, such as those of neighbourhood, the workplace, or even kinship, into relationships that are at once necessary and elective, implying durable obligations subjectively felt (feelings of gratitude, respect, friendship, etc.)' (Bourdieu 1986: 249–50). This makes this form of capital more of a relational phenomenon than a tangible, or easily quantifiable, resource.

In this overall model of the relations of capital, understanding economic and social outcomes is achieved through analysis of the interaction between the three different forms. This we attempt in what follows, focusing on areas of inner London and the economic and cultural resources, social networks, and normative structures through which they have been gentrified. We examine how differing sections of the middle class strive to create and maintain urban situations for the consolidation of prosperity and also to realize varying ideals of city living. These are understood as core aspects of the necessity for middle-class groups to develop strategies of self-protection and cultural reproduction in increasingly competitive circumstances. Although we are well aware that middle-class social networks tend to be extensive rather than local (Wilmott 1987; Allan 1989), we focus here on those situated patterns of affect and reciprocity clearly associated with, though by no means inevitable in, contemporary gentrification processes.

Examples of accumulating economic capital and buying convenience generally include appropriate investment in transport (particularly private cars and increasingly 'people carriers' that can enable several children to be moved safely), childcare, leisure and cultural services and consumption to maintain psychological health and distance. In many cases, the purchase of a second home has also been an appropriate 'coping strategy' to maintain some literal distance from the city, particularly for those with children – although as the children grow older this can become somewhat of an albatross around their neck. Examples of accumulating and protecting cultural capital include the following:

- children being assisted through educational credentials and other advantages to become themselves middle-class subjects;
- to delineate and maintain shared symbolic universes with others of similar ilk; this is related to the accumulation of social capital;
- to achieve distinction and social status relative to other groups – both middle class and non middle class. The notion of distinctiveness is partially spatial.

The mechanics of achieving this, almost by definition, are largely, although by no means exclusively, directed through children, such as by:

- Identifying good pedagogic practices – this operates particularly at primary schools and provides a counterweight to an over-reliance on league table performance. It involves what might be termed the 'expressive order of the school';

- inculcating individualised notions of personhood into children at a relatively young age, particularly when mapping out appropriate educational careers for them;
- Identifying schools and nurseries and developing particular networks based around children;
- Exposing children to appropriate cultural/leisure activities.

This last point reinforces one of the original reasons for wanting to continue to live in the city – its cultural infrastructure and the enjoyment of this infrastructure. Many of the tools for interpreting and participating in this were acquired through higher education and it is this link that parents are keen and able to pass on to their children as part of a more generalized strategy of cultural and social reproduction. For those with children many of these issues are refracted through the children but, in reality, only reinforce their own lives. The issue of cultural capital, in which almost by definition gentrifiers are well endowed, is a critical link between the possession of economic capital and the deployment of social capital in social networks, which again are usually mediated through the household's children. This should not be regarded as being restricted to those with children. There are life-cycle effects here but those without children are also able to deploy and consume their cultural capital more directly.

Finally, we need to consider the different ways of developing social capital, which differs from economic and cultural capital in that it can only be realized in the context of social relationships and particularly networks. These are the mechanisms that *can* enable a middle-class community to cohere; examples might include:

- the formation of local groups to address middle-class concerns about local infrastructure, environment and services;
- informal school-gate type interactions and recognition of mutual interests at an individual level;
- tacitly supporting and maintaining symbolic norms of house/self, public presentation and patterns of public consumption;
- maintaining and participating in non local networks based on shared identifications and networks – this reflects back to the issue of cultural capital, which is accumulated and realized often in public and national-level settings and institutions.

The details of these assumptions and their theoretical underpinnings are identified and spelled out in the next chapter, but what is proposed here is intended to inform how we have approached the study of the gentrification of London and, in particular, the ways in which the middle classes have coped in a fast-changing world in which the focus on flexibility has dealt them both opportunities and threats.

Note

1. This has been changing recently with for example the transformation of Clerkenwell and Shoreditch, both on the fringes of *The* City (of London – the financial centre) which has seen a large number of formerly commercial properties converted into residential spaces ('lofts') or 'live/work' spaces (particularly in the somewhat cheaper Shoreditch, which is in the deprived area of South Hackney as opposed to Clerkenwell, which is on the Islington borders).

–3–

Spatial Difference and Strategic
Middle-class Activity

The focus of this chapter is on the theoretical-interpretive approach, which we adopt in the task of trying to situate and concretise processes that have hitherto been largely considered in the abstract. Our approach places particular emphasis on interactions between place and social networks, patterns of middle-class 'asset' deployment and cultural reproduction across the four core social 'fields' of *housing, employment, consumption and education* (Bourdieu 1984). The centrality of the first two of these requires little in the way of re-articulation at this stage. Of particular interest here, given its often central role in these processes, is the sphere of education and, indeed, children in a more general sense. The relative neglect of households containing dependent children in analyses of gentrification has represented a missed opportunity in the attempt to develop a detailed picture of the practices and strategies through which distinctive middle-class groups are being formed and maintained in different parts of the city. This neglect we intend to remedy, both for the reasons outlined and in the interest of pursuing more general – and fundamental – questions about relationships between class, social consciousness, models of the person and place. We hope also, in this respect, to avoid the individualist presuppositions of much contemporary social analysis (van Krieken 1997) by situating social agency, where possible, in the dimension of inter-generational time.

The discussion in this chapter, then, focuses on the research in hand, drawing only occasionally on the quantitative analysis of London's contemporary demographics (Champion and Ford 1999; Ford and Champion 2000), which informs the anthropological aspect of the study. The second half, as it were, of the equation – the extensive out-migration of London's lower middle- and working-class populations – is beyond both the remit and scope of the present work. Although not discussed here in any significant detail, it has been a critical backdrop for the emergence of gentrification and should be borne in mind as a core aspect of the social transformation of London over the last twenty years or so (Robson 2000). The necessity for future research into its causes and characteristics is, of course, strongly indicated.[1]

The general purpose of the research is to determine whether there are patterns of connection between specific occupational groups, household types, housing market strategies, patterns of consumption and particular areas of the city. The context in which this enterprise is set – the contemporary fragmentation of the middle classes (Savage, Barlow et al. 1992; Butler and Savage 1995) and the re-emergence of London as a global metropolis (Sassen 1991; Fainstein, Gordon et al. 1992; Buck, Gordon et al. 2002) – is one of considerable complexity, generating a range of conceptual difficulties and ambiguities in matters of definition and interpretation. It is hoped that the research will go some way to clarifying these as well as developing concrete discussions of relationships between middle-class formation, culture and place.

The over-arching hypothesis is that there are a variety of significantly different, patterned gentrification-processes currently unfolding in London, and that these are becomingly increasingly central to and characteristic of the social structure and future of the city. The hypothesis implies a range of core research questions:

- What are the central characteristics of contemporary processes of middle-class formation?
- How can the central characteristics of particular groups, whether emergent or relatively stable, be typified?
- How is the identity of a London locality 'produced' or 'reproduced'?
- How is the settlement and redefinition of urban space implicated in more general processes of class/group formation?
- What are the connections, in all of this, between social class background, employment, housing market strategies, household type and life-cycle?
- What kinds of inter-class interaction characterize particular areas?
- How do the disparate elements of 'lifestyle' (economic, social, symbolic) interact in the formation of coherent, shared and, perhaps, spatially situated identities?

The issue of relationships between class, place and identity is, of course, of central significance. In addition to the questions outlined, the research focuses on an area hitherto neglected by a sociology of gentrification overly preoccupied with the young and single: the role of children and parental/pedagogic practices and strategies in general and specific processes of middle-class cultural reproduction (Butler 1997). Of interest here are the specificities of economic and cultural asset deployment (Savage et al 1992; Lockwood 1995) characteristic of different groups in their struggles to maintain or improve long-term advantage and status across the variety of competitive social fields. Education is one of the – perhaps *the* – most important of these, and an analysis of the way in which local educational 'circuits' (Ball, Bowe et al. 1995) are strategically manipulated by middle-class parents is a key aspect of the research.

Schools, nurseries and colleges are therefore absolutely central to the infra-structural ecologies of many gentrified areas. The specificities of local educational 'markets' (Byrne and Rogers 1996; Conway 1997; Taylor 2001) are in this sense integral to the mapping of a range of localities with which the research is concerned. In the following chapters detailed profiles will be drawn up of all six areas on the basis of educational circuits, local housing-market histories and patterns of settlement, public and private services, markets and facilities and general cultural/ spatial characteristics such as parks and leisure spaces.

The next step is to examine, as precisely as possible, just how representative sections of middle-class populations inhabit and interact with their localities. How connected or otherwise are the different groups to what is immediately around them? To begin with we need to know the extent to which middle-class groups cohere to the point of working, collectively and instrumentally, to change or 'remake' (Wright 1991; Massey 1995) the area in which they settle, via neighbourhood and amenity associations, parent teacher associations and so forth. The tendency to do so implies a level of social interaction – if not cohesion – with 'locals' in some areas that may not be characteristic of others. For this reason we will be working with a provisional continuum of middle-class engagement-disengagement with the people and institutions of their localities. We will be looking, in other words, at the extent to which localities become transformed primarily by social activity, brute physical change (as in Docklands – see Smith 1989; Foster 1999), or varying combinations thereof. It is anticipated that levels and varieties of transformation will vary widely across groups and areas.

Examining patterns of association, leisure and consumption for their spatial characteristics will extend our understanding of the extent to which middle-class Londoners may be living relatively independently of pre-existing local services, resources and social networks. The aim is to build up a comprehensive picture for each locality, attending to both general strategies and the minutiae of everyday activity. Data from personally administered questionnaires enable us to present information about respondents' activities and strategies in the already indicated core fields of housing, employment, consumption and, where relevant, education: the primary contexts in which assets and forms of capital are deployed.

Middle-class Assets and the Metropolitan Habitus

The overriding priority, where the analysis of middle-class formation is concerned, is to avoid simply reading off different groups from their 'objective' class/ occupational positions. Processes of formation are, rather, better understood as emerging out of the dialectical interplay of varying forms of social capital and habitus on the one hand, and the distinctive opportunities – across a range of fields – offered by metropolitan marketplaces on the other. Our research, given this, is broadly situated in the paradigm of middle-class formation and reproduction developed by Savage et al. (1992) on the basis of Bourdieu's (1984) work on class, status, 'taste' and cultural reproduction. Adapting Bourdieu's ideas to the British context, Savage et al. propose a broadly typological schema of 'liberal professional/ascetic', 'corporate/undistinctive' and 'post-modern' middle-class fractions on the basis of their differential engagement in occupational and consumption/leisure fields in addition to their differing modes of material and cultural asset-deployment. It is the latter that is particularly important in inter-generational cultural reproduction. We will be working in the spirit, if not the exact forms, of this early attempt to typify the main groups emerging from the fragmentation of the middle-classes; the third of Savage et al.'s categories, in particular, appears so broad and imprecise at times to denote merely an absence of membership of the other two. Nevertheless, it points to a broad set of novel social behaviours and phenomena that may well contain important insights into some of the 'crossovers' in occupation and lifestyle in contemporary gentrified London. The stable emergence – or otherwise – of this incoherent, non-integral and consumption-led middle-class 'lifestyle' is something we will be looking at very closely in order to determine its dimensions and characteristics. It is envisaged that an analysis of the connections between new groups classified under the rubric of 'new cultural intermediaries' (O'Connor and Wynne 1995) and life-cycle stages may be to the forefront here. Before developing our critique and subsequent use of Savage et al.'s (1992) typology, we first discuss briefly Bourdieu's concept of the habitus.[2]

The Habitus

The habitus, centrepiece of Bourdieu's conceptual paradigm, is one of the most important conceptual tools in contemporary social thought. *Habitus* refers to the ways in which processes of class formation – and reproduction – are facilitated by the storage and (transposable) transmission of core cultural dispositions in the individual. Jenkins (1992: 67) sees theory as 'thinking tools' and, in Bourdieu's case, the three most important legs to this are: practice, habitus and field. We will briefly discuss these in order, although more space will be devoted to field than the others because it is key to our approach to gentrification.

> [Bourdieu] replaced the notion of rules which govern or produce conduct with a model of social practice in which what people do is bound up with the generation and pursuit of strategies within an organising framework of cultural dispositions (the habitus). (Jenkins 1992: 39)

Bourdieu does not believe that people are consciously thinking about what they are doing all the time, they take it for granted for much of the time. There is not, in other words, a 'Fordist-era' trade union/management rule book that governs all actions. Jenkins questions this and suggests that, in fact, some practices are *taught* whilst others are *imbued* and argues that most actions do have a purpose even if these are not conscious. In a sense, and it is a point that Jenkins returns to often in his short book, Bourdieu (contrary to what he says) takes a Weberian position of purposive action but dresses it up in the somewhat trendily contemporary term 'strategy' although, as he points out elsewhere, all this really does is lift the term from a business environment where it often serves to provide a gloss for normal business behaviour (Jenkins 1992: 83).

The *habitus* however is the crucial term because it acts as the bridge between, on the one hand, individual decision making about lives and, on the other, the structures that constitute society (Jenkins 1992: 74). In other words, the habitus enables sociologists, more or less, to resolve the troublesome dichotomy between subject/object and structure/agency. The habitus is rooted in the body and exists through the practice of actors and their interactions with each other and their environment. It does not just comprise manifestations of social behaviour but is integral to that behaviour and a combination of the personal and the systemic (Jenkins 1992: 74). It is the 'dispositions of the habitus' that are 'generative of practice' and these are not mechanically determined but work through individuals and provide a basis for what people do; they often work across fields, the prime example being gender. Jenkins is highly critical here of the relationship between the habitus and practice and accuses Bourdieu of determinism because of the way in which he links 'subjective expectation to objective properties'. Provocatively, but with some justification, he likens Bourdieu's approach to that of Talcott Parsons as being essentially teleological and conservative in that norms are internalized and so become the source of social stability (Jenkins 1992: 81). This is the nub of Jenkins' criticism of Bourdieu – that for all the rhetoric, social action is determined by the limits put on it by the structure and, as such, it is a top-down model. However, the same reading can be made of Marx and indeed Jenkins draws attention to the notion of 'class in itself' and 'class for itself' distinctions in Bourdieu's work. He suggests that 'strategizing' might form a useful link between habitus, practice and field (Jenkins 1992: 83): 'to use Bourdieu's own expression, we are slipping here from a model of reality to the reality of the model. Strategies appear to be more his creation than his research subjects' (Jenkins 1992: 84).

These criticisms notwithstanding, which we find largely convincing, we remain committed to Bourdieu's approach, which, as Jenkins concedes, is one located in practice, doing and a commitment to empirical research (Jenkins 1992: 176). We find it particularly attractive in trying to 'think with' the problem of gentrification, which is a highly empirical (and empiricist) concept and particularly one that combines social and spatial aspects. The notion of *field* is a key concept here.

Field

A field, in Bourdieu's sense, is a social arena within which struggles or manoeuvres take place over specific resources or stakes and access to them. Fields are defined by the stakes which are at stake – cultural goods (lifestyle), housing, intellectual distinction (education), employment, land, power (politics), social class, prestige, or whatever – and may be of differing degrees of specificity and concreteness. Each field, by virtue of its defining content, has a different logic and taken-for-granted structure of necessity and relevance which is both the product and producer of the habitus which is specific and appropriate to the field. (Jenkins 1992: 84)

The field involves recognizing the centrality of social relations to social analysis – according to Bourdieu

'I define a field as a network, or a configuration, of objective relations between positions objectively defined, in their existence and in the determinations they impose upon their occupants, agents or institutions, by their present and potential situation . . . in the structure of the distribution of power (or capital) whose possession commands access to the specific profits that are at stake in the field, as well as by their objective relation to other positions . . .' (quoted in Wacquant 1989: 39).

A field is a structured system of social positions occupied either by individuals or institutions; it also comprises forces that exist between these positions – the nature of which defines the situation for their occupants. A field is structured internally by its power relations – domination, subordination or equivalence, and by the nature of the relationship they offer to the goods or resources (capital) which are at stake in the field (Jenkins 1992: 85).

The social world can be conceived as a multidimensional space that can be constructed empirically by discovering the main factors of differentiation which account for the differences observed in a given social universe, or, in other words, by discovering the powers or *forms of capital* which are or can become efficient, like aces in a game of cards, in this particular universe, that is, in the struggle (or competition) for the appropriation of scarce goods of which this universe is the site. It follows that the structure of this space is given by the distribution of the various forms of capital, that is, by the distribution of their properties which are active within the universe under study those capacities capable of conferring strength, power and consequently profit on their holder . . . These fundamental social powers are, according to my empirical investigations, firstly *economic capital*, in its various kinds: secondly *cultural capital* or better, informational capital, again in its different kinds; and thirdly two forms of capital that are very strongly correlated, *social capital*, which consists of resources based on connections and group membership, and *symbolic capital*, which is the form the different types of capital take once they are perceived and recognized as legitimate. (Bourdieu 1987: 3–4).

The nature of positions is to be found in their relations to the particular form of capital:

> The *existence* of a field *presupposes* and, in its functioning, *creates* a belief on the part of the participants in the legitimacy and value of the capital which is at stake in the field. This legitimate *interest* in the field is produced by the same historical processes which produce the field itself. (Jenkins 1992: 85)

More complex societies have more fields and the boundaries are shifting and determined by struggles in which agents strategise to preserve or improve their position with respect to the defining capital of the field. Using Bourdieu's concept of field in research entails three distinct operations:

1. The relationship of the field in question to the 'field of power' (politics) must be understood. The field of power is thus to be regarded as the dominant or pre-eminent field of any society; it is the source of the hierarchical power relations that structure all other fields.
2. Within the field in question one must construct a 'social topology' or map of the 'objective structure' of the positions which make up the field, and the relationship between them in the competition for the field's specific form of capital.
3. The habitus(es) of the agents within the field must be analysed, along with the trajectories or strategies that are produced in the interaction between habitus and the constraints and opportunities that are determined by the structure of the field

We find this approach very useful in thinking about, and undertaking research into, the way in which different gentrified areas are constituted and how these are the outcomes of the interactions of the four different fields (occupation, housing, consumption and education). It is the deployment of these different forms of capital that distinguish the nature not only of gentrified areas but of the particular fields in those areas. To this extent, we support Bourdieu against Jenkins' charge of economism in the use of the term 'capital', because as Bourdieu argues, it is a matter of interest of which there are many and these are not just reducible to the economic or rational. There are, in effect, as many interests as there are fields to be maximized. Jenkins doubts whether it is possible to imagine how an actor does anything other than pursue an interest – particularly in a situation in which Bourdieu denies to the social scientist the role of deciding what constitute the actor's interests (Jenkins 1992: 87–8).

Calhoun (1993) explains the multiple dimensions of capital helpfully:

> Economic capital is essentially that which is 'immediately and directly converted in to money' (Bourdieu 1986: 243), unlike educational credentials (cultural capital) or social

connections (social capital) . . . He [Bourdieu] has made particular strides by recognizing how much of cultural capital presupposes embodiment of distinctive and distinguishing sensibilities and characteristic modes of action. Thus it is that he is able to show how the labour of parents is translatable into the 'status attainment' of their children in ways not directly dependent on financial inheritance or even better on schools. Such parental labour depends on the availability of free time from paid employment, however, which shows the dependence of the other forms of capital on economic capital (ibid: 253). The importance of this sort of cultural capital is greatest, moreover, where for some reason it is advantageous to deny or disguise the inheritability of position (ibid: 246) . . . his sociology does not offer much purchase on the transformation of social systems. It is geared towards accounts of their internal operation. (Calhoun 1993: 70)

Jenkins (1992: 89) argues this is not particularly novel – how, he asks, are fields to be identified or determined; what is the model of institutions? Bourdieu, he claims, does not distinguish sufficiently clearly between people and institutions:

there is in Bourdieu's social theory a gap which is only partly filled by the notion of the habitus, between micro level of practising agents and the macro level of fields and the social space. A theoretical model of institutions is required to fill this gap. (Jenkins 1992: 90)

The relationship between field and habitus is also not clear – does each field generate its own habitus or do actors bring them to the field? What happens when an actor only comes across a habitus as a fully formed adult? How can a field have its own habitus if habitus is the property of embodied individual agents? Basically Jenkins suggests Bourdieu's is a model of stability similar to the structural functionalism of Talcott Parsons with which it shares some of the same weaknesses. Notably, how does change occur when power and authority flow from the top down? Despite Bourdieu's enthusiasm for resistance, Jenkins claims that there are not many examples of this – it is about the success of domination and reproduction. It is a universe in which things happen to people (Jenkins 1992: 91). According to Calhoun (1993: 72):

Bourdieu has rightly protested that his work is by no means bracketable as a theory of reproduction *tout court* . . . but he is centrally concerned with how the various practical projects of different people, the struggles in which they engage, and the relations of power which push and pull them nonetheless reproduce the field of relations of which they are a part. 'The source resides in the actions and reactions of agents who, unless they exclude themselves from the game, have no other choice than to struggle to maintain or improve their position in the field, thus helping to bring to bear on all the others the weight of constraints, often experienced as intolerable, which stem from antagonistic coexistence.' (Bourdieu 1990: 193)

Our approach is, in the spirit of Bourdieu, one of empirical investigation in which the problems raised by Jenkins, whatever their abstract validity, are mitigated by the validity of the approach in undertaking empirical work. However this does produce some problems for us when operationalizing the concept of social class because, as Jenkins once more points out, the field of employment dominates and although, in the spirit of Savage et al. (1992) we wish to embrace the range of lifestyles the definitions tend to be over-determined by those of employment and occupation.

Middle-class Divisions

We are provisionally retaining (as judgements to be confirmed or rejected) the 'ascetic', 'undistinctive' and 'post-modern' categories proposed by Savage et al. (1992:) on the basis of Bourdieu's (1984) work on class, status, 'taste' and social reproduction. Even on the basis of the most cursory examination, it is clear that at least two of these groups are very heavily represented in gentrification processes. The 'ascetic' culture of public sector professionals appears to be strongly represented in some of our research localities, whilst ambiguously 'undistinctive' (or 'traditional') milieus characterize others. However, a convergence between the two is noticeable in many areas and 'fit' well with Savage's concept of the post-modern. It remains to be seen whether more detailed and precise categories are required for the rendering of social experience in middle-class inner London. Although we will be proceeding, very broadly, according to the principles of this approach, there are some important issues to be thought through in terms of its operationalization – particularly in light of Savage's more recent re-evaluation of both his own work and of approaches derived from Bourdieu in general.

The first and most important thing to note here is Savage's more recent analysis (Longhurst and Savage 1996) of some of the shortcomings of his previous work. These are to do, broadly, with the non-contextualization in the 'everyday' of many market-research style studies of (individual) consumption, and an insufficient interest in axes of similarity, as well as differentiation, within the middle classes. To take the second point first, Longhurst and Savage observe that middle-class individuals may exhibit more complex and contradictory forms of consumption than the attribution to them of straightforward habitus types allows for. It is argued that Bourdieu's focus on patterns of variation leads him to overlook commonalities across apparently differently structured groups and generate definitions of habituses that may be misleading in their construction of the boundaries around each example. The caution here is against simply setting up in the business of habitus-mapping, as the 'search for variation needs to be placed in direct relationship to the related need to examine patterns of commonality' (Longhurst and Savage 1996: 287). This is illustrated by some interesting findings about the uses of television.

Abercrombie (1996: 48) notes, in an analysis of research into television in *Social Trends*, that the proportions of time spent watching different types of programme are almost constant across the different groupings within the audience: 'in many ways this is a remarkable finding. In other fields of activity, generally speaking, one finds that different groups have very different social behaviours.' Halle's (1991) work on the display of decorative art in working- and middle-class households is also mentioned for having shown, despite some important differences between groups, general patterns that spanned classes, ethnicities and genders. Finally, and in connection with Bourdieu's classic use of the *Well Tempered Clavier* as an indicator of habitus, Longhurst and Savage note that this music is generally unpopular, and that this is the case even among the most culturally privileged groups. These issues may serve to indicate large areas of unexpected commonality and what might be individual experiences of fractured and/or synthesized habitus.

This leads on to the second point about connections with everyday experience. Variations may not in themselves be of any particular significance. The crucial point is not simply to establish that variation exists but to 'bring out the relational character of such variation or in other words that the existence of tastes is directly related to the absence of given tastes elsewhere' (Longhurst and Savage 1996: 288). A focus on the questions of everyday life is therefore thought important in order to gauge the significance of cultural practices in their context. The call here is for analyses of consumption to be more sensitive to the interplay between subjectivity and context, more sophisticated and flexible in their rendering of consumption practices and exploring this field in ways that are less concerned to base such practices in occupational class divisions. The interactive dynamics of households, particularly where gender relations are concerned (Wacquant 1991; Warde 1991; Crompton 1995; Massey 1995; Breughel 1996), and the collaborative, unintended and 'subversive' uses to which consumed products might variously be put constitute this sense of the everyday. The authors are, in short, suspicious of the attempt to derive straightforward correlative connections between class and culture.

Warde (1996) suggests that these considerations imply the further development, rather than the rejection, of Bourdieu's paradigm. Calling, like Longhurst and Savage, for future studies of consumption to be characterized by case studies of specific social practices, Warde sees the next step as involving the examination of the ways in which particular groups operate in particular fields and the ways in which those fields themselves differ in their internal logics (for example housing, education and, in a recent analysis, personal finance – Aldridge 1998). Ultimately, the aim must be to examine 'both the behaviours of different social groups and the behaviours entailed by different types of activity' (Warde 1996: 310).

These points should perhaps make us wary of adopting too simplistic a framework of correlative relationships between class and consumption; of being too eager to map out patterns of closure and cohesion where they may only tenuously exist; and to bear in mind the possibility of important but easily overlooked commonalities among middle-class groupings. Such significant variations as we identify will no doubt have to be vigorously argued for and demonstrated, but a good deal of mileage can be derived from staying with the concept of habitus – as a heuristic device with great analytical/interpretive potential, if nothing else – if some of these well-taken points about fracturing and, perhaps more interestingly, synthesis are incorporated into its use.

Savage's suggestion that the focus in matters of consumption practices should be shifted away from occupational divisions is an important one to think through. Spending too long agonizing over the dimensions of specific varieties of middle-class habitus may be as counter-productive as being overly preoccupied with the minutiae of class definitions. Following Savage into a belief in the significance of interactive household/local practices might mean adhering to a view of class as a relatively broad 'social fact' (Lee 1994) in a more Durkheimian[3] (less economistic) sense. This is consistent with Goldthorpe and Marshall's (1992) call for analyses to proceed without the requirement of a reductionist theory of generic-class based collective action; Goldthorpe and Marshall argue, intriguingly, for a more limited project focused on the continuing likelihood of relatively stable groupings in which 'identity', for the most part, precedes 'interest' (see also Devine 1998).

This kind of approach is important, where consumption is concerned, as a corrective to simplified conceptions of the relationships between consumption and social identity (see Lee 1994 and, for example, Campbell 1995; Douglas 1996). The role of consumption in contemporary processes of middle-class formation might therefore be thought of – especially among the more 'mature' groups – as less significant as an indicator of 'self-creative' individuality than the drawing of well-defined, complementary formal boundaries around already distinctive identities. Consumption can, in this sense, take its conceptual place among the range of 'informal' strategies of middle-class formation in which the research is interested. Lockwood (1995) asks some relevant questions about the significance of relational aspects of middle-class formation: to what extent can classes be identified through their more or less 'exclusive patterns of informal social interactions'? How significant are inter-marriage, friendship networks and associational memberships as compared to formal economic and 'status' boundaries? Patterns of consumption may be thought of as significant for the symbolic shape they give to these processes; they are not so much indicators of novel and increasingly heterogeneous identities, but may be strategic aspects of the ongoing agonistic struggle of groups to define who and what they are not (Douglas 1996).

This view is, of course, quite consistent with the general shape of Bourdieu's conceptual apparatus, and we will be looking – caveats accepted – at the ways in which the particularities of middle-class habitus(es) find reproductive bases in economic activity and social practice. The key question here is the extent to which the spatial component of these ongoing processes is of central rather than marginal significance for particular groups. Put differently, how important is the locality in streams of culture that have hitherto been largely understood as being relatively independent of the spatial, and more centrally characterized by broader patterns of associative 'community' and action (Argyle, 1994; Willmott, 1987)? What differences, in this respect, are there between different groups – or fractions – of the contemporary middle classes and ideas about, and experiences of, 'locality' and 'community'? Our preliminary suggestion is that such divisions do exist between specific groups, and that it is possible to map these, as processes, onto London's patchwork of culturally and economically heterogeneous and promiscuously juxtaposed locales (Lyons 1996; Butler 1997).

As far as the local dimension is concerned there is, in addition to employment, housing and consumption, a fourth, critical, social field to be negotiated on the terrain of middle-class formation: education. This is frequently so significant a factor in the location choices made by middle-class households that to overlook its significance is to do extreme violence to the attempt to develop a rounded account of the causes and mechanics of London's social transformation where issues relating to children and asset deployment are, it is argued, absolutely critical to particular processes of group formation.

'Our' Four Fields: Employment, Housing, Consumption and Education

In this section, we outline briefly a description of the four fields and how they relate to the four forms of capital introduced above. Employment and housing are considered in rather more depth than education and consumption; education is considered in Chapter 7 and much of Chapter 6 addresses consumption. The fields are introduced here as a basis for the following chapters, which describe our research areas and their inhabitants.

Employment

We have already drawn attention to a weakness in Bourdieu, to some extent replicated by Savage et al.'s (1992) approach to divisions within the middle class, in which attempts to create lifestyle categories tend to revert, to a greater or lesser extent, to employment and occupation. Nevertheless we are sticking with this approach and we recognize that occupation remains a potent force in understanding how lifestyles are constructed – not just because of the consumption that they buy but also because they remain broad indicators of attitudes, values and aspirations as well as of association. We are nevertheless mindful of Bagguley's (1995) argument that we need to pay close attention to the direction of the causality in the relation between values and occupation. He demonstrated convincingly that many of the middle-class radicals of the 1960s chose certain occupations (social work and teaching, for example) because of their pre-existing ideological orientations and not vice versa. So the habitus brought to the field of employment is one that is formed during the long years of middle-class education.

It is not simply that cultural capital, in the form of credentials, permits access to the desirable professions and occupations but also the conditions under which that cultural capital was gained have implications for the manner in which it is deployed. This is also likely to have spatial implications in terms of where to live in a situation where people are able to exercise choice. It might appear that this will be an outcome of the operations of the housing market and therefore indirectly of employment via the differential ability to raise housing finance. It is, however, possible that decisions about which areas to live in and what employment sectors to work in are the outcomes of previously reached decisions about higher education and occupation. In other words, it may be that views of symbolic capital have a role in shaping definitions of desirable positions. That is to say, occupation might be seen as an expression of cultural (as well as individual) personality. Finally, economic, cultural and social capital support children through their educational careers and into desirable jobs. It is likely that the particular mix will vary; for example, those with sufficient stocks of economic capital may deploy it to buy their children cultural capital, which is then realized inter-generationally. Savage et al. (1992) demonstrate that first generation middle-class managers tend to encourage their children into professional jobs via the acquisition of cultural capital – this strategy applies particularly to girls who are more likely to be excluded from intra-generational mobility through the managerial hierarchy. Professional parents on the other hand, are more likely to be able to deploy their cultural capital via social networks of like-minded parents directly to the benefit of their children – for example, by accessing selective state schools and thereafter elite universities. The role of cultural capital in social reproduction ('symbolic violence') has been subjected to rigorous investigation by Sullivan (2001) who, whilst finding that cultural capital in the home environment has some influence on GCSE performance, concluded that other factors such as social class and material wellbeing are also powerful.

Housing

Economic capital buys and renovates houses and, as suggested above, the higher the stock of economic capital, the greater the choice of areas in which to purchase housing – although there is clearly an area/housing type (or size) trade-off. It is likely that symbolic capital is involved in the meanings ascribed to localities and location choices and that this will be related to quality and quantity of cultural capital. A contrast here might be between new-build gentrification in Docklands and a north London terrace in Islington. In areas where the 'collective action' model of gentrification (Warde 1991) is in play, social capital is likely to play a central role in the process of turning a stock of 'devalued' housing into a new and redefined neighbourhood. The deployment of social capital, which is only realized in social interaction, is most likely to be the case where relatively modest stocks of economic capital have been available. This refers both to the 'pioneer' phase of gentrification and to the notion of the marginal gentrifier (Rose 1984; Williams 1986) although it has been argued (Smith 1987) that when the gentrification steamroller starts moving so do the marginals and that they are more likely to be permanent fixtures in the novels of Margaret Atwood than the downtowns of major cities. Nevertheless this view is not likely to prevail as cities become more gentrified and more diverse, and we need to be able to understand ways in which housing becomes emblematic of differences within the middle classes. On the other hand, high levels of social capital or indeed symbolic capital are not inevitable in the process of locality transformation, where private and/or public economic capital working through the land or property markets can be primary.

Consumption

Gentrification is essentially about consumption and so are the economies of cities. 'Consumption' and 'social reproduction' are not, as some early theorists assumed synonymous (see, for example, Smith 1979). At its crudest level, economic capital enables individual consumption; the higher the economic capital the greater the choice over consumption. However, it is not simply an issue of 'how much' because, as we have already seen, the gentrification of Islington in the early days was seen as the display of 'ostentatious thrift'. In other words, differing modes of symbolic capital influence attitudes towards display; for example, ascetics do not go in for conspicuous consumption and are likely, even if they can afford it, not to buy large and expensive cars – quite apart from the fact that they are invitation to vandalism in some of the streets in our fieldwork areas. Urban consumption, as Zukin (1995) has shown, involves culture and, whilst this is often 'free' in terms of physical entry, it requires varying levels of cultural capital to access.

We speculate that social capital – in so far as commonly held values and dispositions may be connected to it – plays a role in defining and maintaining norms of display and presentation. We will discuss examples of this in chapter four but the issue of gentrification kitsch – absence of net curtains and bare floorboards

(Raban 1974) and Victoriana (Jager 1986) – are perhaps examples of this in the literature. Where, if at all, do *distinction* and symbolic capital merge into social capital?

Education

Economic capital, at its simplest, buys private education and hence privileged access to inter-generational cultural capital and social reproduction: the higher the economic capital, the greater the choice of schools. As we have already suggested however cultural capital a) provides children with the necessary credentials for success and b) imbues children with the scholarly and social confidence to succeed.

Cultural reproduction, in its cultural capital aspect, equips children with the personal and cognitive skills for success – independence of mind, a capacity for abstract thought and action, flexibility, adaptability and reflexive social control.

Social capital, especially where the 'private option' is not being widely taken up, may have an important role to play in the development and maintenance of 'circuits of schooling' (Ball, Bowe et al. 1995). This is particularly likely to be the case in areas where community building and primary school colonization have gone hand in hand. This will no doubt aid the 'strategizing' link between the habitus and practice.

In the next chapter we map out how these conceptual tools apply across the metropolis of inner London.

Notes

1. A good place to begin would be an analysis of trends in social/spatial mobility identified by Fielding (1995). Fielding professes surprise, in an otherwise exemplary analysis, at the large numbers (24 per cent) of 'blue collar' individuals moving into the 'petit bourgeois' category. Indeed, the latter category is 'now so working-class that it questions whether this is now a middle-class category at all' (1995: 173). There can be little doubt that trends in working-class out-migration are implicated in this neglected, and largely unexpected, strain of social mobility. We need to know much more about the dimensions and details of these processes.
2. This is not intended to be in any way a comprehensive discussion and we point the reader towards the many books devoted to this concept (such as the Web site

maintained at Massey University New Zealand, which is probably the best source: www.massey.ac.nz/~nzsrda/bourdieu/home.htm); for sympathetic overviews Robbins (1991), Harker, Mahar et al. (1990) and Lane (2000) remain useful. In our view, the best introduction remains Richard Jenkins (1992) study. Whilst sympathetic to Bourdieu's 'project', this remains an essentially critical approach, which raises some fundamental criticisms of Bourdieu which have informed our approach. Jenkins also gives useful advice on a strategy for both reading and using Bourdieu towards the end of his book.

3. The domination of class analysis by Marxist and Weberian perspectives has left little room for much in the way of what might be called the Durkheimian sensibility. This must partly be due to the relative disinterest shown in class analysis by Durkheim himself, but it might also be the case that emphases on relations of production and status-stratification have obscured some of the more general ways in which class could be thought of in a more metaphorical sense, as having to do with questions of group identity not reducible to clearly apparent and rationally accesible material phenomena. This is not to argue for an updated Durkheimian model of class analysis (although that might be interesting!) but for an acceptance of particular aspects of class consciousness (or unconsciousness) as somehow factual, durable and relatively transposable across material contexts. Such an idea is at the heart, after all, of Bourdieu's entire project.

The case of the late Basil Bernstein, himself a neglected inheritor of the Durkheimian project, is interesting to consider. Although his 'restricted' and 'elaborated' schema address issues of production, exchange, occupation, power and so forth, it is also possible to interpret them as a metaphorical attempt to render forms of solidarity and consciousness that are real, profound, continually reproduced and *easy to ignore* from conventionalist class-analytical perspectives. Although this is most obviously the case in connection with differences between middle- and working-class consciousness and personality types, it is a more general argument for seeing, in addition, the generation of particular class-related types of culture and personhood as having achieved a significant degree of independence, autonomy and internally logical coherence.

−4−

Mapping the Neighbourhoods

Introduction

In this chapter we demonstrate the ways in which different middle-class groups are operating strategically across the fields outlined in the previous chapter – employment, housing, consumption and education. We identify the *habitus* of the different areas and note the deviations and dissidences from them – this is one of the best ways of identifying the habitus. We also look at the habitus of different social class backgrounds and of different employment fields. We relate these to the housing, education and consumption possibilities in each of the areas as ways of 'realizing' the 'potential' forms of habitus that are waiting to be made collective through living in the area. There need to be some channels for this realization to take place, which is where strategies and constraints come. Our findings indicate that people apparently want to be able to swim in these for some time.

We introduce 'ACORN' clusters as a way of characterizing the consumption characteristics of the areas in which we undertook our research and so introducing them to the reader. These clusters are a popular marketing analysis tool that groups particular *types* of areas by their known consumption characteristics. These typologies are accessible via postcode data and can be readily accessed through Web sites such as www.upyourstreet.co.uk. Interestingly, all of our areas fall into a restricted number of ACORN clusters.

Having mapped the areas in this way, in the following section we spell out in more detail the *habitus(es)* of the agents in *fields* in each of the areas along with the *trajectories* and *strategies* that are produced in the interaction between the habitus and the *constraints* and *opportunities* that are determined by the structure of the field. However it is, as we learned in the previous chapter, necessary first to construct a *social typology* of the objective structure of the positions that make up the field and to analyse relationships between them in the competition for the field's specific form of capital (Jenkins 1992: 85). This operation will constitute the second major section of the chapter.

The Fieldwork Areas

We eventually chose six areas in which to undertake our fieldwork, which we felt confident encompassed, on the one hand, the 'gentrification by collective social action' and 'gentrification by capital' dichotomy whilst also containing, as it were, a 'natural history' of inner London's gentrification process over the last forty years. Our choice of areas was influenced by an analysis of census data, through informal interviews, non-participant observation and extensive walkabouts. Following this, we were reasonably confident that we had also incorporated the range of social class typologies indicated by the Savage (1992) model discussed in Chapter 2. One important decision was to ensure that a significant proportion of the fieldwork was undertaken south of the river Thames, which, we felt, had been neglected in most previous work.

Although we were looking for difference, on the lines outlined above, it is important to stress that the areas were likely to be quite similar in important respects. This is confirmed by the subsequent research but also by the ACORN classifications, which are good indicators of lifestyle patterns in ways not dissimilar to the Target Group Index used by Savage et al. None of the areas are what might be termed middle class in conventional understanding – nearly all are ethnically mixed, home ownership is in a minority, there are more poor people than those with high incomes and two car ownership is below average. What comes across despite this is a greater tendency than the national norm to vegetarianism,

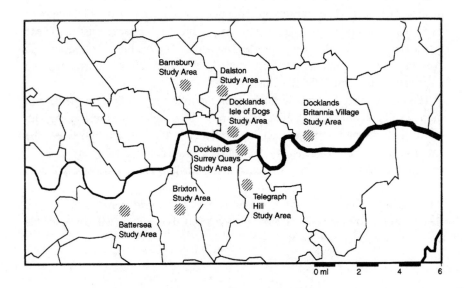

Figure 4.1 London showing the study areas

to exotic and far-flung holidays, a marked predisposition to read the *Guardian* and not to watch or listen to commercial television or radio and finally to drink gin. There are important nuances of difference but the greatest contrasts are probably with the middle class as a whole – this is an urban middle class that practises, as the journalist Nicholas Tomalin (the original model for the Marc Boxer cartoon in Islington) put it, 'conspicuous thrift' (Carpenter and Lees 1995: 298). This is an urban middle class in the making, which, much to the frustration of the marketing profession, has to be teased out from under the urban poor with whom it apparently co-habits spatially. We now describe each of the areas in some detail drawing upon our own observations and the consumption characteristics thrown up the ACORN analysis.

Barnsbury

It would be difficult to find a more classical or attractive gentrified area in inner London than this. Having now had something in the region of thirty years to stabilize and 'mature', Barnsbury represents perhaps a yardstick by which to

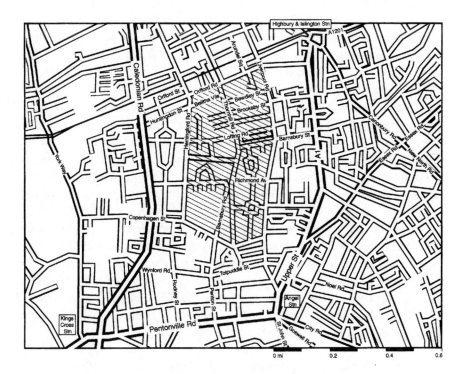

Figure 4.2 Barnsbury study area

measure other settlements of its (broad) kind. The highly desirable houses and cottages, many of them beautifully, almost perfectly, renovated, line spotless, ordered and cared-for streets; the area would appear to be all but beyond further improvement – on a mild spring day the ambience is almost luxuriously idyllic.

There is little sense here of threateningly insalubrious, ungentrified encroachment. The council estates are screened-off from the central part of the area, and in any case their denizens have to reckon with one of the most stable, confident and charmed gentrified enclaves anywhere in London. It might be difficult to imagine much in the way of local/incomer strife in the area as a whole – at first sight, there is an absence of any fragile, borderline atmosphere to the settlement such as characterizes other localities in the city. On the other hand, Barnsbury is shepherded between two iconic streets: Upper Street and the Caledonian Road (also known as 'the Cally'). It is probably not possible to imagine a greater contrast between the worlds represented by these two 'edges' to the area (Lynch 1960). Upper Street to the east represents the affluence of gentrified London with its shops with twenty-five varieties of exotic bread whilst the 'Cally' is rooted in the exclusion of working class Islington and home to the prison populations of Pentonville and, only slightly removed, Holloway gaols.

Barnsbury, then, is our 'control group'; we know from Lyons' (1996) work and elsewhere (see, for example, Carpenter and Lees 1995) that many gentrifiers have put down roots here, and that the phenomenon is therefore, to some extent, intergenerationally stable. Modes of identifying with, and living in, the area might, given this, be of a quite different order from those in some of the other areas we will consider. It also affords us a very good opportunity to have an in-depth look at connections between place, cultural reproduction and childhood. Our presumption might be that Barnsbury, along with Telegraph Hill and, perhaps, Battersea, will be particularly significant in this respect. There are a number of primary schools in the area but no single one that *serves* the area – although probably Thornhill is the most central and important. It would seem that although some are favoured by the local middle-class residents a number are shunned – there is a lot of to-ing and fro-ing at the beginning and end of the school day. There are, however, relatively few community venues other than restaurants, bars and pubs, which are increasingly geared to private consumption by those with the necessary credit cards and have thus become a powerful symbol of social exclusion.

Punching the postcode into www.upyourstreet.co.uk and going to the ACORN[1] pages largely confirms these observations *as far as the middle class is concerned*. ACORN puts Barnsbury in Type 21, 'prosperous enclaves, highly qualified executives', which it goes on to describe in the following terms:

Outside Inner London, and to a much less extent Outer London, this ACORN Type is rarely found outside university towns such as Oxford and Cambridge, and high status provincial centres such as Edinburgh, Brighton, Cheltenham and Tunbridge Wells. These are very affluent neighbourhoods containing well-educated, mobile, younger professionals living in flats. (http://www.upyourstreet.co.uk/inf/msc/det/index.php3? location1=N1+1EB 17/4/02)

This undoubtedly underplays the contemporary affluence of some of the inhabitants that we have observed ('conspicuous thrift' notwithstanding) who, whilst possessing the 'cultural capital' of those living in some of the above mentioned cities and towns, also have [very high] incomes that the academics of Oxford and Cambridge could only dream of. It also ignores the many deprived people who make up the area's majority population. The profile points to high numbers of graduates (four times the national average) and professionals (twice the national average). It further suggests that these people take care of themselves both in terms of what they eat (a high propensity to vegetarianism) and by taking exercise. Car ownership is below average, but the tendency of those with cars to buy new and expensive cars is above average. Unsurprisingly perhaps, they buy CDs and hardback books in much greater than average numbers and the proportion earning over £40,000 a year is more than double the average and they are well provided-for with pensions. 'By far the most popular daily paper is the *Guardian*' with five times more than normal '*never* watching independent television'. They take longer holidays in 'far flung places' and tend to eat and drink out but shun traditional British food. Playing sport and visiting galleries, theatre and the cinema are 'all also enormously popular' and by a long margin they are gin drinkers. It is only necessary to spend a short time in Islington to confirm that this judgement is likely to be accurate for the most part – we are however less than convinced that you would find 'gin alley' here, much more likely a crisp chardonnay.

Telegraph Hill

Telegraph Hill is an enclave surrounded on two sides by extensive council housing, on two others by large areas of more differentiated, mixed housing. It has a readily identifiable central core made up by four main streets. These slope up from New Cross Road to Telegraph Hill Park. These four main streets, and the smaller ones that cross-cut them, are of substantial, and by now mostly renovated, Victorian stock. The central area has a quiet, leafy and overwhelmingly calm aspect, with very little in the way of pubs, shops, and so forth. There is one primary school in the central Telegraph Hill area – Edmund Waller – which is the area's 'school of choice'. It has a strong middle-class atmosphere and is an important institution of the local public sphere. The voice of local parents in the running of the school is strong, and a high proportion of the children go on to 'Askes'. Child-centred networks appear, in general, to be very strong in the area, and represent perhaps the

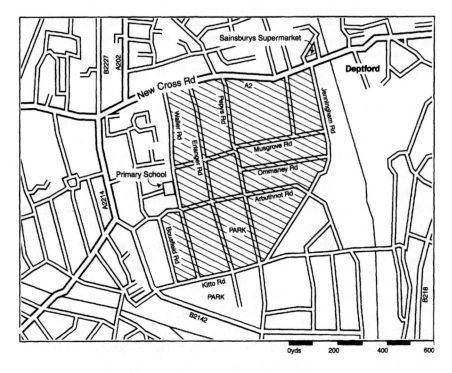

Figure 4.3 Telegraph Hill study area

most important means by which adults make and maintain connections. Haber-dasher's Askes School, which is divided between a girls' and boys' section, has City Technology College status with a very strong reputation. Children travel to the school from all over south-east London, although children from local homes are strongly represented – but not as strongly as many parents would like, which, as we will see, is an important issue locally.

Very close by, a five minute walk away is Somerville Adventure Playground, one of the busiest and most popular in London, which is nevertheless barely used by middle-class children. Its constituency is drawn from the surrounding low-density council estates. The one pub in the area, *Kelly's*, is barely used at all by middle-class Telegraph 'Hillers'.

Telegraph Hill Park hosts at least some degree (although it is difficult to quantify how much) of interaction between the area's different class groups. The Under Five's Club situated there appears to be used by all groups. Down the hill, on the other side of the New Cross Road, is a large Sainsbury's, well-used by local people of the middle-class Telegraph Hill, working-class and Goldsmiths-student varieties. Goldsmiths College, part of London University, is a five-to-ten minute walk from the central Telegraph Hill area in New Cross towards Deptford. There is only a marginal middle-class presence on the rather less select shopping parade in New Cross Gate, just at the bottom of Pepys Road.

At the top of the hill are the church and a community centre, which is strongly associated with the Telegraph Hill Association, an overwhelmingly middle-class initiative that holds its own annual arts festival. The Association is an expression of the very active organizational activity through which Telegraph Hillers define and maintain their sense of community. The Association has, for example, recently held open meetings with Lewisham council and London Transport on the future of the East London Line. The term 'Telegraph Hiller' is probably not one with which local working-class people would readily identify.

ACORN allocates Telegraph Hill to 'Type 24'; these areas are described as 'partially gentrified multi-ethnic areas' and are found 'almost exclusively in inner London. These highly cosmopolitan neighbourhoods contain a mix of rich and poor and people from different ethnic backgrounds living side by side . . .' (http://www.upyourstreet.co.uk/inf/msc/det/?location1=SE14+5LX 17/4/02).

What is striking about these areas is the under-representation (by 40 per cent) of people of retirement age; single and large households are over-represented and those in between under-represented. This probably fits Telegraph Hill where there are a lot of students from Goldsmiths either in bed sits or renting out houses. We are further told that those with academic qualifications, particularly degrees, are over-represented as are those in higher status occupations including professionals. The *Independent* and the *Guardian*, on the one hand, and the *Mirror* and the *Sun*, on the other, are the papers of choice, which is indicative of social differences within the area. Converted flats make up a large proportion of homes – twelve times the national average. Whilst car ownership is low – 56 per cent of adults having no car – there are more than five times the national average owning a car costing more than £20,000. Income is polarised with greater than average numbers in the under £5,000 and over £40,000 bands. Whilst they have a tendency to go to 'far flung' destinations for holidays, residents are also four times more likely than normal to have a holiday home. They are twice as likely as average to be vegetarians. They are no more likely than average to go out to eat or drink but are 50 per cent more likely than normal to spend time at home drinking wine, which is 'by far' the most popular drink ahead of both beer and gin. Finally, they are 'not particularly sporty' but culture is popular – visiting cinema, theatre and art galleries 'more than average'.

Brixton

Brixton is a busier and far more culturally diverse area than Telegraph Hill. Long thought of as the centre of Britain's Afro-Caribbean community, it is now more socially and culturally heterogeneous in terms of ethnicity and social class than it was even at the beginning of the 1990s. The boom in middle-class settlement in the area at the turn of the century was preceded by previous waves that, however, failed to gain the momentum and solidity of contemporary processes of gentrification. The most significant of these were in the early and late 1980s. In the first period, following the civil disturbances of 1981 (Scarman 1982), property prices were low enough to attract a core of adventurous 'pioneer' middle-class incomers. The second, originating in the housing boom of the late 1980s, was caught in the housing slump of the early 1990s. It has picked up since, however, accelerating dramatically since 1995. Brixton's more recent status as an internationally renowned, cosmopolitan lifestyle centre – with an expanding commercial infrastructure of bars, clubs and restaurants – is clearly implicated in the more recent gentrification of the area, with many incomers attracted to its vibrancy and fashionable prestige. There is also evidence that the growing desirability, respectability and housing-market competitiveness of Brixton is attracting an 'overspill' of middle-class incomers priced-out of more solidly gentrified surrounding areas such as Clapham and Balham.

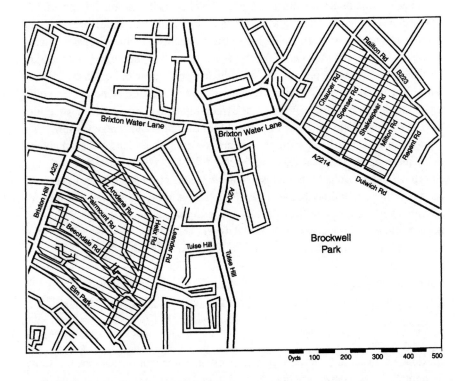

Figure 4.4 Brixton study areas

There are two residential areas involved here in our study – Tulse Hill to the west, Herne Hill to the east. Each abuts onto Brockwell Park. The latter, however, is not a part of Herne Hill 'proper', but an area close to central Brixton re-christened by estate agents in recent years as 'Poet's Corner'. This small network of streets (Milton, Spenser, Shakespeare and so forth) has now been designated a conservation area, and contains a range of highly desirable and architecturally interesting properties. The area as a whole runs parallel to Railton Road, Brixton's notorious 'front line' of the 1970s and 1980s. The process of gentrification here makes this, perhaps, the most dramatic in all our areas. Streets adjacent to one of Britain's best-known symbols of urban disrepair and revolt have been settled and largely transformed over the last decade by comparatively high-income professionals reclaiming its increasingly 'sought-after' properties. Tulse Hill, its counterpart on the other side of Brockwell Park, is a larger area containing mostly terraced streets of housing, less spectacular but solid, desirable and more easily accessed form the centre of Brixton. It is more socially mixed than Poet's Corner but, in its interior, is comparatively calm and ordered. Both areas therefore offer residents dense, but relatively peaceful, environments close by one of Britain's most vibrant and volatile inner urban areas.

Unlike Telegraph Hill, and perhaps more like Barnsbury, there are few public institutions that are the focus of the middle-class communities. There is no single 'school of choice' for example. By far the best performing school – Sudbourne's – is on the west side of Brixton Hill and its catchment area is restricted to the few surrounding streets. Brockwell Park is an important resource for the area but it is not in any way as intimate as the park in Telegraph Hill nor is there a significant local amenity association. Rather Brixton is known and valued for its hedonist infrastructure – the clubs are well-known not just across London but also Europe, for instance the best known (The Fridge) has a currency converter on its Web site. Its cinema (The Ritzy) is one of the best known 'independents' in London. The attraction of Brixton lies its public persona, which is rooted in a form of funky multiculturalism. It is this that is leading to the increasing use of the term 'sought after street' in the estate agents' windows. The area west of Brixton Hill along Acre Lane is also gentrifying rapidly (this includes the Sudbourne's catchment area) but here the impression is that this is more of a 'spillover' effect from Wandsworth rather than for its innate qualities.

Tulse Hill, like Telegraph Hill, is a 'Type 24 area – partially gentrified multi-ethnic' whereas Herne Hill is a 'Type 20 area – gentrified multi-ethnic' like Battersea our next and more upmarket area. This probably describes the differences between the two areas quite accurately; Poets' Corner is better established and rather more affluent, whereas the streets in Tulse Hill are more mixed and the gentrifiers more marginal. The differences between the two are somewhat arcane but the proportion of professionals in Type 20 areas is higher (70 per cent above average) with three times the national average of degrees. The two types share a lack of people over 65 but Type 20 areas are less likely to have young people than Type 24 which again probably describes accurately the difference between the two areas in Brixton. These are solid *Guardian* reading areas, however *The Times* and the *Independent* are also favoured. Whilst the proportion earning over £40,000 is greater they appear to be even more 'conspicuously thrifty' with a tendency to have cars that are over five years old and to buy less expensive and smaller cars. However they are into keeping fit with 51 per cent more than average buying keep-fit equipment. They are also more likely to play sport and to go out to eat and drink than Type 24 areas and are equally likely to go out for cultural purposes. When they do drink at home it is gin which is twice as popular as average (http://www.upyourstreet.co.uk/inf/msc/det/?location1=E14+3EN_17/4/02)!

'Between the Commons' Battersea

'Between the commons' in Battersea in the London Borough of Wandsworth, or less reverently 'Nappy Valley', is a well-defined, quiet, attractive and well-ordered area of *very* desirable housing. The locality abounds with both modest and rather grand terraced and semi-detached Victoriana with a few period cottages and other 'nuggets' (to use the estate agents' hyperbole) scattered around. There are also a

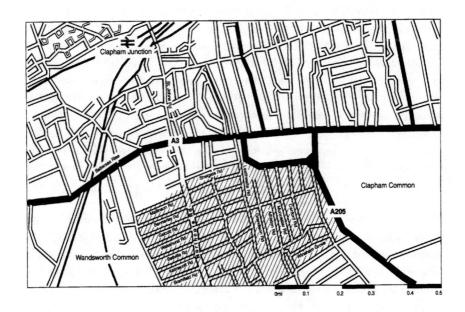

Figure 4.5 'Between the commons' Battersea study area

few tastefully upmarket new-build developments. Many of the locals appear to conform to Lyons' (1996) portrayal of them – this is clearly corporate/City country. There is, without doubt, some 'fairly serious money' around; City suits and cut-glass accents are evident even in the daytime. The area's focus is Northcote Road, which runs like a river along the valley bottom into which the residential streets decant their inhabitants like mountain streams to consume its pleasures. Battersea was one of London's best-established working-class areas between the wars; its borough council was one of only three to give support to George Lansbury when he was imprisoned in Brixton gaol for refusing to cut wages and benefits (Branson 1979). More recently it was epitomized as the home to 'cheeky chappy' South London working class in the book and film *Up the Junction*. It became a multi-ethnic area in the 1960s and 1970s with a large African Caribbean population. Some of the longer established residents remember when most of Northcote Road was given over to a daily street market with many of the stalls selling West Indian fruit and vegetable produce. Having been down to one or two stalls at weekends, it is now ironically on the up again as the local middle-class seeks out authenticity in its eating and cooking.

Battersea's gentrification began in the 1970s – probably to some extent as a spill-over from the traditionally upper middle-class settlements of Chelsea and Fulham (Munt 1987; Lyons 1996). It was aided and abetted, uniquely in London, by the local authority, which in the 1980s became an iconic Thatcherite borough. Wandsworth used its powers, particularly in planning, to facilitate the development of the infrastructure for gentrification – ranging from street enhancements to the building of new private schools. It took full advantage of changes to the legislation affecting housing and education to encourage market solutions. As a consequence, Wandsworth not only became a rapidly gentrifying area but this spread extensively across much of the borough – although, as the ACORN data for Type 20 areas (the same classification as for Poets' Corner) suggest, it remains a socially and ethnically mixed area. Like Barnsbury, yet more so, the disadvantaged 'other' remains largely invisible. Its good communications, from London's busiest over ground station at Clapham Junction and the underground from Clapham Common and Clapham North stations, ensures ten minute access to London's financial centre in the City and its West End commercial and governmental centre via Waterloo and Victoria stations. These good communications work in both directions: not only do they enable residents to get to work easily but they also allow others to come and sample the restaurants and bars of Northcote Road for an evening out.

Northcote Road has been transformed; almost all of the originals shops associated with a traditional London shopping street have now closed – often displaying sad notices such as in the one in the last 'greasy spoon' café whose lease expired in 1999 because its owners simply could not afford to renew it. It has now joined the ranks of the themed bars (*Slug and Lettuce*; *All Bar One* and so on), the mushrooming restaurants, the estate agents and the kitchen and bathroom shops. The area is constantly busy with women and children during the day (a mixture of mothers and nannies one suspects) pushing elaborate buggies or loading them in and out of 4x4s[2] (which are favoured here over the people carriers of Barnsbury or Telegraph Hill) or careering around on the school run. In the early evening there are people stopping off on the way from work for a quick one and later the restaurants are full. On a summer evening much of this activity spills outside and the atmosphere feels friendly, safe and continental – as it is designed to. No wonder this is a favoured area. What is surprising is that ACORN still persists in categorizing this as a gentrified multi-ethnic area alongside Poets Corner – it seems, and our data later confirm, that they could hardly be more different. Leaving aside attitudes and attributes, the on-street affluence and display is very different and there is little evidence here of conspicuous thrift. This is the nearest we have in gentrified London to Neil Smith's revanchist city being 're-taken' by the forces of affluence from the poor and dispossessed (Smith 1996).

London Fields

This is a mixed, 'patchwork' area with something of a 'frontline' atmosphere. There is a good deal of eminently gentrifiable property around, much of it already worked on and improved.[3] The houses are modest in size and are often described as 'artisans cottages' – usually two floors (as opposed to the usual North London three-floor terrace) with an 'L-shape' design out the back. Much of the housing is, however, very seedy and awaiting attention and, even from a fairly casual walkabout, it is clear that many houses are still privately rented. On some streets highly desirable period houses are interspersed with very shabby council estates. Parts of the area therefore have an appearance of random social promiscuity in terms of the demographic mix, with many gentrifiers' houses 'un-enclosed' in either spatial or social senses. This may or may not be engendering some interesting 'social cohesion' characteristics. There are some broad parallels with Brixton here – in particular the close proximity of gentrified and seedy houses of similar ilk. Parking seems a nightmare but the cars are modest with relatively few new or expensive models – in fact, as gentrification proceeds, it is possible that the density of cars might decrease as multiple occupation gives way to single-family dwellings with only one car per household.

The relatively well-defined and bordered area adjacent to London Fields – between Graham and Queensbridge Roads – forms the basis of the research area. Perhaps three broad constituencies have a noticeable presence here: relatively solid bourgeois gentrifiers; multi-ethnic working class; and 'alternative Hackney' types. On the other side of the railway tracks, but accessible from London Fields, there

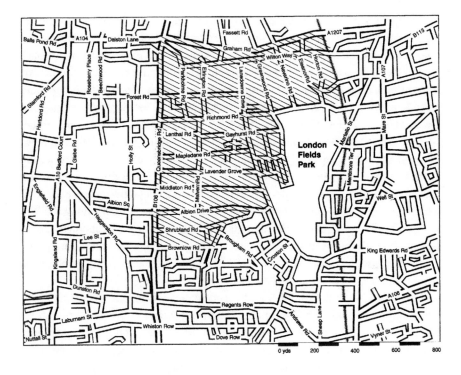

Figure 4.6 London Fields study area

are some purpose-built 'artists' studio spaces – which would seem to indicate the presence of a significant population of people interested in such premises. The linkages between the early stages of gentrification and artists and alternative types is well documented (Rose 1984; Zukin 1988).

The area has some physical similarities to Telegraph Hill, notably the clear grid plan layout of the streets and the proximity to a local, relatively small park. It also does not have a gentrified consumption infrastructure, although there are a few 'local' shops and the beginnings of a more alternative one driven by the development of an arts economy. However these are very nascent and the area contrasts with Telegraph Hill in the lack of hegemony that the middle classes have achieved. It is still a mixed social area and this can be seen on the streets and in the park where no one group dominates. Unlike Telegraph Hill, the impression is left that the middle classes feel ambiguous about establishing themselves over 'the locals'; there is a high degree of ambiguity, which might explain why it has apparently retained a 'pioneer' ambience for so long. This is clear in London Fields (the park) which is clearly not middle-class territory, in stark contrast to Telegraph Hill Park. Many people have moved up and on – to Islington or elsewhere in Hackney whilst others have stayed precisely because they value this uncertainty. It shares this 'alternative', and indeed oppositional, culture with Brixton but without the commercial and hedonistic infrastructure – although the development of one built around the 'arts' is a possibility for the future. The attractiveness of Brixton, apart from its relatively cheap housing, lies – as we have seen – in its multiculturalism and ethnic diversity, whereas in London Fields, which is also highly multicultural, the attraction appears to lie more in Hackney's image as a *working-class* borough with a (largely illusory) tradition of political radicalism.[4] We will return to these images later in the chapter but they are core to our argument about what makes the areas attractive to incomers. What Brixton and London Fields do share, however, is that neither offers a satisfactory solution to schooling, not only at secondary level which is a universal inner London problem, but also at primary level. Unlike Telegraph Hill there is no single school that all the middle-class supports nor, as in Barnsbury or Battersea, is there a choice to be made from a number of improving schools or readily accessible private schools. Unlike Brixton, many respondents are sending their children to private secondary schools.

This ambiguity in London Fields is reflected when we consult ACORN which allocates it to 'Type 38: multi-ethnic areas, white collar workers' (http://www.upyourstreet.co.uk/inf/msc/det/?location1=E8+3LL 17/4/02). This probably indicates that we are dealing here not only with the usual socially mixed gentrified area but one in which the middle classes are less well paid and of a lower economic and social status. The ACORN report describes these areas as being concentrated in the under 45 age range, with a disproportionate number of ethnic minority people – making up a third of the population. There are high numbers of single person households. They are described as being generally unhappy with their standard of living and much more likely than average to be vegetarian, although the two are not linked. One of their more likely purchases is ski clothing, which is perhaps indicative of an 'aspirational' middle-class population. There is an income peak of £30,000–40,000 per year which is interesting in that in most of our other areas this peak occurs at over £40,000. In terms of newspaper readership there is the now-familiar split between the *Independent* and the *Guardian*, on the one hand, and the *Mirror* and the *Sun*, on the other – interestingly however, it is the *Independent* that is the most popular (2.3 times the average compared to the *Guardian's* 60 per cent). The population diversity is indicated by holiday behaviour – overall the proportion taking holidays is 13 per cent less than average but those who do, like the other areas we have described, tend to go further for longer and often in the winter. Like Telegraph Hill, they are less likely to eat out in the evenings or go out for a drink but they are heavily into sport and cinema and art galleries (not theatre like our other areas). They tend to be beer drinkers but also go for vermouth, port and gin.

Docklands

'Docklands' refers to the area of the old London Docks that was developed by the London Docklands Development Corporation (LDDC) in the 1980s and 1990s (Brownill 1990; Foster 1999). The gentrification of Docklands can be characterized as having been undertaken by capital as opposed to collective social action (Warde 1991). We focused our research on three sub areas (The Isle of Dogs, Surrey Quays and Britannia Village) in each of the three boroughs that constitute Docklands – Newham, Southwark and Tower Hamlets. We interviewed smaller samples in each, which made up a cluster of a similar size to the areas already described. We expected Docklands to be different: almost by definition, these were people buying into a marketed idea of inner-city living compared to making their own neighbourhoods. This became apparent when we began to research the areas, partly because they were so new and incomplete. However, what was even clearer was the interactions between Docklands' three worlds – those of the old working class, the Bangladeshis rehoused from the north of Tower Hamlets and the new

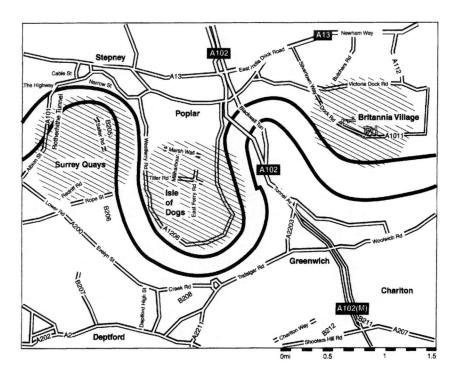

Figure 4.7 Docklands showing Isle of Dogs, Surrey Quays and Britannia Village

middle class – were largely mediated (often violently) through 'race' (Cohen 1996; Eade and Mele 1998; Foster 1999). As we have seen, all the other areas of collective social action were apparently constructed around their whiteness but in ways that were more managed and mediated. In Docklands, the old East London working class and the new economy were juxtaposed physically and socially in ways we simply did not see elsewhere. The juxtaposition between the old white working class and the Bangladeshis was even sharper and had a small but noticeable contagion effect – nowhere else did we ever encounter *explicit* levels of antagonism amongst the new middle class. It was also only in Docklands that we got the physical polarization of 'gated communities' in which the new rich locked themselves in and 'the other' out. In reality, the two white groups were largely invisible to each other: the new middle class appear in the morning, hurrying to work, and come back in the evening although this was usually staggered over many hours – during the middle of the day they were all but non-existent. We now briefly describe the three fieldwork areas.

Britannia Village is at the western end of the Royal Docks complex. This is a new build development with an inner-urban, 'lifestyle' atmosphere. Bounded on one side by the Royal Victoria Dock (giving, apparently, good sailing and windsurfing) this is a discrete, indeed hermetic, development being marketed by Wimpey as a centrally located urban village – although it has nothing by the way of internal infrastructure. There is, however, a community centre (with doctor), and a new primary school has recently been opened. Residents are directed, by the site brochure, towards Canary Wharf and the Isle of Dogs in general for their consumer needs. To get a newspaper or pint of milk necessitates a car journey to the nearest petrol station although the recent opening of the ExCel centre has provided new possibilities for convenience shopping.

Dwellings, which are for the most part of the standard riverside-condo variety with a smaller number of 'town houses' alongside, started at a hundred thousand pounds (in 1998), making them more affordable than those in better-established and more central riverside developments. We knew, from previous work, that their buyers are young urban professionals with little interest in 'gardens and things like that' (Butler and Rix 2000: 79); the emphasis in the marketing brochures is very much on local water sports and easy access to the metropolitan core. The surrounding visual landscape would, in a sense, fit this typology; a mix of well-preserved dockland icons like cranes and, a little more distant, the grittier post-industrial vista of shattered-looking warehouses and factories (used as backdrop for the film *Full Metal Jacket*) – many subsequently developed with a studied regard for their historical role (such as Peru Quay). In terms of social cohesion, there seems to be little in the way of a 'local' population in the immediate vicinity to interact *with*; the 'Village' is, in any case, designed to be exclusive – spatially and socially. The development's planning consent required that part of the site was given over to social housing, which was developed by the Peabody Trust behind a large separating wall – although no developer would admit to calling it that.[5]

Britannia Village is the least developed of the Docklands areas – the eastern end being the site of City Airport, a new campus for the University of East London and the new ExCel Exhibition Centre. This relatively unformed nature reflects in the ACORN profile 'type 53: multi ethnic estates: severe unemployment, lone parents' which would suggest an ungentrified area housing Newham's poor and displaced. It does note that such areas 'also include, however, small pockets of much more affluent residents'. This comes through in the analysis when it observes that, although the readership of *The Times* is over four times higher than average, 'by far the most popular Sunday newspaper is the *News of the World*, indicating perhaps [that] the more affluent residents of these inner city neighbourhoods are only present during the week'. This points to one of the characteristics of Docklands which is that it is an area in which many residents have their city pied à terre with all of its connotations for (lack of) commitment, time and obligation to the area and the neighbourhood. ACORN notes the generally low incomes but with 'a peak in the income profile in the £40,000+ band' and, despite overall low car ownership, 'the above average proportions of both large and expensive cars'. Consumption is driven by the large deprived populations (few holidays, lager drinking, heavy smoking and convenience foods) however this might also reflect a rather different kind of middle-class resident who is not only partially resident but who pays less attention to issues of taste and distinction, more of Savage's mainstream undistinctives as opposed to ascetics. Sixty per cent do not have a holiday in these neighbourhoods. (http://www.upyourstreet.co.uk/inf/msc/det/?location1=E8+3LL 17/4/02)

Isle of Dogs. The southern part of the island (which, as can be seen from Figure 4.7, is not really an island at all) is a hive of residential building activity, as what must be the last of the viable waterfront spaces are developed. The new developments are taking their place alongside the existing sweep of top-of-the-range riverside condominiums, some of them on a very large scale. The emphasis, in contrast to Britannia Village, appears to be more on these than smaller scale urban 'villages'/townhouses and so forth – but this could be an impression created by the sheer size of some of the former. One makes the journey from such places to down-at-heel council estates and generalized shabbiness very quickly here. This gives an appearance of a patchwork of socially distinct and physically juxtaposed localities, some with hard-looking 'edges'. Indeed, some of the more 'select' locales seem not to be quite as exclusionary as they might like in socio-spatial terms. There is probably a general demarcation line, represented by Manchester and West Ferry Roads – these follow the 'coastline' around the island and the gentrified/developed parts are overwhelmingly on the narrow strip between these and the river. The central part of the island, between the Greenwich-facing desirable areas and Canary Wharf to the north, appears largely untouched by the developers.

The ACORN classification of the Isle of Dogs is 'Type 20 – Gentrified Multi Ethnic areas', which puts it into the same category as *Between the Commons* and *Herne Hill*. This is probably testament to the extent to which the Isle of Dogs has become established as a middle-class area since the late 1980s. It bears similarities to Between the Commons in the sense of people working in the City but probably at a very different stage in the life cycle – singles, couples with no children, empty nesters and those with a main home in the country treating it as a 'pied à terre' near to the City (Crilley, Bryce et al. 1991; Hall and Ogden 1992). What comes across, whichever way it is looked at, are issues of inequality and polarization, old and new. This is more sharp edged here than in Battersea where it is better hidden. The well-off in both areas are both comfortable and very comfortable with it, but in the Isle of Dogs little is done to hide the dispossessed.

Surrey Quays. This is Docklands 'south of the river' (Thames) which has changed almost out of recognition since 1980. It has been comprehensively redeveloped and re-branded and is a real anomaly in the context of the broader area – perhaps the last extensive swathe of an entrenched white working-class in London (Robson 2000). The Bermondsey/Rotherhithe area has always been *very* serious, the nodal point of 'traditional' south-east London. Although it is considerably more heterogeneous than it was, Surrey Docks south of the tube station still hosts huge tracts of run-down council estates. It is north of this old heartland that gentrification has taken place, and this gives the area in general the appearance of being fairly neatly divided into two halves – although it is a little more complex than this.

Along Salter and Redriff roads, on the archipelago-like circuit that mirrors the Isle of Dogs, is what we take to be the most extensive dockland development south of the river. There has been an enormous amount of prestige building along the riverfront here, with new developments still coming onto the market. Along the river itself, the majority of the buildings are of the condominium variety, some offering luxury apartments at what seemed extraordinary prices. On the other side of the strip of road which follows the 'coastline', there are a number of Wimpey/ Barratt/Fairview 'village-style' developments, offering more modestly priced dwellings. The area as a whole is now very green, quiet and calm – and retains a characteristically 'dockland' end-of-the-world atmosphere.

A little further north into the peninsula something very interesting begins to happen; the condos become more interspersed with cleaned-up and (at least visually) reclaimed council estates, some of which are now in the hands of housing associations. Here, right on the river, is an extraordinarily dense and socially promiscuous patchwork of new and old housing and people. The becalmed and isolated atmosphere that permeates the area makes it somewhat difficult to 'read', giving rise we assume to some interesting social dynamics, as far as *cohesion* (or its absence) is concerned.

The key site of public interaction is the turn-of-the-decade Surrey Quays shopping complex, on the border, as it were, between the northern and southern parts of the area. In the afternoon the central interior area is, more or less, (performatively) 'controlled' by adolescents truanting from school, with the non-locals moving somewhat gingerly around them. No other place in south London exhibits so stark a mix of locals and in-comers – stuck together in an out-of-the-way and hardly cosmopolitan area. Its great virtue for the latter, one imagines, is its very close proximity to the City. This perhaps reflects in its ACORN classification which, like London Fields, is a 'Type 38: multi ethnic areas: white collar workers' – intriguingly it probably couldn't be more different in terms of attitudes but the mix of old and new is equally juxtaposed. Our impression is that the multiculturalism is considerably more hard-edged and reluctant than that of London Fields but that it is extraordinarily promiscuous in terms of its ethnic and class mix in which the newer housing will almost certainly contain the upwardly mobile white new working and middle classes.

Thinking about the Social Typologies and Building the Habituses

In this section we set out our notion of the metropolitan habitus in London and relate that to the four fields we have identified as the focus of our investigation: consumption, education, employment and housing. We begin by making some general remarks about the metropolitan habitus and its constituent fields and then move on to an examination of how each of these fields relates to our fieldwork areas. We examine the different social typology of each field in each area by discussing the different combination of capital which respondents are able to draw on and how they pursue different strategies – this is particularly important in the case of education. In all cases, the nature of the habitus is constructed in terms of the objective capabilities of individuals and their prior socialisation. It is this which we believe goes to constitute the different habitus(es) that make up the metropolitan habitus – in other words each area, to some extent, has a distinctive habitus (or mini-habitus)[6] but so does the metropolis as a whole as far as the middle class is concerned.

First, as Bourdieu reminds us, we need to construct a *social typology* or map of the objective structure of positions which make up the field and to analyse the relationships between them in the competition for the field's specific form of capital.

Mapping the Social Typologies

Taking each of our fields, we argue that they are each divided between metro-politan (in effect centred – in all senses of the word – on the City and the West End), sub-regional and local components. In everyday language these would be referred to as 'markets'. Clearly the division is not the same between them although, in the case of the employment (or labour) and, to a slightly lesser extent, housing markets, these are defined by London's metropolitan status. In other words, London's emergence as a key node in a globalized services-driven economy has meant that not only does it concentrate high level functions at a national but also at a regional (European) and global level (Sassen 1991; Fainstein, Gordon et al. 1992; Buck, Gordon et al. 2002).

This has had the effect of detaching London's labour and housing markets from the rest of the UK and, to some extent, from the rest of the metropolis – they are both focused on the centre. This is also partly true in terms of consumption although we will argue that one effect of this has been to refocus some at least of this away from the 'West End' to satellite consumption centres – of which two (Battersea and Islington's Upper Street) are centred on areas in which we conducted our research. In relation to education, whilst London remains the focus of high level academic research and development and at least some of the most prestigious undergraduate and postgraduate teaching programmes, this does not generally apply to compulsory and immediate post compulsory education. It might even be argued that there is an inverse gradient and the quality increases with the distance from the centre, although in fact it is more complicated than this. The employment field, therefore, is driven almost entirely by London's metropolitan status and is focused on the metropolitan centre, whereas the housing market is dominated by similar considerations at a meta level but is mediated by local factors such as price. Consumption is more equally divided between the metropolitan considerations (such as museums, theatres, restaurants and specialist shops), sub-regional (entertainment, shopping and eating) and local (shopping and eating and in some instances entertainment). In education, sub regional and local factors dominate. These are summarized schematically in Figure 4.8.

Education

The field of education has most spatial autonomy and is least constrained by 'global' factors and most by local factors. This can largely be explained in terms of the structural changes that inner London experienced in the post-war period and the associated changes in educational policy driven by the former Inner London Education Authority (ILEA) with a strong commitment to equality of opportunity

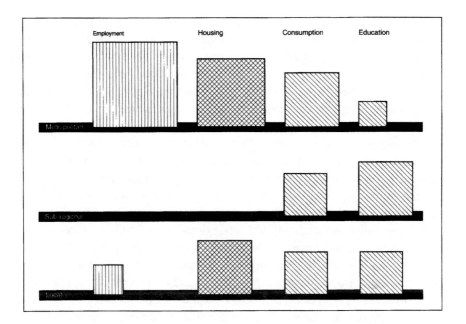

Figure 4.8 Distribution of fields across the metropolitan markets

and provision. In effect, inner London schools became increasingly working class. Subsequently, with the flight of much of the white working class from inner London during the 1970s and 1980s these schools lost many of their traditionally upwardly mobile members. Inner London schools became increasingly multiracial and began to reflect the deprived and disorganized nature of the communities they served. We discuss the issue of education in detail in Chapter 7 but two points need to be established here.

Firstly, that education performance at primary and particularly secondary level in London, and in particular inner London, is amongst the worst in the country, which is a massive disincentive to middle-class parents to invest their time and cultural capital in supporting their children in such poorly performing schools. It is not just the poor educational outcomes in terms of credentials that worries such parents but also the 'expressive order' of the schools, where there is perceived to be an unsuitable climate to enable learning and social reproduction in the widest sense. The traditional sense of a middle-class hegemony over the education system is regarded as having been lost and there is no longer any guarantee that the school will speak in the same 'extended code' in which middle-class parents talk to their children (Bernstein 1975).

Secondly, during this period 'parental choice' has become enshrined as an increasingly formal principle in education. To a greater or lesser extent middle-class parents have always been 'choosers': not only for example between private and state education but also about living in the vicinity of 'good' schools. This became increasingly important after the abolition of selective 'grammar' schools and the move towards comprehensive education – a process more fully carried out in London than elsewhere. The 1988 Education Act formalized the principle of parental choice and increased the menu of schools available – particularly at secondary level. The effect of this was to put a premium on information and the presentational skills that could seek out and gain access to the 'best' schools, which were usually defined in terms of a sub-regional area and sometimes at a London wide level. This period has coincided with London's gentrification, which has increasingly been focused on those working class boroughs which have experienced displacement of their skilled working classes and witnessed high levels of social exclusion (Atkinson 2001). There has, however, been significant variation in these education markets even on a sub regional level. The impacts on locally gentrified areas in turn have been influenced by differences in the middle-class habituses in those areas (for example: predilection for, and antipathy towards, private education) as well as the actual quality of provision. Overall this has led to quite different strategies to maximize benefits of social reproduction. In Table 4.1 we outline the various education markets available in our different fieldwork areas

We are able to identify three major strategies that are pursued in the field of education which appear to be related to the habitus of the individual areas and the deployment of resources available to those living there.

Firstly, there is the deployment of economic capital through the purchase of private education; this strategy appears to be used in four areas with different degrees of enthusiasm – Battersea, Barnsbury, London Fields and Telegraph Hill.

Table 4.1 Educational fields and fieldwork areas

Area	Local	Sub-regional	Metropolitan
Barnsbury	None	Strong private network	State and private
Battersea	Strong private and state selective	n/a	n/a
Brixton	None	Under-developed state network	n/a
Telegraph Hill	Local state selective	Strong private and state selective network	n/a
London Fields	None	Under-developed network of state selective	State and private
Docklands	None	None	Private

Note: reference is to the schools regarded as available and not to actual presence of schools.

In the former, which probably has the 'best' locally available circuit of state education of all our areas, this is a function of the habitus and a belief in the market. There is almost a sense of obligation to invest economic capital in social reproduction to acquire the necessary cultural capital to enable the next generation to realize this in appropriate employment markets. In Barnsbury, London Fields and Telegraph Hill the situation is more complex and constrained by the availability of appropriate state education together with a greater commitment to non-private modes of reproduction. In Barnsbury the perception however is that there are no appropriate secondary state schools and this either necessitates accessing highly selective state schools on a metropolitan basis (Latimer Upper School in Enfield, The Oratory in West London and somewhat nearer the Camden School for Girls) or 'going private'. The sought-after private schools are also highly selective and someway distant (Channing or Highgate for example), which often means that – unlike Battersea – parents send their children to the private preparatory schools that feed these schools and prepare them for the Common Entrance examination. In Telegraph Hill private education is more of a 'fall-back position' if they are unable to access the local and sub-regional circuits of selective state schools. There are a number of private schools in the sub regional area and this is a strategy pursued, albeit reluctantly, by many parents. London Fields, like Barnsbury, is entirely reliant on a metropolitan circuit of education. The City of London School for Girls (at the Barbican) is the only private school that could be remotely classified as nearby.

The second strategy is to deploy the cultural capital that professional middle-class households possess (the best single indicator of gentrification being the possession of a university degree and usually a higher degree and/or professional qualification). Instilling cultural capital into the children is believed to lead to successful children; this is often done through the acquisition of symbolic capital (such as visits to museums) which leads to 'on-side' children who are motivated and capable of successfully applying to selective state secondary schools. These strategies are often mapped out for individual children and are not exclusively oriented towards performance but the perceived normative mapping of the individual child (Ball, Bowe et al. 1995; Reay and Ball 1998). This strategy is adopted in all areas although this is less the case in Battersea than elsewhere – partly because of a belief in private provision, partly because of the relative feast of choice and partly because, as a group, they appear less inclined to the acquisition and deployment of symbolic capital. Some respondents in Brixton and London Fields felt ambivalent about using this approach partly because their levels of cultural and symbolic capital were lower than elsewhere but also because political principles about privileged access to social reproduction infused the local middle-class habitus. Often this was resolved by considering a move from London to areas where the educational divide was less sharp.

The third approach, which was compatible with both of the others, was to transform the performance and ambience of a primary school(s) in the locality. This was achieved through the successful deployment of cultural and social capital in Telegraph Hill and in Barnsbury but failed conspicuously in Brixton where the middle-class children remained 'an isolated group'. In Telegraph Hill this was a necessary strategy partly because many parents did not want to send their children to private school and also because many did not have the economic capability. Strong social networks were, in the case of Telegraph Hill, formed around the primary school and over the years transformed its ethos into one of a middle-class school even if their children remained a statistical minority in a school with a socially deprived majority. The local circuit of education traditionally included access to Haberdashers' Aske a long-established secondary school but, following the 1988 Act, this became a City Technology College. As a result it was now required to recruit more widely and across ability bands, which meant that many local middle-class children failed to gain entry. In the last few years, there has been a sustained campaign to build a new Telegraph Hill school that is truly comprehensive and recruits locally. The chair of governors from the local primary is one of the prime movers for this and it is modelled on a similar and successful campaign in neighbouring Southwark. At the time of writing the outcome is unclear even if the strategy behind the campaign of combining social and cultural capital is not. In Islington where less than half the children in its primary schools go on to secondary education in the Borough, the residents in Barnsbury have similarly been influential in transforming the performance and ethos of a number of primary schools – in one of the more successful the head teacher resigned over the conduct of Key Stage Two in 2001 tests where the results were 'withheld'.

These strategies therefore concern the ability to re-create cultural capital on an inter-generational basis in which competition in the 'field' exists to create prestigious and useful credentials. These depend largely on the ability to deploy economic, cultural, social and symbolic capital in different measures.

In private education, economic capital is transformed into cultural capital through the ability to pay fees but also parental input and the ability to impart cultural capital and draw on symbolic capital deriving from distinction and good taste.

Selective state education primarily involves the ability of parents to impart cultural capital. The parental input therefore is of greater importance than in private education but it is also often necessary to back this up through the deployment of lesser amounts of economic capital by purchasing private tuition at strategically important stages. Economic capital may also be important in determining the ability to purchase property in the desired catchment area. In this model cultural capital reproduces itself but, in so doing, draws on economic capital and symbolic capital to give their children the 'edge' at crucially competitive periods.

The non-selective secondary school in inner London has become increasingly rare as a middle-class 'option'. The ability however to colonize primary education by 're-inventing' a school is becoming more familiar. In this situation, social capital is converted into, or used to consolidate, cultural capital; social capital is realized in social networks that enable this to be deployed in ways that enhance it compared with the cultural capital of individual households. This depends on a collective awareness which is partly mediated by lack of economic capital but is also a function of the habitus with its narrative of equality of opportunity and meritocracy. In Figure 4.9 we outline the possible positions in the field of education across the metropolitan middle-class habitus. We relate this to our division of the metropolitan middle class (following Savage, Barlow et al. 1992) into corporate/undistinctives and liberal/ascetics and post-moderns. The model suggests that there will be different proclivities to prioritize particular capital stocks in order to meet the primary goal of social reproduction and the enhancement of their children's cultural capital.

How might this social typology for the field of education relate to social relationships? We believe that this is a key to understanding the logic of the current metropolitan habitus and its spatial dimensions – which appear to be otherwise under-recognized. Figure 4.10 proposes some of the main elements in relation to the field of education in an attempt to map the habituses of the various areas in relation to the key fields and in particular to posit a possible relationship between employment, housing and education.

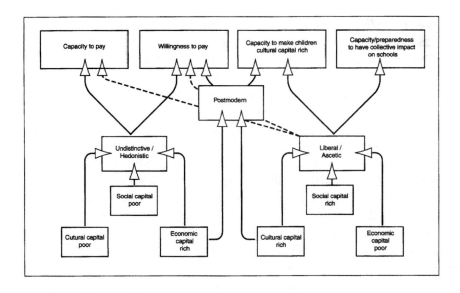

Figure 4.9 Possible positions in the field of education

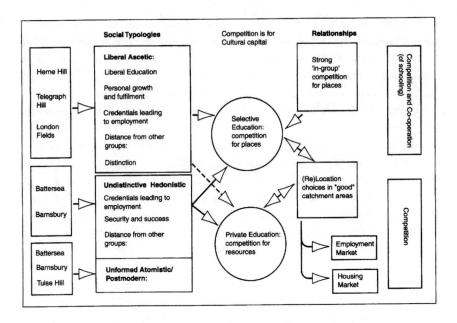

Figure 4.10 Social typology and relationships in education

Housing

As we have previously noted, the metropolitan housing market is tied into London's world city status and, whilst moving in relation to the UK housing market, it is also influenced, at least at the top end and in its core, by other global cities such as New York and Paris. This sector of the housing market is also heavily influenced by the City of London and the financial services industry and particularly the level of annual bonuses; these people do not generally rely on mortgage finance. Moving out from the traditional core of upper class housing we come to the inner London gentrified belt, which is the subject of this book. This is a diverse set of sub-regional and local housing markets that have a complex set of economic relationships to each other and the London, South East and UK housing markets. As we have argued, individuals pursue complex strategies towards these housing markets, which are influenced primarily by their stocks of economic capital but also by decisions about the nature of the area's habitus – or perceived habitus. This is often articulated in terms of the 'attitudes, beliefs and feelings' held by individuals, which, in many cases, are the outcome of their period of compulsory and post-compulsory schooling and primary socialization. For example, we asked people about their house-buying strategy which, it turned out, almost always favoured

Table 4.2 Metropolitan housing field characteristics

Area	Socially Produced	Economically Competitive	Symbolically Desirable
Barnsbury	✓	✓	✓
Between the Commons		✓	✓
Brixton			✓
Docklands		✓	
London Fields	✓		
Telegraph Hill	✓		✓

place over price; in other words people decided roughly where to live and then found a house or flat they could afford.

In the field of housing, the competition is over economic and symbolic capital. The competition is for the most desirable and/or appropriate properties in desired and symbolically meaningful areas. This is accomplished through the deployment of economic capital but areas themselves become desirable through their cultural and social capital 'use values'. We have crudely typified our six areas in Table 4.2.

Housing has been the most valuable means of asset accumulation in the UK over the last half-century and nobody in London loses out in the medium or longer term, but some areas are more likely to be constituted through economic capital than other areas. This applies particularly to Battersea and Barnsbury where not only access to the local housing market but also its norms are governed by the deployment of economic capital; it is this that then buys access to the social networks. We also believe that Docklands, by definition as an outcome of gentrification by capital, is dominated by considerations of economic capital; as we will argue this is deployed in order to avoid the obligations of social capital. Docklands has an element of symbolic desirability but one that would not generally be regarded as distinctive elsewhere in gentrified inner London. Barnsbury, as the table indicates, is the most complex, in that it scores highly on all three dimensions – we argue later that in Barnsbury economic capital is now deployed to access the 'laid down' social capital of previous rounds of gentrification. In other words, what is being purchased is what is perceived as a social-capital-rich social environment; this is not the case in Battersea.

Social capital as a live resource that is actively deployed through contemporary social networks predominates, we would argue, in Telegraph Hill, London Fields and Herne Hill in Brixton but is largely absent in Tulse Hill where once again there is a flight from social obligation and norms in the kinds of ways outlined in classical urban sociology by Wirth (1938) and Simmel (1950). This is associated with the salience of symbolic capital which is highest in Bansbury and Battersea, in a mainstream variety, but is also present in a 'vulgarized' version in many of the riverside Docklands developments and in a counter or transgressive mode in Brixton and to a lesser extent in London Fields. Symbolic capital is also present in Telegraph Hill but in relation to a form of 'in-group prestige'.

Employment

One aspect of employment as a field that has changed considerably in recent years is the relationship between economic and symbolic capital – class and status as Weber would have it. In particular, the private sector has become 'sexy' in a way not previously imaginable, at least to liberal/ascetics; the public/private sector boundary is now considerably more permeable not just at the level of individuals but also because of the influence of neo-liberal economic policy, which has subjected much of the public sector to the market directly or indirectly.[7] This is probably also changing work practices and leading to a convergence in the work culture. Of those working in the private sector, this is almost exclusively in services (as opposed to manufacturing) with a clear bias towards professional or marketing as opposed to managerial or technical 'situses'. Increasingly the job content between the various employment sectors in London has converged around the possession of specialized knowledge. We would expect to find powerful evidence for the intersection of the employment and housing fields but in perhaps surprising ways.

Consumption

We will discuss consumption briefly, not because it is unimportant, but because its status is somewhat different from the others. Consumption in the sense of spending one's money on goods and services can take place in a number of different locations in a major city such as London and, indeed, it is this that is so attractive to many living in gentrified areas – compared to the 'sterile' suburbs in which they were brought up. It is often argued that gentrification is the ultimate expression of

Table 4.3 Absence/presence of cultural infrastructure

Area	Consumption Infrastructure
Barnsbury	Yes
Battersea	Yes
Brixton	Yes – alternative
Docklands	No
London Fields	No – although incipient 'artsy'
Telegraph Hill	No

consumption – taste and distinction to remodel housing from a previous era that has fallen into disrepair and it is this that distinguishes the gentrifying middle-classes from those buying ready-made, post-modern dwellings elsewhere – or indeed in Docklands (Wright 1985b; Jager 1986). Even in mainstream gentrified areas the notion of consumption is an important source of differentiation and a major distinguishing feature between our fieldwork areas was whether or not there was a local consumption infrastructure, as indicated by Table 4.3. We will return to this issue later but we believe that it relates strongly to the social typologies developed in relation to the housing and employment fields.

In the next chapter we introduce the subjects of our study, which will add some flesh to the rather abstracted claims made here about the nature of the metropolitan habitus, its constituent fields and the axes of commonality and difference.

Notes

1. ACORN produces 54 'ideal type' profiles of post coded areas for the United Kingdom which are agglomerations of housing and social mixes and are not based on any single area.
2. Sports Utility Vehicles (SUV) in North American parlance but with exactly the same social cachet and meaning in relation to the protection it affords against the trepidations of the urban jungle. People Carriers translate into Mini Vans in North America but perhaps come with less suburban connotations.
3. It is also not a particularly recently gentrifying area: Tony Blair and Cherie Booth had a house there before they moved to Barnsbury in a classic manoeuvre of upward mobility.
4. It is worth noting that during the years of George Lansbury's radicalism, the leader of Hackney Council was none other than Herbert Morrison, Peter Mandelson's grandfather, and himself an ultra realist who did his best to spike most of Lansbury's actions for the working-class poor in London.
5. As the editor of *Rising East* I got into some trouble with the Peabody Trust, one of London's largest and most progressive providers of social housing, for illustrating an article by Phil Cohen on my university's new campus with a photo of such a wall! Cohen, P. (1998). 'Urban regeneration and the poly-versity: the road to Beckton Pier' *Rising East: the Journal of East London Studies* 1(3): 24–51.
6. I am grateful to Gary Bridge for this term to describe our approach.
7. The Private Finance Initiative (PFI) under which private capital undertakes to build and in some cases run public institutions such as hospitals over a longer period is just the most recent example of this.

–5–

A Class In and For Itself?

In this chapter we introduce the people – our respondents – who are at the heart of this study; in the following chapter we examine their characteristics, attitudes and so forth in terms of the quantitative data we gathered but here we allow them to tell us about the areas in which they live. We return to this qualitative data in Chapters 7 and 8 but here we draw on it in a largely descriptive sense to get a 'feel' for the areas in which they have decided to live. We start with Barnsbury, if for no other reason, than that is where gentrification was first spotted in the literature and has informed much of its subsequent study. We then work our way around the study areas in an anti-clockwise direction to London Fields before looking at the three sub-areas that make up our Docklands study area.

Barnsbury

There are two main themes about Barnsbury, which intersect and are at least partially contradictory. The first refers to its material and cultural infrastructure of consumption and the second to its 'social capital rich' reputation and the networks associated with this.

> It's now very vibrant, with a great 'street' life – a choice of restaurants, bars, theatres etc ... recent gentrification is a result of changes in the City. It's more attractive now for young singles, lots more businesses attracted to the area, which has benefited wider populations and the whole area is much smarter. (BY20)

> The housing stock has been massively improved by private owners and there are far more amenities, a wonderful diversity of eating out places – unparalleled, I should think, anywhere in London. Business is thriving, nothing is left derelict – this brings prosperity to the area. The specialist shops have improved, I particularly like the new interior design shops. (BY25)

> This is quite a close knit area socially. This street pulls together, we have meetings if there's a problem. (BY29)

Children can be much more independent in an area like this. My son can get to plenty of friendly families in the area should he get into trouble while he's out and about. It has that kind of networks. (BY5)

I like the people who live round here, the left wing feel – it can be a very supportive community when things go wrong. (BY8)

Many residents felt that they were able to have the best of both worlds, to be centrally placed yet able to get away to their second home

It's very pleasant here, well provided with parks and lots of things to do with small children. It's nice for us because we're well off, less so for others – we are able to get away, leave London. We can get out of here, e.g. for long summer holidays. (BY43)

For many, centrality was one of the major benefits of living in Barnsbury – both to the West End and to the City. Lawyers could 'pop' into their chambers on a Sunday if they had forgotten to bring home the right boxfile for a case on Monday morning.

It's not central to London, it's *in* central London, and the West End's accessible for cinema, theatre, shopping. We can walk into town. Not having to commute is the main thing. I can have breakfast with the kids – that is worth an unquantifiable amount. Being with the kids is just not a problem. That's the main thing for me, more than the local commercial infrastructure . . . I like the local school, it has a good atmosphere with a good mix of social classes and people, quite artistic people around. (BY50)

It's great to be central, close to things. I know the area very well, and have a lot of good friends in the neighbourhood. I enjoy it – just here it's peaceful and green, I like the trees and squares of Barnsbury, and their proximity to the West End and Upper St. It's a nice place to live . . . There are an awful lot more lawyers around, only they can afford it. Upper St was an ordinary high street when we came here . . . Islington has become a fashion item, which is pleasant enough. (BY39)

Many respondents contrasted the city buzz of London and the 'human' scale of Barnsbury although this was often mediated by an awareness of the 'other', however well-hidden by the leafy streets of owner-occupation

It's central, close to the theatres, West End, Barbican. I can walk to the galleries. This is a tremendous advantage, the source of all positives, you feel like you're living in the heart of London, you have the city buzz. London's a wonderful place . . . the street is quiet with great architecture. It's a delightful, villagey place on a human scale. We have wonderful neighbours. But beyond the area there's Barnard Park – no thank you very much – the area is shabby beyond our locality . . . (but) it might be more difficult to live

here if we didn't have the escape to Somerset that we have, the house down there . . .
(BY53)

This contrast between the buzz of the centre and the quiet of the local is expressed
by both long term and more recent residents. This respondent is in his late sixties
and has lived in the area for forty years:

I certainly wouldn't move from here willingly – I've lived here now for more than half
my life . . . the best thing about it is the centrality (my natural habitat is the centre of
London) . . . to live in a very quiet street in a relatively safe, agreeable and attractive area
is a great blessing, and I count myself as fortunate in having found it . . . (BY46)

This thirty-one year old woman has lived in Barnsbury only a few years:

It's very quiet, though central, and great to be so near the City and West End – nowhere
in inner London is quieter, as far as I know . . . it's a nice community, with an awful lot
going on. There are lots of little theatres around us. The borough has a fascinating history
. . . (BY41)

Most respondents cross the city/local divide with its implications of a social gulf
easily:

It's convenient for work and close to cultural centres. The community is a good cross
section. The local facilities are very good; there is a very lively eating scene. It's a
comfortable place to live . . . but it still has a good atmosphere, overall, it's not alienated,
there's no antipathy. (BY48)

This sense of community is, as we have indicated, one of the enduring themes
about living in Barnsbury. We remain somewhat sceptical how far this notion of
community – which was assiduously built by the first generation of gentrifiers –
persists. One respondent, for example, having thanked us for sending her feedback
on the initial survey data, said that she was initially a little upset by our speculation
that social cohesion might be weakening but recalled that she and some friends had
recently been mugged returning home late one night. She felt that this was now
increasingly 'par for the course'. Many respondents were now concerned that the
stark contrasts in wealth might be having a malign effect. A recurring theme was
to relate social cohesion to the architectural style of the privately owned housing:

I like the proximity to town, the local history, the built environment itself, I like all these
things. The approach to planning in the area has been good, generally, and the place feels
connected to the past – in a sense it feels quite undeveloped . . . the place does somehow
manage to maintain a balance of extremes: even the rich lawyers have been of the 'right

sort', though I do fear that money is now driving the place in a different direction. (BY54)

We have good, like-minded neighbours, something that was sorely lacking when we lived in Surrey Quays. It's a lively area, with lots of small shops rather than the bigger things. It's central, with good transport, and lots of cultural activities (cinema, theatre, galleries) . . . it's a mixed community . . . we like the architectural style of the place very much . . . it's very different here to Surrey Quays. There seem to still be a lot of very heavy old south London types around in the area we were in, although everybody there mixed in together. We had all sorts of things happening around us – people's houses being burned down, robberies, all sorts. It could be really nasty . . . it seems much better round here, though the rougher types are still around, on the estates. (BY55)

The diversity and difference of the area is an enduring theme although there seems an implicit contradiction between the way in which respondents welcome both its 'groundedness' in a 'local' economy and, at the same time, the 'improvements' in the housing stock:

There is a strong sense of community here. The visual aspect, the architecture, is very pleasant. The arts are well represented. There are lots of things for young children . . . Upper St has a lively nightlife, which is pleasant, the presence of young people and lots of activity. (BY66)

The area has gradually become much more pleasant – it was very slummy when I first came. There is a friendly, communal atmosphere. (BY1)

It's very friendly and very mixed – it's got diversity and a nice community feel about it. This is one of the nicest places in London – I have strong feelings about it. (BY3)

It's an extremely cosmopolitan, interesting area which retains its long-term identity . . . it's very mixed, with a nice local atmosphere. It's easy to live in. (BY38)

This is a close knit area socially – this street pulls together, has meetings if there's a problem . . . on the whole, the area is getting better, nicer to live in . . . I'm glad to see the progress, it's nice to see houses being renovated. Much less demolition than in the past. (BY29)

Generally, the housing stock has been massively improved by owners. There is a wonderful diversity of eating out places. Unparalleled, I should think. Business is thriving, and nothing is derelict. (BY25)

The social divisions in the area are well summed-up by the distinction, referred to previously, between Upper Street which is the village main street for Barnsbury's middle classes and the Caledonian Road which runs parallel half a mile to the west and remains resolutely 'unimproved':

> It's very pleasant environmentally – wide, tree lines streets etc. The Cally [The Caledonia Road] is really grotty, but there is a good mix of shops on Upper Street, including three good book shops. (BY65)

> The Cally and here are two different kettles of fish . . . when I first came here it was quieter, but in the past year there have been a lot more kids hanging round in the park – in fact, the police were called to them today. There's a lot of shouting and yobbery now – this is much more of a problem than it was in Stoke Newington. The kids come over from the Cally, from the estate, and congregate in the bushes. I don't feel safe anymore. I'm reluctant to let my son go out there without an adult. (BY36)

The two streets bound the area and each represents one of the two communities in Barnsbury in a way that is not replicated in any of the other fieldwork areas. Although many respondents could be seen as in some form of 'denial' about the polarization of their area, others were highly aware of it and many saw it as a problem, particularly in terms of children and education (which we discuss in some detail in Chapter 7). Many of the more 'reflexive' comments came from the longer term gentrifiers and we return to this in Chapter 8 when we consider the significant issue of re-gentrification. Nevertheless, even the younger and more recent incomers refer to the differences as social polarization – both the following respondents are in their early thirties:

> There's a huge imbalance between poverty and wealth in Islington. It's strange to see such a huge gap – you really see it at school. Some of the wealth is pretty extreme, the extremes. (BY2)

> It's no longer just gentrified at the city end, it now spreads further up, all the way up Upper Street, not just the Angel . . . too many white, middle class single people. This is an issue with council tenants whose kids can't afford it, can't stay in the chain . . . Schools is an issue, the posh people are taking the best state places. (BY12)

On the other hand, some of the incomers resent the challenge to their lack of 'authenticity' and right to belonging which goes with the 'settler' analogy. The middle-class versus working-class model is not one that they recognize in the division between private and social housing:

> There's a perception of a high level of crime, and growing aggression between the skilled and the unskilled. The local papers have more and more letters from council tenants complaining about rising prices and claiming that the middle classes put nothing back

– but I do contribute to the area, it's my home. I resent (after ten years) being called a 'settler' by a correspondent to the *Islington Gazette* . . . we in [street name] have absolutely nothing in common with the other people in the area, who in fact are *not* working class, more an income support underclass . . . Islington has 14% unemployment, on the fringes of one of the richest places in the world, I wish we could do something about it. There's a much harder interface here than in Brixton, where we lived before. Islington is very harsh compared to Brixton, which was leavened by a range of different groups. (BY13)

Perhaps not surprisingly, many respondents identified the problem as a managerial one with a council that was failing to get to grips with it. The borough council came in for a large amount of criticism, which was only exceeded by the vitriol heaped on Hackney council by respondents in London Fields. In Islington they were perceived as pushing an outmoded socio-political agenda which benefited nobody – as the following bit of analysis indicates:

money is driving the place in a different direction; we are getting different types of people here now. The proximity of the city is crucial here . . . there is a good deal of unease, locally, about the direction of values . . . the regime in Islington has not grasped the issues in a managerial sense, have not taken account of the practical outcomes as well as the ideological issues – education is a long term by product of this problem. There is a weakness of delivery that can't be explained away by indices of social problems, the issues are of competence and management. (BY54)

Another respondent expresses the frustration rather less clinically but reflects a common cluster of attitudes that encompass both broad social views as well as those that are much more instrumentally oriented to their own individual concerns:

The negatives here are lots of rubbish and dogshit, stupid property prices and a stupid council . . . there is a huge imbalance between poverty and wealth in Islington. It's strange to see such a huge gap – you see it most at school. Some of the wealth, the extremes, is pretty obscene . . . the council is particularly crap – I've had loads of problems with them, ground rent and council charges are in chaos. They are unhelpful and abusive. Nothing is ever straightforward. (BY3)

The council is seen as largely failing to resolve the contradictions in the area and therefore to be responsible for them. This displacement of responsibility comes across in the accounts of many respondents. Despite this, Barnsbury is a place for which respondents feel great affection and loyalty and it meets many of their needs for city living; it is close to the centre of work and play, has a consumption infrastructure and plenty of 'people like us'. Clearly the issue of social polarization is a concern; many originally moved to the area because of its 'social capital rich' discourse, which they now see as being disrupted by global and local factors for which they hold themselves, and people like themselves, as partially responsible. This infects much of their discourse, which reflects a concern about authenticity and their place in the city. However, at a material level their investment in their jobs and their housing is such that they appear to be determined to 'tough it out'; this becomes apparent when we look at issues concerning children and education in Chapter 7. It is a subject on which they had much to say.

Battersea

The continuities and contrasts between Barnsbury and Battersea are endless and fascinating. The two areas are the most affluent in our research and both are based around a consumption infrastructure – Upper Street and Northcote Road – that serve not only their own populations but are, in both cases, a satellite centre respectively for North and South West London for an evening out. Both are also tied to the City although, as we shall see in later chapters, in different occupational sectors. Finally, both are also what might be loosely termed global places: high on the option list of any multinational executive contemplating a London posting and needing somewhere for him (usually) and his family to live. What seems so different between the two areas is the 'feel': Battersea has less of the 'urban concern' of Barnsbury, economic capital and relations of the market seem to be much more important than those of social obligation or concern. Families seem to dominate in both areas and whereas the concern with safety is reinforced by a sense of 'edginess' in Barnsbury, safety and security appear to infuse Battersea not as an issue but as a given. If Barnsbury is focused on consumption and cohesion, then Battersea is about amenity and accessibility.

> We like it very much. It is very safe, and has all the amenities one could want . . . We still enjoy what London has to offer, and our friends are here. There is good shopping, and plenty of space . . . and it has a vibrancy, a buzz, there is a zing to living here . . . things have really changed in London: black cabs will now come south of the river. (BA1)

> Extremely good transport links – this was our original motivation for coming here. Good local primary schools. Open space, good facilities. (BA2)

> It's very pleasant and incredibly popular. Everything is here, you haven't got to go over the river for everything you want – we have our own department stores. It's very safe, very middle class. (BA3)

> I like it here very much – we can get up to the Kings Road very easily, Sloane Square is accessible. So transport and access to the centre are excellent . . . being able to walk on the commons is wonderful. (BA4)

In contrast to Barnsbury where everybody was apparently celebrating being able to be part of the city (but at the same time not being part of it) and where people took the long view about continuing to live there, one of the striking things about Battersea was the incipient anti-urbanism. They had to live in London because of jobs but most hankered, one received the impression, for the country-side and would willingly swap most of the facilities for a pair of green wellies. Although the connections with the city and the upper class villages of Chelsea and Fulham were big plus points, again and again there was a refrain about being able to get out of London easily and also about how they would be moving on in a few years – if things went well up in the City being the implication.

It's a good place to live – it's quiet, the people are nice, it's clean and it's safe. The facilities are good, and there are the parks . . . Transport is good, it's easy to get out of London. It's just nice. (BA7)

It's safe and friendly, and there are a lot of people with a shared outlook, which is important to me – I had nothing in common with the people in West Hampstead, where I lived before. There are a lot of people who are here for 3-5 years, before moving on. It's a kind of staging post . . . It's convenient for the rest of the world, and people like coming here – it's attractive to outsiders. (BA54)

It feels good and open, with a good neighbourhood feeling . . . it's great actually . . . more and more people with kids are using the area as a stepping stone before going to the country. (BA32)

Battersea residents are also not unselfcritical of the area and themselves (as a social group) but, whereas in Barnsbury this is displaced off onto the new rich who have bought into the social capital rich environment but are not prepared, as it were, to put in the hours, the auto-critique of Battersea is more of a self-parody of the middle class.

It's not really my favourite place, I'd prefer Chelsea. This falls in between too many stools. There's too many people going round pretending this is the country, which it's not – it's neither town nor city . . . The houses all look the same – and the people are all too samey, there's no diversity. I hate that – we're all the same, no characters . . . it's becomes very middle class, private schools, public school backgrounds, far less black people than there were. (BA44)

It had a different feel before, now it's much more 2.4 kids. The types who were around before were more varied in outlook and background. Now it's the huntin', shootin' n' fishin' set, much more homogenous . . . what this area really needs is a good tennis club. (BA49)

There is a similar issue of authenticity of belonging, as in Barnsbury, but in Battersea it is mediated through shopping – the infrastructure is almost entirely devoted to consumption and is not leavened by the 'culture' of Barnsbury. There is no Almeida Theatre, Kings Head or Screen on the Green. It is door-to-door restaurants, bars and trendy shops. What is a positive is also, for some, now a negative:

> It has a nice, local feel – in London but not of it, relaxed . . . I've got to know people, so I feel part of a community, which is rare in London. There is good shopping, restaurants, bars, green spaces all around you; very pleasant . . . It's changed a lot in the 7 years I've been here. Northcote Road has changed out of all recognition – there were a lot of boarded up shops, one or two restaurants, and now it's gone very upmarket . . . the street market has diminished, sadly, but overall the place has improved dramatically, it has a sense of life. (BA18)

> People don't talk to each other, there's no neighbourhood feel . . . it's gone upmarket with the fashionable chains of pubs and restaurants coming in. This has generally been a good thing but it's gone far enough now – any more and it will be to the detriment of the area. (BA48)

> The similarity [to us] of the other people around is both good and bad, but it does mean that there is a prevalence of families like ours, with young children. It is architecturally attractive, and has a reasonable amount of green space. It's quite close to the important cultural centres, and there's an interesting variety of local shops. It also has a large number of good schools. (BA63).

Whilst it has its auto-critics, for the most part what respondents value about Battersea is its 'villagey' atmosphere in which they feel safe and 'comfortable':

> It's a very good place – two large commons, good shops, good transport (so we don't need another car) . . . It's very villagey, I do a lot of talking to people in the street . . . it's a nice lot of people, a lot of self-employed people like film makers, architects, wine merchants – it doesn't have the uniformity of Chelsea . . . it's a very safe area. (BA5)

Whereas in Barnsbury it was the architecture that was elided with its attraction, in Battersea, although the houses are pleasant enough, it is the spatial ordering that is commented on, which, it is generally felt, the local authority – Wandsworth – has used its powers to enhance. The contrast in attitudes to the local government could hardly be greater and is in contrast to Barnsbury; it is seen as providing genuine choice of private and state education on the doorstep. The local primary school prepares children for the Common Entrance examination for entry into private schools as well as grooming them for state selective schools. Time and again, respondents talk about it as the ideal place in London to raise children, primarily because it is perceived as safe and provides all the public and private services that families need

> A thriving community. It's good socially, we're always bumping into people, talking to shopkeepers. I know this is almost a cliché, this thing about community atmosphere, but we do have it here . . . there is an atmosphere of safety, no security grills, nobody shutting themselves away. (BA29)

> The commons and parks make it feel good and open. It has a good neighbourhood feeling . . . it's great, actually. (BA32).

> I feel safe in the area – there is relatively little burglary and plenty of security cameras. It has a real community feeling, chatting to shop owners and so on. (BA34)

> All the things I need are on the doorstep, so I walk everywhere. The shopping is good (though the market is deteriorating) . . . it's safe, and quiet in the middle of the day. (BA39)

> We worked out very carefully why we wanted to live here before coming: very good school; huge amounts of open space but with proximity to the vibrancy of central London; good transport links and great facilities for families. We are very much amongst friends, having lived here for as long as we have. (BA43).

> It's wonderfully convenient and almost crime free – it's very central but without any inner-city feel. (BA46)

> The facilities are brilliant; it's pleasant, safe, not at all threatening. (BA48)

A defining issue then is the provision of education, which contrasts directly with Islington as we shall see in chapter seven. Even at this stage, the contrast is clear however. Whereas in Islington, there is a stark private/state choice with many feeling forced into an early decision to go private although they are unhappy about sending their children to fee paying schools, in Battersea one gets the impression of a genuine choice being available. The irony is that in Battersea there is less need to use private schools because the state provision is regarded as more than satisfactory. Where the decision to go private is made, then the local council has ensured that good private schools are on the doorstep – unlike Islington where it is necessary to commute.

> With kids, the perks of living here are fantastic – the schools are great, nurseries, private – a huge choice . . . The local shops are great, I can get everything I need locally . . . it's very family oriented. (BA70)

Even many of those who sing the praises of Battersea are aware of what they see as the contradiction of their presence – in transforming the area into what is almost an inner city suburb in which the 'old locals' have no voice or presence. With this, the shops and diversity that once made this a working class area and, so, a little different, have disappeared. One of the older respondents now in her mid-sixties regrets this:

> It's becoming very boring. The sense of community is disappearing – this is the self protecting middle class. Very few of the other people are now remaining . . . The market was sensational 23 years ago – they were very real characters, the market traders. It's dwindled since Sainsbury's came . . . we've lost a lot by gentrifying – people don't look at you or talk to you in the street in the way that they used to – I couldn't get anybody to join in with the VE day celebrations recently . . . There are too many wine bars and restaurants (though a Mexican wouldn't go amiss!). I miss the old shops. There was a hardware shop, a small stationers . . . (BA12)

> I'm moving soon. The life has been sucked out of it [the area] . . . the old street market, the vibrancy, are gone . . . and this was one of my main reasons for moving here originally . . . There seems to be no daytime provision now, nothing for the local people . . . the main thing was the presence of a wonderful local community, a village community, and I felt part of it. This was very special, and they need to try and retain something of this as the area changes . . . But Northcote Road is more anonymous, and anonymity is a poor side effect of gentrification. (BA13)

In many ways they have become so ubiquitous, socially if not actually, that the middle class has tended to have stopped hearing itself and has, to all intents and purposes, become Battersea. For many this is not a problem, but others feel that it is not what living in the city should be – however much they appreciate its assets otherwise:

> It's not a multicultural area, it has very simple norms – it's very easy to stand out here . . . there are far too many restaurants catering for the braying classes . . . there used to be many more elderly, old-style Battersea residents – there is now a regrettable absence of these types. There are a lot of rugby club parties, that sort of thing. It can be very noisy now, with all these bars being so busy. It's a strange situation, with all the different bars attracting particular groups all along Northcote Road . . . the school based social networks are extensive, but they are not the ones that I would choose. (BA46)

For many people of course, this is precisely the attraction of Battersea and a testament to its successes that it has remade an old working-class area in its own image as an uncontested middle-class settlement. This produces a yearning in some, and not just older long timers, for a past where there was some difference.

Not having to worry about the downsides of that difference, such as education, is, however, worth a lot and one good reason to be grateful for the London Borough of Wandsworth; not a situation that applies to the London Borough of Lambeth, which hosts the Brixton study area.

Brixton

Brixton is not a place to feel at ease in, and not many people came there to do so. It is the difference, the frisson, the edginess that are its attractiveness to those who have bought houses there – although there is a newer and more recent group who can be seen as housing market refugees from plusher bits further to the west in Battersea, Clapham and Balham. This group tend to have settled the area around Acre Lane on the west side of Brixton Hill; our study areas are to the east of Brixton Hill. Tulse Hill runs off Brixton Hill to Brockwell Park whereas Herne Hill (also known as Poets Corner) runs East between the Park and Railton Road (the so-called frontline when Brixton was the nearest Britain could do for the racialized inner-city war zone). What both areas share is the relative calm of their 'interiors' in contrast to the buzzy disorder of central Brixton.

> The immediate area is nice and quiet, there's never any hassle. It's secure and safe, with lots of families with kids. Central Brixton is the opposite, it's youthful, with lots of things going on – pubs, cinema, restaurants, clubs. The atmosphere is youthful, trendy in some way. (BN26)

> I love it – we have great neighbours and people are generally very friendly. It's central but quiet, and there is actually lots of wildlife . . . It has a nice buzz to it, it's a good place to go out (though we tend to go to Clapham more) . . . But it has a good atmosphere, I like seeing all the characters around the tube station and central Brixton . . . the centre of Brixton has really been cleaned up, and it's a lot more lively. It feels quite safe now, I'm not at all bothered . . . people look out for each other here, tend to respond to alarms – unlike in some areas. (BN27)

Whilst many might dispute the communal aspect of the area, what unites almost all the respondents is the tremendous buzz and vibrancy of it as a place to live (both words appear frequently in respondents' accounts).

> It's close to the West End, which is good, but nice and high up – the opposite hill to Highgate, in fact – so we have a terrific view of the metropolis . . . it's friendly and vibrant with a great, mixed, market. On the whole, there is more racial integration than anywhere else in London . . . Brixton still has enough of a downside to limit the number of pine strippers who might want to live here. Though the Brixton middle class *is* a real

feature, as I see at my daughter's nursery, I don't see it becoming gentrified as quickly as somewhere like Chiswick . . . the area has improved in lots of ways. The market is unbelievably vibrant, with the African influence much stronger than it used to be . . . we have a kind of social ease here – it's much more relaxed than north London. Things are much easier, just talking to our (West Indian) neighbours, there's a lot of give and take. Neighbours look out for one another's kids – unlike in North London. (BN35)

However it is the mix of multiculturalism with an alternative consumption infrastructure that is the attraction of Brixton for many. It shares with Battersea and Barnsbury an engagement with the global economy but one that is much more 'full on' and raw; it is not somewhere that an itinerant banker would be expected to live (although some do). The relative tranquillity of the residential zones in our field-work areas contrasts with the energy of the entertainment district of central Brixton, which radiates out from its underground station.

This road is quiet, it's a friendly neighbourhood, but there's plenty to do nearby. It's just good, I like it – the cinema, parks, centrality . . . I like the cultural diversity, the weird and wonderful vegetables and so on . . . The Afro-Caribbean flavour is great. So hopefully the improvements will affect everybody. (BN21)

For many the clubs, the independent cinema (the Ritzy) are what make Brixton such a wonderful place to live

The best things about Brixton are its people, its parks and its cultural side . . . it's a lively, young person's place (which is why I came to live here originally, but it's obviously not so relevant now). I actually met my wife in the Fridge! . . . these last couple of years the place has just been *heaving* at night, everything is packed out all the time . . . A slightly different type of person is moving here now – the type of people who live in Clapham are spilling over to here. It's less run-down, derelict feeling. (BN3)

The attraction is also quite serious, not just that of a hedonistic ageing youth culture; the multiculturalism is attractive not just because it signals an open-ness to differences of 'race' and ethnicity but more generally.

The people here are great – it's still a community. The neighbours are wonderful, friendly but not too friendly. My daughter is mixed race, so it's very comfortable for her to be here. (BN6)

Importantly, the multiculturalism doesn't work through as intermingling but as a toleration and celebration of difference which largely works through groups ignoring each other – as the following extract indicates:

I like the tension that exists here, and the peculiarity of enjoying this kind of inner city atmosphere while surrounded by people like ourselves – I really enjoy this tension (we've had no trouble ourselves). It's not multicultural, it's black *and* white – I like the way that people live together *and* ignore each other . . . the area is not entirely predictable. It's a genuine model of city living . . . the edginess of central Brixton is a buzz – I enjoy the madness of it, if I'm not too tired. It's sort of mad, but I love it. (BN15)

We describe this relationship as 'tectonic' (Robson and Butler 2001), whereby people move across each other like the plates in the earth; in some ways this metaphor can be extended to describe the relations between class groupings in middle-class London. In Brixton, this certainly works and is a tension-management device that ensures relatively stable relations in an essentially unstable social structure.

We came across more openly gay respondents in Brixton than anywhere else, many of whom felt it was an easier place to place to live than elsewhere in inner London

It's the best place I've ever lived in London. It's very comfortable for me as a gay man in central Brixton – though it can be tense, there is a strong gay and lesbian presence. It's also very ethnically mixed, which makes me feel comfortable. I feel comfortable with the diversity . . . It took a long time to connect with people in the street at first, probably because we were two men living together, but it's a lot better now . . . Brixton doesn't feel like it did in 82/83, around the time of the riots. There's not the same desperate atmosphere as there was then . . . (BN39)

It's a pleasant and safe area. It's very quiet even though there is a lot of activity in the area is general. There's lots to do close by, so I don't need a car; Ritzy, restaurants, fabulous things. And the population is very diverse – we don't stick out here as 2 women living together. (BN15)

Some of the longer term residents feel that the inexorable march of gentrification is now having an effect and that what makes it attractive is now under attack:

The longest-term residents are the friendliest. The newer type of yuppie resident is less friendly. This is worrying, the kind of people now moving here from Clapham . . . the area is becoming much whiter – lots of the older people selling up and going back to the Caribbean, so it has a completely different racial picture. Their kids can only afford to stay in the area if it's in a council flat. (BN23)

Brixton is very crowded socially, which is a negative . . . and the different communities have moved further apart. This locality is becoming increasingly white and sane (as a psychiatric social worker I had a lot of black clients here formerly) . . . I had thought that the area would be more mixed, which was a reason for deciding to come here, but it no

longer is – it has much more of a frightened, middle class atmosphere than I'd imagined
. . . (BN19)

Whilst the affective side of Brixton was its main attraction for many, if not most, the logic of the metropolitan housing market is at work here. Simply, there is more space for less money than in many areas of London and this has, as we have noted, attracted some of the Battersea aspirants who find the area harder to take.

> It's a good value for money area – you can still buy a big property without it costing the earth . . . it's become much more gentrified over the last 10 years. Railton Road, especially, has changed: the black unemployed no longer congregate there in the way they used to . . . So the reputation of the place has changed, we now say that it's Herne Hill in Brixton, not Herne Hill in Dulwich! (BN18)

The flip side of this is that fewer Afro-Caribbeans are remaining in the area which means that in a sense its iconic diversity is becoming increasingly 'virtual':

> A lot of the area is getting much nicer, much cuter . . . A lot of the older Afro-Caribbeans are selling up and going back. We are part of the move that will change the area, make it less interesting. So we are very much a part of the process (though we are very aware of the contradictions in our position). (BN15)

This is particularly, it seems, a source of regret to the longer term respondents who feel they have 'invested' in the area and are now seeing that taken away by a younger and less committed group:

> More and more middle class people have moved in – these streets are less multicultural than they used to be. The whole point of city life is multicultural living. This street used to be friendly – people really came together here during the riots – but now a lot of people have moved away and you hardly know anybody. People on the whole are much younger now. (BN8)

> More middle class, white, thirty-ish people are moving into the area. A newer sort of people, actors, media people and so on. I wouldn't want this to carry on as I value the mix we've always had here – black, white, young, old. (BN6)

Many respondents are very much aware of what is happening now in their area and the longer term implications:

> Lots of West Indian people have sold to white middle class people and moved right out of the area or gone home. There is an incoming white middle class, definitely more affluent people coming in, almost on a monthly basis – lots of people carriers. Ordinary

families have been priced out of the area; kids can't buy a house in the same area as their parents. It's becoming much more like north London areas where there are rich and poor communities with nothing in between, which are just polarized. . . the character of the area has changed as it's been done up . . . Things like youth services are closing up, but [middle class] people like us are popular with the council – they give us the kinds of things we want, like recycling schemes, which are now prioritised ahead of adventure playgrounds. This is all happening at a rate of knots . . . I'm really worried about the ghettoisation of the city, with all the non-wealthy families ending up in the outer city. (BN9)

The local council is a matter of concern to many respondents, and it is largely held in contempt both on grounds of managerial incompetence and, as we have seen above, for its policy stance. It is seen as not having learned the lessons from Islington. Whilst not wishing to embrace residential gentrification like Wandsworth, it has decided that the funky, hedonistic and alternative night-time economy is its 'unique selling point' and has gone some way to building an economic strategy around this. As such it has more or less alienated every con-stituency: many of the more recent gentrifiers do not want to see rich white youth around, and the local black youth are increasingly being squeezed out as are the black club owners who now find their licences not being renewed for the sale of alcohol. There is a widespread antipathy towards attempts to institutionalize what was essentially a culture of resistance and some real fears that this is precisely what makes it attractive; sanitizing Brixton's culture may simply not work. These tensions are now, some argue, working their way through into the community and inter-group relations:

I don't go to the market anymore, it's full of idlers . . . you can't see what you're doing, the streets are full of idlers. I don't like it. If I want fresh fruit or vegetables I go down to East Street [two to three miles distant]. I walk up to Herne Hill and catch a bus, go down there. (BN03)

The last round of changes seem to have had more effect. It's much more culty now, a Mecca for young people. But this is causing tensions, the area being taken over by a white-led youth culture. I think relations between black and white people are becoming more strained . . . there's a lot of aggressive racism on both sides. My son and his friends – black and white – are very vulnerable. He's been badly beaten up twice by black boys. (BN77)

Brixton is therefore a very different kind of area to Barnsbury and Battersea; its attraction to many lies in its diversity and multiculturalism although this is more 'ideal' than lived. In reality, most respondents valued the fact that where they lived was relatively quiet and cut off from central Brixton. They took pride in saying that they lived in Brixton; it said something both to and about them. Those who had been there a long time wore their residence with pride. They regretted both what they saw as its passing and the emergence of a new Brixton that traded on its past but that was now in retreat before the twin forces of a property driven gentrification and a commercially marketed night-time economy that appealed to white audiences attracted to its bad past.

Telegraph Hill

Telegraph Hill could not be more different from Brixton, Battersea or Barnsbury in one crucial respect which is that, whereas these three have embraced the city through consumption – albeit in very different ways, Telegraph Hill has kept that aspect of the city at arm's length. There is no such consumption infrastructure and that is what people like about the area – what is celebrated publicly elsewhere becomes the focus of the private household in Telegraph Hill. Consumption takes place within the home rather than on the street. The resources that make Telegraph Hill work are its middle-class social networks and this is what people value about the area. In common with respondents in Barnsbury and Battersea, many respondents here made a point of linking the social environment with its built context:

> We like the conservation aspect . . . We're into architecture and keeping the original features. The trees and mix of people mean a lot to us, the social mix, actors, artists, people from all sorts of backgrounds. There's a lack of stereotyping, they're not all working in the city, or as solicitors. It's an intelligent group of people, on the whole. So the environmental and the social go together. (TH12)

At face value, the habitus in Telegraph Hill is similar to that of Brixton – a celebration of diversity and difference but, as this respondent hints, it is a different diversity that is being sought out. It is actors and social workers rubbing along with solicitors endogenously within the middle class. We are looking here at a very specific group of middle-class people to whom 'getting along with the neighbours' matters, not just because that is how village life ought to be but because it also provides the social networks that can help them negotiate their way through the potentially hostile waters of living in one of the most deprived areas of South London, which is still, in many ways, inflected with a white working-class culture (Robson 2000). The Den, the home of Millwall Football club and iconic of an old way of life is not far away and the fact that many of its supporters have fled to the whitelands of outer south-east London and Kent does not stop them returning during the week in white vans to do the building jobs on gentrified housing.

Middle-class life is a struggle and nowhere perhaps more strongly than when it comes to education and social reproduction. Telegraph Hill, as we shall see, is more home-centred than any of our areas and also, given the relative lack of economic capital of its residents, one of the more fragile. What is lacking in economic capital is compensated for by the strategic deployment of social capital through culturally capital rich networks – 'The best thing about this place is the people' (TH23). Two aspects are emphasized by respondents: the pleasing physical aspect of the area and the sense of belonging to a community of fellow spirits. This is often contextualized within a discourse about difference and diversity but there is a tension here: it is a diverse area but the impression comes across that this is a backcloth to the actual interactions that take place amongst a remarkably homogenous middle-class group.

> It's a friendly, green, family-oriented sort of place, with a good mixture of people . . . it feels like it's really coming up. There are a lot of self-employed, arty people coming into the area – it's a flux, not static. (TH17)

> Huge gardens with plenty of wildlife – only 3.5 miles from the centre of town, and travel can only get better with the new extensions (to the Jubilee line and DLR) . . . a nice, mixed community, not exclusively middle class or one ethnicity. (TH19)

The area is undoubtedly pleasant, as we have indicated previously, particularly in contrast to the 'mean streets' aspect of much of the surrounding deprivation of New Cross and North Peckham that make up some of the roughest areas of South London. The streets are wide and tree-lined and the houses generous with wide, sunny gardens – often in contrast to much of gentrified north London where the terrace style leads to long, narrow and often sunless gardens. The juxtaposing by most residents of the physical pleasantness with the social closeness is remarkable:

> It is an oasis of calm, with a calm, green, quiet atmosphere. Community spirit is good, lots of people I can socialize with. My daughter has good friends here . . . it's central, with good transport links. (TH65).

> I like the parks, the physical aspect of the area. It's quiet and orderly . . . the local school is a big plus . . . there is a nice mix of people, we know quite a lot of people through neighbours, and take part in activities in the area, etc. (TH67).

> The best part of my day is coming back in over Blackheath, seeing the buses, the noise, the pace of life along the A2 at the bottom of the road. I like the ethnic diversity. I need to deal with diversity – I have known people who have moved further out and have become very suburban. (TH29).

It's a very attractive area, with a lovely view. It's like a haven, with tree-lined streets and an almost country feel – but it's close to the centre, so it can also have a city feel, which I really love. (TH42).

There are a lot of positives to life here: a good mix of people; good facilities; good schools; good parks; and good access to central London. And there are a lot of people like us around, lots of journalists and so on. (TH43)

Telegraph Hill is a small community, near to the school, a close knit area. We socialize with people from school who live in the area as well . . . we've got the jazz festival, the arts festival, there's lots going on. (TH44).

I love living here, really like it. Architecturally it's super, and the environment is lovely. You have, on the hill, a mixed atmosphere, and the people are lovely . . . I like living in the city, having lived in Kent . . . (TH33).

Like Barnsbury, this is a reflexive group of people who are aware that they are having an effect on the area not just for others but for themselves as well. The increased awareness of Telegraph Hill's gentrification is seen as having a potentially malign influence on the area and its ethos.

a newer neighbour in the street said to a group of us recently 'does anybody need an au pair, we have two'! – more of that kind of outlook here now. (TH49).

there are signs that house prices are getting to the point where the kind of people we identify with socially won't be able to afford it . . . would have preferred if the area hadn't become expensive . . . (TH55).

The balance has shifted too far in favour of the white middle class, there's too much of an artistic bent – that kind of ethos is too powerful . . . having an arts festival has lent more dominance to the white middle class artistic community we have in the area now. (TH13)

It can be a bit isolated and parochial – there are a lot of 'arty' types around, and a fair bit of snobbery . . . (TH42)

Enormous changes since the 70s – it was perceived as a very poor area then, not at all well off – and then the middle classes moved in. We felt isolated to begin with, but then the Telegraph Hill Association got off the ground, there was the festival, and it began to feel much more comfortable, with much better networks . . . (TH49)

It's getting smarter. I would guess that people moving in now have higher incomes. Almost all the houses have been improved now, and are in a good state of repair. It feels more prosperous and comfortable, but I suppose more polarized, as is the area as a whole – but certainly more middle class-professional than it was when we first came here. (TH65).

There seem to be more young people with families coming in, my impression being that some of them are in a higher income bracket – some journalists, even City types. The appearance of the area has certainly improved, the houses are better maintained – or at any rate, more of them are. Almost all, now. The last few black and working class families seem to have been edged out. House prices are rising *very* fast. (TH67).

It can be difficult, socially, as the finger of gentrification is pushed outwards . . . on the edge of the area the mix between the working class and the middle class is tense . . . there is a disparity of expectations of local service delivery (e.g., a lot of kids from the poorer families are on the at risk register, whereas social services are hardly relevant at all to middle class families) . . . local authority services are poor and getting worse. Heavy handed policing contributes to ethnic tension in the area, and they do nothing for community security. Over the last 18 months it's been getting far worse, the 'downtown Bronx' mentality of the police. (TH36)

There is a fear of crime, which partially reflects the contradiction between, on the one hand, the ideal of a reflexive middle-class community celebrating its diversity and, on the other, the fear of the real South London at the bottom of the 'Hill'. This is expressed more strongly here than in any other area – and has some basis in reality if the number of yellow police boards are anything to go by.

The street is much busier than it used to be, with more people passing. There is the occasional murder at the bottom of the road . . . I've been burgled three times and mugged once, though these things come in waves and it seems to be better now . . . (TH9).

Crime is always a worry . . . (TH40).

The fear of crime is really quite strong, I do worry about the crime rate . . . (TH14)

Environmental concerns and the fear of crime go together in the same way that the majority link the positive environmental aspects with the sense of the 'reflexive middle-class community': 'traffic pollution, noise, graffiti are all terrible in the surrounding area, and crime is a real issue – there *have* been muggings, burglaries etc.' (TH49). For some at least, the local authority mediates these concerns in so far as it can: 'it's a Labour borough, with good priorities, which cares about things that really matter i.e. the elderly . . . ' (TH19).

Others might question the last claim and indeed relations with the local council are now very fraught over the issue of building a new secondary school (which we discuss in Chapter 7) which in effect would provide a follow-on secondary school for the local primary and has become a major issue for the local area. Nevertheless, at a practical level, relations with many of the officers are quite good and have resulted in a number of environmental improvements to the area, such as traffic calming, and there is none of the much greater antagonism witnessed in Islington, Lambeth or Hackney. Nor however, is there a meeting of the minds as in Wandsworth. Interestingly the views on the council are much more split than elsewhere, as the following two comments indicate:

> The quality of life here is influenced by the local council, which is very good. It was the first in London to grasp the new culture of Local Authority and the Citizen's Charter – the cleanliness of the streets and general upkeep are very good. (TH33)

> The character of the area is slowly being eroded by the council not being watchful about new building and building regulations . . . also, the Hill is going steadily upmarket – regrettably, a lot of property developers have been coming into the area, buying up the houses and bastardising the properties for all they're worth, for multiple occupation. This is not good for anybody, it's exploitation. (TH2)

There are, of course, views contradictory to the general ethos; some people welcome improved communications, decry the lack of 'decent restaurants', welcome rising house prices but overwhelmingly this is a group that does not wish to become part of the global city in the manner of Barnsbury, Battersea and Brixton. Whilst they like the 'arty' atmosphere that somehow leavens the overwhelming seriousness of middle-class professionals, many do recognize that this is part of the growing mechanism of social exclusion that makes it increasingly hard to talk of the Hill as a diverse community. The arts and particularly the Telegraph Hill festival are a means of mobilizing cultural capital into social networks and as social capital. The people, local institutions and geography all appear to work together to this end: 'it has a good community feel, people brought together by the school and park and things like the annual arts festival put on by the Association' (TH20).

London Fields

London Fields, although perhaps the least 'socially defined' of our areas, is a reasonably well defined geographical area based on a grid-plan of streets running off Queensbridge Road towards London Fields, which is, as the name suggests, a green space. Unlike the 'parks' in our other areas it appears to be a contested space and not one that has been appropriated by the indigenous middle class. In this sense, it fits a more general sense that the middle class here have not exerted cultural or social control over the area – London Fields feels less of a middle-class space than our other areas despite its bijou artisan-type dwellings. This is, in part at least, because this group is far less certain that it wants to hegemonize the area than elsewhere. It bears similarities in other respects to Brixton and Telegraph Hill. Like Brixton, it is a diverse and multi-cultural area but it lacks the hedonistic ambience of central Brixton and the consumption infrastructure. In this respect, it is more like Telegraph Hill although there are, as mentioned elsewhere, the beginnings of what might develop into an artistic mode of production – not only are there many artists' spaces in the area but also it is near to the developing cultural quarters of Shoreditch and Hoxton. It is much less formed than either of these two areas and it is difficult to assign it an identity. We have speculated that its location in Hackney is important, as a symbol of a working-class place that has recently become home to other socially-excluded groups. Not surprisingly, managing to sustain middle-class life exerts considerable pressures and respondents describe its positive and negative features accordingly but both, in a sense, bear on Hackney's deprivation and image as Britain's 'poorest borough' (Harrison 1985).[1] One of its original attractions was that it was cheap, which appealed to many – particularly those without large stocks of economic capital:

> It was an absolute sink when we first came here (twenty years ago) . . . when my husband said that we had £45k to spend the estate agent replied 'which half of Hackney would you like to buy?' (LF2)

It would however be a mistake to see this as the main reason why respondents moved there; as we have argued in relation to other areas it is variations in the metropolitan habitus that seem to be the most important focus for why people choose to live in particular areas of inner London. The same respondent goes on to say:

> The diversity of the area is why we live here – it's brilliantly colourful and international . . . we will NEVER live anywhere else . . . we love the dynamism, particularly of the ethnic mix. It never stays the same, it's become much more African and Turkish in the last twenty years, and there's always new things in the mix. (LF2)

Time after time, respondents stressed the friendliness of the area, its diversity and the fact that it was 'improving'

> It's very friendly, there are a lot of people you can really like and get on with . . . friends living locally . . . the pubs are good and it's convenient for town . . . it's more expensive and definitely improving – traffic calming, parking restrictions, new developments like the library, a new playground . . . everything finally seems to be on the up, rather than that feeling of decay. (LF6)

It's not suburban, I like the urban feel and the cultural mix . . . there are a lot of arty people around, things are just starting to happen in the area, but it's not *too* upmarket. There is a sense of community, other parents around who are teachers, lots of like-minded people around . . . but the important thing is the mix; my son is mixed race, and it's good that there are a lot of people like him around, which is very important . . . there are more restaurants and a slight feeling of the area going more up market, but it's it's not a case of obvious gentrification – I like the rough edges. (LF7)

It's a very friendly place and familiar to me now. It's mixed and interesting, unlike Tunbridge Wells, where my mother lives; that funny kind of monoculture seems strange now. I spend an afternoon there with her and her friends and after a couple of hours I'm running back here, screaming. If gentrification goes too far it will be a shame, though I *am* middle class and I like the new shops, etc. (LF1)

It's an attractive and friendly neighbourhood, with its own 'London Fields' identity . . . the physical appearance of the place has improved enormously as a result of the activities of the newer buyers . . . social housing has, by and large, improved, the newer developments are much better than the 70s monsters, and the older ones have been improved, so a general improvement in the look of the place overall. (LF15)

Holly Street has changed considerably, having a benign effect on the area . . . there is an emerging community, I know neighbours now . . . (LF22)

The observation that the improvements 'have not gone too far', together with references to the flagship regeneration under the New Deal for Communities initiative of the Holly Street Estate, which is on the borders of the area, indicate some of the problems but also what appears to be a genuine wish to live in a mixed area and work through the problems.

The mix of people is lovely, really excellent, smashing neighbours . . . it's quiet and the space is great, plenty of room in the parks . . . we were made to feel very welcome when we moved here, which was a concern . . . We've had no problems with neighbours (old working class and middle class alike), so it didn't really conform to what might have been expected, our moving here and settling in. (LF36)

Green space here is better than the London average . . . the mix of people is good, especially for the kids, who see so many kinds of people they think it normal. (LF25)

It's not a trendified place, it still has quite a lot of character, which is quite unusual for London . . . there are some nice houses and interesting buildings in a mix of styles . . . it's close to areas that I like and relatively quiet . . . (LF29)

The general neighbourliness of the whole community – this is the major part of my life, now . . . there is great diversity, a range of 'cultural' things to do, a 'buzz' . . . I sometimes visit my mother in [a picturesque south coast village] (if you know that little picture postcard place) and it seems so strange to me now, all those blue rinses looking the same, talking the same language . . . after a while I'm desperate to get back to Hackney, the kind of richness you have here is now my normality. (LF37)

Most of the frustrations about living in London Fields are visited on to the local borough council, which is universally vilified for its alleged corruption and undoubted inefficiency which not only make middle-class life difficult but represents an act of betrayal towards the under-privileged.

There is a poverty overload in the borough, and the council is uniquely politically unstable and inefficient. It's very disheartening, the way people in local government fight among themselves in the midst of so much poverty . . . Education and the health services are a shambles. (LF30)

It's unpleasant to lock shutters, doors with mortice locks etc., but it is necessary . . . I was mugged on the doorstep. It occasionally feels a bit heavy on the streets. This is why I began to drive, to alleviate that feeling of discomfort on the street . . . I dislike Dalston itself intensely, it's filthy, shockingly shabby, and it's been dumbed down to the nth degree, everything to the lowest common denominator. It's absolutely horrible, but I'm privileged enough to not have to wallow in that . . . as an onlooker, I can see that education has certainly failed to improve since the council took over . . . this is a major priority for the kinds of people who live round here, but their children are really being failed by Hackney . . . why the hell are they selling school buildings to property developers? . . . it feels less tense in terms of policing. There is much less aggro between locals and the police than there used to be, there used regularly to be marches on the police station and riots and so on, but this has calmed down . . . The situation is dealt with more carefully by the police now, there's not the same sense of being in a potentially difficult situation . . . the helicopter is used now with much more restraint. (LF44)

The council appears to have no pride in the area; they're grossly arrogant and careless. They have an absolutely lackadaisical, 'anything goes' kind of attitude . . . it's as if they don't understand the concept of civic pride and its knock-on effects across the population as a whole – it does not lead by example . . . dealing with social services is a nightmare; personnel are not properly trained, ignorant and non-cooperative, they have no social or people skills, no sophistication or capacity to interpret and deal with people – they are unapproachable and useless . . . there is a general feeling of a lack of money in the area, recycling and cleaning are a shambles and there are no police on the beat . . . this instigates a lack of trust or hope in local people . . . Holly Street is the one bright achievement . . . (LF46)

Despite the grime and crime, most people feel that the diversity of the area is what made it where they wanted to be and that just sufficient change has taken place for both them and other residents to make it place where they continue to wish to live.

> I'm gay, which gives me a much wider acquaintanceship than if I were married with kids – I can enjoy the full diversity of the area, though most of my friends have in common a university-educated, middle-class background . . . in this particular corner I have noticed a phenomenon which has been accelerating in the last two years, of the older long term residents cashing in and moving on. I know four people who have done this – a lot of these people are older Afro-Caribbeans and so the area is becoming whiter and more middle class. You need to be pretty affluent to get in here now . . . but everybody mucks in pretty well together . . . there are still a few real old timers around from when this was a predominantly Jewish area, a few archaeological remnants; when I go to antique dealers out in Essex and give a lot of the Jewish dealers my card, they can't believe my address, in the old neighbourhood . . . this happens to me a lot, it's very strange. (LF24)

As we will see in Chapter 7, education remains a huge problem for middle-class people but this is dealt with in a different way from other areas – the accommodations which are reached with the system seem to be much more individual and taken as part of a general strategy about living in a deprived and multi-cultural area. It is as if respondents have more self-confidence in their cultural capital to deal in a long-term and considered way with the problems that are thrown at them by living in an area like London Fields which is run by what was, more than once, described as a 'crap' council.

> I come across a lot of people unlike us through their children . . . it's the childminding mafia that really runs the area, loads of activity, and they're Sikh, black, Scottish, underclass, everything, and our children all end up playing together . . . so I have plenty of contact with all sorts of people not like me but we all recognize that there are lines that can't be crossed. There are huge chunks of my life that can't be discussed with them, and vice versa . . . so even though I spend a lot of time with those people and have a good rapport, we don't get close – we all know where that line is. (LF43)

The lines in Docklands are, however, far more impermeable.

Docklands

Docklands is different in most respects from the other areas that we have looked at mainly because it constitutes an area that has been gentrified by a combination of private capital and state policy – what Warde (1991) has termed gentrification by 'capital' as opposed to 'collective social action'. The previous five areas that we have been describing in this chapter were all the outcome of the latter process in which there was a complex interaction between people and place. In Docklands, the relationship is that much more straightforward: the place has largely been constructed by capital and largely at the direct expense of people. It is then marketed on to other people as a commodity redolent with social meaning and cultural cachet. This has two implications. First, that the relationship with local people is much more brutal; they are crudely a problem that stands in the way of the successful transformation of the area. Second, that by buying into an area with a marketed place identity people are generally indicating their willingness to forgo their involvement in place making. This might be seen as an assertion but if so, it is one that is generally borne out by what respondents have to say about the area and what they like and dislike about it. What are perhaps of equal interest are the differences and similarities between the three sub-areas – to some extent they have already been indicated by our observations and by the ACORN typologies but there is clearly a Docklands hierarchy emerging, largely based around proximity to the City and length of time since they were developed. More generally, however, what emerges out of the study of the Docklands areas is the lack of a metropolitan habitus; we begin to sketch this in this chapter and then develop it in the ones that follow.

The Isle of Dogs for many people *is* Docklands, but was just the first and probably most brutal transformation of what was an archetypal working-class dock community into a residential and business district. It is this combination of functions, legoland riverside condominiums and the Canary Wharf complex that distinguishes it from our other two areas (Britannia Village by City Airport and Surrey Quays on the south bank of the River Thames). Nonetheless nearly all respondents recite the attraction of the area as those of 'easy living', not having to get involved in social obligations to others.

I like being near the river . . . the Isle of Dogs is peaceful, less trouble than Whitechapel or Bethnal Green. (ID2)

Easy journey to work – I WILL NOT sit on a train – though a lot of the people around here tend to disappear at weekends. A lot of people just keep working flats on the Island, but we choose to make it our home . . . it's just a lovely environment . . . there were still a lot of empty plots when we came here (3 years ago), now it's finished. It's all coming together, filling in – definitely improving . . . I much prefer it too where I lived before, in Clapham, Putney. (ID3).

The same views are generally expressed by those living in Britannia Village, which is more isolated and almost entirely lacking in any form of infrastructure or social economy.

> I like it because it's not congested – we don't need the services so the quality of the provision doesn't bother us. We like the anonymity – I don't know whether the people I see around the place are my neighbours or not. I can't tell. (BV7)

> People seem very friendly; I'm excited about what could happen here in terms of community . . . I like living close by these discrete East End areas with their own lifestyles . . . (BV8)

To some extent, the responses almost mirrored the marketing brochures with their pictures of waterside cranes, empty docks and modern 'fresh-as-a-daisy' housing:

> If I'm going to live in London I need to be near water, so this is good. (BV10)

> I like the architecture of the place, and the flats are clean and low-maintenance . . . living on the side of a dock gives it a special quality . . . the place has dramatically improved over the last three years, I really like living here. (BV14)

More people in Docklands than elsewhere talked of their property as an investment that would accumulate and saw it as having an exchange value that was at least as great as its use value – a claim that 'collective action' gentrifiers went to great pains to deny.

> There will be a complete infrastructure here eventually . . . as an investment it could hardly be bettered. (BV15)

This was particularly the case in Britannia Village, which, at the time of the interviews in 2000, was still being completed and was almost entirely lacking in anything to sustain physical wellbeing or social life. The reaction to the social mix of the area is almost faux-naif at times:

> It's a good place to come back to. I like the ethnic mix of the area in general, the teenage girls pushing prams – some of the twenty rear olds have three kids . . . the way people dress. (BV19)

Surrey Quays to the south is rather more settled and central than Britannia Village but more socially mixed than the Isle of Dogs. Its inhabitants again stress ease and the ongoing fascination with a riverside location but also the fact that it is grafted on to an existing urban structure. These are made to seem positive factors.

> The good thing about this place is that it's close to the centre of London but not *in* it. This makes it relatively stable . . . (SQ23)

> It's both very peaceful – the river in particular is beautiful, a real pleasure to live on – but also incredibly dynamic . . . more and more leisure facilities, many, many more conversions. (SQ24)

Predictably enough the problems centred on issues of polarization, which are in part focused on cultural conflict and social mobility or lack of it:

> The local pubs are out of bounds, I just don't use them . . . they're full of old 'gorblimey' east end types (the kind of people I originally left London to get away from) . . . there is a lack of any kind of village atmosphere here, which I don't think will ever happen . . . it's very polarized on the Island, it's either very east endish or people in very expensive places, a lot of wealthy people . . . that's why I socialize elsewhere, there's no-one on my wavelength here . . . (ID5)

> there is vast polarization between the haves and the have not, and you can feel very isolated here . . . there is absolutely no choice in education, which doesn't effect us personally . . . (ID10)

Elsewhere, however this has a harder edge

> The immediate area has improved considerably, with the new building and the shopping centre . . . but the area in general has declined considerably . . . the 'ethnics' have taken over south London, they're all here to claim asylum or exploit the situation, and they've got nothing in common with us . . . we like it round here, it's very quiet and nice, but south London as a whole has gone to the dogs, definitely . . . they call it a melting pot – I call it a cauldron. It's got to explode. (SQ8)

> We both feel threatened here – my nephew was beaten up on the doorstep last week . . . the Island will not take off socially, there is an oil and water problem here, two very different worlds . . . The hard core of the population are docklanders, surrounded by a fluffy periphery of new developments. These are two completely polarized forms of life and activity or, if you like, it's the difference between Asda and Tesco Metro (at Canary Wharf). These two extremes make it hard to provide a common leisure service in the area which will work for everybody, and so there is no public or commercial sphere whatsoever . . . . . . Too much immigration has been allowed to concentrate in London, especially in this area . . . (ID11)

Although the expression of these views was restricted to Docklands' respondents they are not atypical of many of this group. There was a contradiction between 'buying into' the (optimism) of the marketing image whilst retaining a depressingly pessimistic evaluation of how the current social polarization might work through:

London is heading in this direction . . . once this is no longer a village, crime will rise, there may be security problems . . . the problem here is that though more people have come in and it's got busier, they all just live in their little boxes and don't mix. There's an absolute dearth of kids here. Lots of couples but no kids. (SQ22)

It can be quite an abrasive environment, this part of London . . . it sometimes feels dangerous, especially when you're alone. You have to watch your back. (SQ24)

There is no infrastructure for socialising here, nowhere to go – this will become an issue as I get older . . . this is more of an area for younger people who are not putting down roots. (SQ26)

I don't like the changes, all the new people coming into the area (even though I'm one of them!) . . . it is becoming too built-up, overdeveloped, and crime is starting to rise . . . local people are being driven out, and in a way I'm part of what's driving them, even though I identify with them in terms of social background . . . so I'm the odd one out here . . . (SQ28)

Although it was always pleasant, quiet and safe on this stretch of the river, this is beginning to change . . . it no longer feels safe, since the DLR extension connected us up with Lewisham. Now south London people are coming across the river and it's a free-for-all – they're coming here because they know there's no proper police station on the Island . . . a neighbour of mine was mugged on his own doorstep recently. It's no longer quiet and secluded, there are more and more people coming here now . . . there is no place where the different groups on the Island could meet and rub shoulders. This is the fault of the council, who understandably bend over backwards to accommodate business but do very little for local people . . . all these electronically gated and private developments encourage this feeling of isolation and separation . . . there is a juxtaposition of extremely expensive waterfront housing and the council housing – it's still not clear whether they can co-exist happily or not indefinitely . . . there is also a lot of tension between the Bangladeshi and older docker populations on the main part of the Island . . . although it would be misleading to say that all the 'locals' are resentful of the change. I think some of the older east enders are happy that the Island is improving, looking better and so on . . . (ID29)

The question that lay at the back of most people's minds was whether or not this was manageable, could they remain largely detached from what they saw as a hopelessly un-integrated community?

It's a strange place – people like us, the old white working class, incoming Bengalis – all hermetically sealed off from one another apart from when using public transport. (ID17)

I've actually got a house in Essex . . . I just have the flat on the Island as my work base . . . I'm at work all day and usually work-socialising in the evenings. (ID6)

Most respondents felt that docklands really met their needs but these were focused on aspects of lives which wanted no involvement in where they lived. This wasn't always the case but even where it was, there was nearly always a life elsewhere. It was almost as if they were in flight from the metropolitan habitus and gentrified London which they felt put too many demands on them.

Note

1. In fact, it regularly contests this spot on the Department of Transport, Local Government and the Regions (DTLR) deprivation index with Newham and Tower Hamlets.

–6–

Home and Household

Introduction

The individual household is the key variable in this study; in this chapter we 'fix' this by looking at the 'lived experience' of different household arrangements, which we again link to the different areas. There are a variety of households both within and between areas. In the next two chapters, we show how many respondents create carefully crafted strategies to deal with the problems of living and working in the city. We argue that the most significant of these concerns involve social reproduction and the schooling of children, which we discuss in Chapter 7. In this chapter, we look at the organization of the home and how it relates both to the external world of work and also the other involvements in the city, particularly in relation to culture, leisure and consumption. We examine the importance of relations with friends and the nature of the social networks to which respondents belong. We show that much of the social capital on which respondents are able to draw goes back a long way and is often embedded in friendships and contacts made at school or particularly university. There is thus a high coincidence here between sources of social and cultural capital. An important aspect here will be a discussion of those living in Docklands, which is relatively impoverished except for economic capital; there is an almost wilful neglect of social capital.

Population Characteristics

Perhaps the most startling finding about our respondents was their ethnicity, of the 90 per cent who answered the question about their ethnicity, 97.5 per cent identified themselves as 'white' – overwhelmingly as 'white British' although a minority (7 per cent) defined themselves as 'white European' and 6 per cent as simply 'white'. The figures for their partners, where applicable, were similar. Put another way, out of the nearly 400 respondents who answered this question, two people identified themselves as 'Black Caribbean', two as 'Indian' and one as 'Chinese' and five as 'other'. There is no question that almost all of the forty-eight who did not wish to answer this question were also white.

The issue of ethnicity is rarely raised in relation to gentrification, although an exception is Lees (2000) who refers to the role played by 'race' in gentrification research, which has generally seen white gentrifiers displace black and working-class people. Lees finds few instances of gentrification by non-white people. A search of the best academic database threw up three references – in Brooklyn in New York City, Sydney Australia and Puebla in Mexico. All were concerned with the influx of white gentrifiers into existing black areas. The urban black middle class appears to be almost invisible through the lens of gentrification. The apparent homogenization of the gentrification process is an important, yet neglected, aspect of the metropolitan habitus. It is not that there are no ethnic minority members of the urban middle class; it is that they apparently do not live in areas of mainstream gentrification and/or researchers, ourselves included, are blind to the nuances of 'race' and ethnicity.

Anecdotal evidence suggests that there are black and Asian middle-class settle-ments in London (in north-west London, East London and outer South London – for example: Brent, Redbridge and Thornton Heath) but – for whatever reason – they are not part of mainstream gentrification in inner London. It might be argued that housing market considerations apply – that non-white middle-class profes-sionals are not able to afford the house prices but this seems unlikely. It would seem more likely to be a process of inclusion and exclusion operating in the context of the metropolitan habitus. There is a considerable literature on the effect of gender on gentrification (Bondi 1991; Warde 1991; Butler and Hamnett 1994; Bondi 1999), but there is none on the effect of 'race' and ethnicity. Not only does this point to a serious gap in the research literature but also indicates some worry-ing concerns about the nature of the gentrification process and the modes in which it has been studied.

Traditionally the 'others' of gentrification have been the 'displaced', which have almost always been defined in terms of class and/or housing tenure. The apparent homogeneity of the gentrifiers in our research in terms of 'race' and ethnicity is striking, particularly when almost all of the areas in which it has occurred in inner London are multicultural. The 'us' and 'them' are however not ranked just in terms of class and material resources but they are also ethnically and 'racially' asymmetric. This was not an issue that we addressed explicitly in the research but is one that demands reflection. Almost without exception, our respondents – particularly in Brixton, Telegraph Hill, London Fields and, for the most part, Barnsbury – talked about social diversity (in contrast to the supposed homogeneity in traditional middle-class settlements) as being one of the plus points of living the inner city. In Brixton social diversity was explicitly referred to in terms of multiculturalism, elsewhere it was often implied. What seems quite clear is that everywhere it was not something that respondents had any intimate knowledge of – their friends and fellow gentrifiers were universally white and non-whites appeared only as 'local colour' – we refer to this as contributing to the 'tectonic' nature of Brixton (Robson and Butler 2001). We return to this issue of ethnicity in a discussion of the 'metropolitan habitus' in the final and concluding chapter.

Sixty per cent of the respondents we interviewed were female; in Brixton three-quarters of respondents were female. Women accounted for 64 per cent in Barnsbury and 56 per cent in Telegraph Hill; elsewhere they were under 55 per cent. We don't attach any particular significance to this – the reasons were probably different in each case. In Brixton, twenty-two out of twenty-four single-person households were female – elsewhere the proportion was nearer to the overall male/female balance. In Barnsbury women had quite often withdrawn from the labour market when children had been born and therefore we assume had more time to participate in the research.

There was considerable homogeneity in terms of age with relatively little difference between the areas: Brixton was the youngest but not by very much. As Table 6.1 indicates, this was a middle-aged group with a mean age in their forties and a standard deviation of approximately ten years each side of this. It is perhaps of interest that Telegraph Hill and London Fields have the highest average ages and the smallest standard deviations. It is also of interest that there were respondents in their mid to late seventies in each of the areas – other than Docklands

Table 6.2 indicates the composition of the households – there were some missing data that usually resulted from a reluctance to answer the question and we hypothesize might have been unwillingness to indicate same sex cohabitation. The missing data were highest (approximately 10 per cent) in London Fields and Docklands. The data allow us to make a number of interesting observations about differences between the areas. Firstly, the proportion of single person households overall is approximately one third but is particularly high in Docklands and low in Telegraph Hill and Barnsbury. Surprisingly it is around the norm in Battersea which also has the highest number of collective arrangements – usually young people living together. This is probably accounted for by the numbers of relatively wealthy young people living in property bought for them by relatives or trust funds

Table 6.1 Age of respondent

Area	Number of Respondents	Minimum Age	Maximum Age	Mean Age	Std. Deviation
Barnsbury	71	26	79	45.58	12.14
Battersea	73	24	78	43.38	12.05
Brixton	71	27	75	41.51	11.01
Docklands	65	24	68	42.02	11.18
London Fields	70	30	75	47.29	10.33
Telegraph Hill	70	22	77	46.80	10.46

Table 6.2 Household composition (%)

Area	Tel Hill	Brixton	Battersea	Barnsbury	London Fields	Dockland Areas	Total % (n)
Husband/Wife	64.3	34.7	47.9	55.6	39.4	28.6	45.4 (189)
Other sex partner	14.3	15.3	6.8	15.3	22.7	12.7	14.4 (60)
Same sex partner	1.4	11.1	2.7	4.2	3.0	3.2	4.3 (18)
Collective	4.3	5.6	8.2	2.8	7.6	1.6	5.0 (21)
Single Person	15.7	33.3	34.2	22.2	27.3	54.0	30.8 (128)
Total (n)	100 (70)	100 (72)	100 (73)	100 (72)	100 (66)	100 (63)	100 (416)

(similar to the so-called 'trustafarians' who have figured prominently in the gentrification of Notting Hill in recent years). The high number of single households in Docklands fits with our previous description of this as an area focused around work needs with little collective ambience (Hall, Ogden et al. 1997; Ogden and Hall 1998). The area with the highest number of same-sex partner households, by a large margin, is Brixton where this makes up 11 per cent of households compared to an average of 4 per cent. Anecdotal evidence would suggest a higher concentration of gay households here amongst the single householders. Nearly 80 per cent of households in Telegraph Hill comprise either married or opposite sex partnerships, which is nearly one-third higher than the average for all areas and 10 per cent higher than Barnsbury – the next such area. The proportion of opposite sex couple households who are not married is highest in London Fields and lowest in Battersea. This we believe to be indicative of the range of conventional-unconventional social attitudes displayed across the sample. In London Fields over one-third of those living in two-person households are not married compared to one in eight in Battersea. We believe that these nuances in household formation are important aspects of variation in the metropolitan habitus and indicative of wider variations in attitudes and feelings between the areas.

Housing Decisions

Probably the most important, and most symbolic, decision that most respondents made was about *where* to live. Slightly less than one-third lived alone and, of the remainder, for nearly half the respondents this was their first house together although two-thirds of these had previously owned property. Thus the house was an important focus for household formation and the decision to live together. The decisions were long-term ones, for example half the respondents had lived in their previous home for more than five years and half had lived in their current home for more than five years. These were not people who made lots of housing moves – they were part of long-term, considered strategies about whom they lived with and where they wanted to be. As we will see, these were people who were not highly occupationally mobile – most had been in their jobs for a long time and (fantasies apart) reckoned they would still be in them in the longer term. Job changes accounted for very few moves (less than 10 per cent) although some moved to be nearer the job as and when they could afford it (13 per cent). This was usually part of a complex of reasons and often took into account the need to be accessible to two jobs particularly if children came into the household. The main reasons for moving were household related: needing more space, a change in household composition (either children, divorce or new relationship formation) and finally a feeling that they couldn't remain outside the owner-occupation nexus. Two-thirds of those interviewed cited a change in household composition as their main reason for moving.

Ninety-two per cent had *never* considered buying outside London and, of the remainder, the vast majority remained in London because of social and cultural ties. When choosing their house, not surprisingly one determining reason was affordability (50 per cent) but even more so was 'the feel' of the area (55 per cent) and the house itself (38 per cent). Friends in the area (28 per cent) and journey to work (40 per cent) were also important factors. Forty per cent had confined their search to the area in which they now lived. Somewhat surprisingly, given the later importance attached to schooling, only 9 per cent cited schools as a factor in making their choice about living in their present area compared with 19 per cent who favoured the area's 'social mix'. When setting up a strategy to buy, over 60 per cent decided on the area and then looked for what they could afford in the area, which was over twice as many who looked in a range of areas for what they could afford. Clearly, the decision about the area was influenced by price but the focus on area was of prime importance. One-third of those moving house had lived previously in the same area – this was lowest (unsurprisingly) in Docklands (9 per cent) and London Fields (19 per cent). However, what is highly significant is that three-quarters had previously lived in inner London and 90 per cent in London. This is not a back-to-the-city movement of middle-class people; they are metro-politans moving within clearly defined areas of the city.

Whilst not wishing to deny themselves the capital value of their home (which many regarded as part of their retirement planning), capital accumulation was not a major reason for buying where they did or for improving the property. Fifty four per cent denied that capital accumulation prompted their choice to buy; of the two-thirds who had spent money on improving the property these works were undertaken either to maintain the integrity of the building or, more usually, to re-organize the living space. This was an important consideration – there is a gentrif-ication aesthetic that involved 'knocking through' and often making the kitchen the main living and eating space (Jager 1986). Almost all of the houses we visited, and the vast majority of interviews were undertaken at home, had been 'renovated' to provide a large living room at the front. This had usually involved knocking through the front and back rooms on the ground floor. Many had also built extens-ions to the kitchens, which were mostly in the back extensions, often at a sub-basement level.[1] Improvements were more often (70 per cent) undertaken to reorganize existing space than to create additional space (49 per cent). This we regard as significant and the common architecture of gentrification forms, we suggest, an important symbol of the metropolitan habitus – there is for instance rarely a separate dining space. This reflects a fundamental household democracy where both partners are often at work and children are often incorporated into the management of the household and family. The kitchen forms part of the 'command and control' centre from which they all venture out into the city – to work and school.

Most households employed some form of domestic labour (Cox and Watt 2002); for those with children 45 per cent employed some form of childcare, this was predictably biased towards those with younger children. Nannies were the favoured carers in over half the Battersea households employing childcare and a third in Barnsbury whereas childminders were the option of choice in Brixton (43 per cent), Telegraph Hill (33 per cent) and London Fields (57 per cent). Au Pairs (usually for older children) were favoured in Barnsbury (38 per cent) and Brixton (29 per cent). Nurseries were relatively un-favoured (14 per cent) in all areas. The distinction was between those coming into the house to look after the children (largely Barnsbury and Battersea) and those who made arrangements outside the home (elsewhere). These distinctions have some implications in terms of social class; the former strategy kept control by ensuring that all socialization occurred within the home whilst the latter 'exposed' the children to different class and ethnic cultures. It is perhaps somewhat symbolic of some of the issues of difference between the areas concerning social reproduction, which are discussed in the next chapter. Thirty-five per cent of respondents employed at least one person to help with domestic chores, in nearly all cases cleaning although some employed gardeners, dog walkers and people to do the ironing.

Employment and Income

Given the research design, it would be surprising if our respondents were not largely drawn from professional and managerial groups, albeit with a significant

Table 6.3 Respondents' social class

Social Class	Description	Frequency	%
Class 1	Higher managerial & professional	122	33.0
Class 2	Lower managerial & professional	160	43.2
Class 3	Intermediate occupations	23	6.2
Class 4	Small employers & own account workers	19	5.1
Class 5	Lower supervisory & technical occupations	1	0.3
Class 6	Semi routine occupations	2	0.5
Class 7	Routine occupations	1	0.3
Class 8	Never worked & long term unemployed	4	1.1
	Not classified	38	10.3
Total		419	100.0

number of non-professional own account workers. The results were classified according to the Office of National Statistics (ONS) social class categories and are summarized in Table 6.3:

Approximately four out of five respondents were in social classes one and two, which might be narrowly defined as the employed 'service class', an additional 5.5 per cent were self-employed non-manual workers. Almost the entire 'not classified' category was accounted for by women with domestic responsibilities who chose not to participate in paid employment. Insufficient questions were asked to allocate them to a class category on the basis of their previous employment. Area differences between classes 1 and 2 are displayed in Table 6.4.

Barnsbury in particular, but to a lesser extent Battersea and Docklands, emerge as areas with a higher concentration of respondents in social class 1 (senior managers, owners and employed or self-employed professionals). This partly reflects the status of Battersea and Barnsbury as iconic and relatively long-established areas of gentrification and of Docklands as providing a pied-à-terre for well paid 'empty nesters' (an observation borne out by the data). It also represents the reality of the inner London housing market: the cost of property in such areas often begins at approximately £500,000, which puts it beyond all but the better paid, or longer established. It also represents the manner in which these areas are perceived. On the other hand, Telegraph Hill, in particular, but also Brixton and London Fields tend to be populated by what Goldthorpe (1987) has referred to as 'cadet members' of the service class. With reference to the earlier classification of residents, Telegraph Hill reflects the concept of 'welfare professionals' proposed by Savage, Barlow et al. (1992) not just in terms of their occupations but also their lifestyle proclivities, identifications and anxieties. Fifty per cent of respondents in Brixton are also in class 2 – and although the two sub areas 'feel' rather different in this respect at least they are remarkably well balanced with only a slightly higher

Table 6.4 Respondents' social class by area (%)

	Telegraph Hill	Brixton	Battersea	Barnsbury	London Fields	Dockland Areas	Total (n)
Class 1	18.3	22.5	42.5	52.8	32.4	43.8	35.3 (148)
Class 2	56.3	50.7	34.2	31.9	48.5	34.4	42.7 (179)
Class 3	7.0	9.9	8.2	2.8	4.4	4.7	6.2 (26)
Class 4	7.0	4.2	2.7	5.6	7.4	6.3	5.5 (23)
Class 5		1.4			1.6		0.5 (2)
Class 6		1.4	1.4		3.1		1.0 (4)
Class 7	1.4						0.2 (1)
Class 8	1.4	1.4	1.4		1.5		1.0 (4)
Not classified	8.5	8.5	9.6	6.9	5.9	6.3	7.6 (32)
Total (n)	100 (71)	100 (71)	100 (73)	100 (72)	100 (68)	100 (64)	100 (419)

Table 6.5 Total gross annual household income for multiple person households and respondent's income for single person households and for all respondents

Income per annum	Household income multiple person		Income for single person		Respondent's income for all respondents	
	Frequency	%	Frequency	%	Frequency	%
Less than £10,000	1	0.4	6	5.5	17	4.7
£10-20,000	11	4.0	15	13.6	70	19.3
£20-30,000	19	7.0	32	29.1	90	24.8
£30-40,000	38	14.0	14	12.7	64	17.6
£40-50,000	33	12.1	14	12.7	40	11.0
£50-60,000	38	14.0	10	9.1	30	8.3
£60,000-100,000	74	27.2	8	7.3	21	5.8
£100,00-150,000	24	8.8	2	1.8	6	1.7
More than £150,000	29	10.7	5	4.5	17	4.7
Refused	5	1.8	4	3.6	8	2.2
Total	272	100.0	128	100.0	440	100.0

proportion (26 per cent) of class 1 in Herne Hill as compared to Tulse Hill (19 per cent).

There are significant variations here in household incomes that reflect different abilities to participate in the two key markets: housing and education. Table 6.5 indicates the household income of those living in single person and multiple adult households.

Approximately half the two adult households had a household income in excess of £60,000 per annum. In the case of single person households approximately a quarter had an income in excess of £60,000 and 15 per cent of single person households were earning over £60,000. The figures for household income are probably mediated by the fact that more respondents were female than male and that females' incomes were lower than male incomes – this probably underestimates

Table 6.6 Household income for multiple person households by area (%)

Income per annum	Telegraph Hill	Brixton	Battersea	Barnsbury	London Fields	Dockland Areas	Total (n)
less than £10,000					2.4		0.4 (1)
£10–20,000	10.3	6.5		1.8	4.8		4.3 (12)
£20–30,000	6.9	13.0	4.2	3.6	11.9	3.7	7.2 (20)
£30–40,000	20.7	10.9	12.5	5.4	21.4	11.1	13.7 (38)
£40–50,000	12.1	15.2	4.2	10.7	14.3	18.5	11.9 (33)
£50–60,000	12.1	19.6	14.6	5.4	21.4	11.1	13.7 (38)
£60,000–100,000	27.6	21.7	41.7	19.6	19.0	37.0	27.1 (75)
£100,00–150,000	5.2	6.5	8.3	23.2	2.4	3.7	9.0 (25)
More than £150,000	3.4	2.2	10.4	30.4	2.4	14.8	10.8 (30)
Refused	1.7	4.3	4.2				1.8 (5)
Total % (n)	100 (58)	100 (46)	100 (48)	100 (56)	100 (42)	100 (27)	100 (277)

incomes in Barnsbury and Battersea. Nevertheless it is clear from these figures that multiple incomes are of crucial importance to most households particularly in multiple adult households.

The modal category (see Table 6.6) for the household income is £60,000–100,000 in every area except Barnsbury (in excess of £150,000) and London Fields (£50,000–60,000). This suggests that housing market concerns (house prices) may not be the major drivers in determining residential location in inner London. This supports our initial hypothesis that values and lifestyles may drive intra-class fragmentation as much as income and occupation. This once again reinforces the notion of a metropolitan habitus in which such things as feelings, beliefs and values are generative and cannot simply be read off from occupational position. These clusters of factors are often symbolized by decisions about where to live in inner London.

Sixty per cent of respondents owned shares and a similar percentage had building society accounts, less than 20 per cent had life assurance but 40 per cent had some other additional form of savings. Money was not a huge issue with most respondents, for example most denied that capital accumulation on their property (whilst appreciated) played any significant role in their decisions about where to live and when to move. Most were satisfied with their jobs, and even those who said they were contemplating a job move (20 per cent) admitted that this was largely a hypothetical consideration. When asked about their long-term job plans most, after much musing, reckoned that they would still be doing what they currently did.

Respondents' occupations (and those of their spouses) generally reflect the London economy; they are concentrated in the service sector and are largely either professional occupations or senior managers in the civil services or financial services industries. In management, there are two main clusters: those responsible for organizing corporations or the state and functional managers. The latter includes those working in financial services institutions and people such as investment bankers many of whom, in their day-to-day work, tend to regard themselves more as professionals than managers. In the professions cluster, respondents are spread out across the range of professional activity: health, education, law, accountancy, surveying, local government and research. Although there are quite a few in information and communications technology, the remaining science and technology professions are barely represented – no engineers or research scientists for instance. The same observation applies to the associate professions that are clustered in the same sort of way with the important addition of the arts and media which are heavily represented. There were very few people working in routine administrative jobs, the largest category being personal assistants and secretaries.

Managers were most likely to live in Barnsbury, Battersea and Docklands, somewhat less so in Brixton and least likely to live in Telegraph Hill or London

Fields. Senior officials and corporate managers were more likely to be found in Barnsbury or Battersea. All areas, with the partial exception of Brixton, had a similar number of professionals. The divergence in Brixton is explained by a total absence of 'business and statistical professionals' whilst in Docklands there was a more across-the-board under-representation which was compensated for by ITC, which was the highest amongst the sample. What is striking amongst this group of professionals is the extent to which two areas (Telegraph Hill and London Fields) are home to 'teaching professionals'. This group includes those working in higher education as well as schools and colleges. In both cases this group constituted nearly half the professional category and was larger than the next largest group by a factor of nearly three times. This group would be a mainstream component to the 'welfare professionals' referred to by Savage, Barlow et al. (1992).

The under-representation of professionals in Brixton and Docklands is made up, to some extent at least, in the category of associate professionals although in different ways. Brixton, and particularly London Fields, have a high proportion working in the arts, media and design occupations; there is a very large number of people working in the 'artistic and literary' occupations in London Fields (constituting 12.5 per cent of all respondents). Telegraph Hill and Brixton also have a large proportion in this group (8 per cent). Brixton and London Fields also have just under 10 per cent working in the media as either journalists or press and publicity officers. Docklands has none working in the creative and artistic occupations but nearly 20 per cent of its respondents work in business and finance – which is double the proportion in any other area. This group includes brokers in the finance industries, for example. Finally, in the non-professional categories, it is worth noting that the only significant grouping is in the group of secretaries and personal assistants – this is largest in Wandsworth and might be explained in terms of relatively 'well-educated' but under-qualified young women from upper social strata backgrounds.

An alternative way of looking at the professional and occupational status of respondents is to consider their socio-economic status. The data have been summarized into two main groups in Table 6.8 to demonstrate the 'area' effects here, which point to the same conclusions but through a different lens – that of socio-economic occupational status. Looking at respondents this way Barnsbury, Battersea and Docklands emerge as having a 'higher' socio-economic profile than the other areas and Telegraph Hill as having the least in this higher category but the highest in the lower category – interestingly both Brixton and London Fields, which we have termed 'alternative' sites of gentrification, are somewhere in the middle. Telegraph Hill emerges here as a bastion of the lower end of the service class.

In terms of mapping a metropolitan habitus, the nature of occupation is tied up with that of the employer's business. Table 6.9 indicates the main contours of this

Table 6.7 Professional-Managerial distribution by area (%)

	Telegraph Hill	Brixton	Battersea	Barnsbury	London Fields	Dockland Areas	Total (n)
Managers	13.9	18.5	22.4	22.7	12.3	25.0	19.1 (74)
Professionals	69.2	60.0	64.2	69.7	73.9	67.0	67.5 (262)
Admin/Secretarial	3.1	9.2	7.5	3.0	0	2.5	4.1 (16)
Artistic	9.2	9.2	6.0	3.0	13.9	0	7.0 (27)
Other	4.6	3.1	0	1.5	0	5.5	2.3 (9)
Total (n)	100 (65)	100 (65)	100 (67)	100 (66)	100 (65)	100 (60)	100 (388)

division, which suggests that self-employment is the largest single category with the exception of Docklands where it is private sector services. However when the subcategories are aggregated then Telegraph Hill, Brixton and London Fields have the highest proportion working in the public sector, whilst Battersea and Docklands have the highest proportion in the private sector. Barnsbury is much more evenly divided with respondents working across sectors.

Table 6.8 Respondents' Socio Economic group (%)

	Telegraph Hill	Brixton	Battersea	Barnsbury	London Fields	Dockland Areas	Total
Employers in large organizations and higher professionals and managers	17.3	21.2	42.6	52.1	32.0	41.5	34.3
Lower professionals and managers	53.3	49.3	34.7	31.5	47.2	31.4	41.3
Other	14.7	15.9	12.0	8.2	11.2	15.8	13.1
Economically inactive or inadequately described	14.7	13.3	10.6	8.2	9.7	11.4	11.3
Total	75.0	75.0	75.0	73.0	72.0	70.0	440.0

Table 6.9 Employer's business by area (%)

Employer's business	Telegraph Hill	Brixton	Battersea	Barnsbury	London Fields	Dockland Areas	Total
Public Sector: Central Government	1.7	12.1	1.6	6.6	8.8	3.8	5.7
Public Sector: Local Government	25.9	17.2	6.6	4.9	14.0	11.3	13.2
Public Sector: Other	12.1	8.6	8.2	16.4	10.5	7.5	10.6
Voluntary Sector	8.6	8.6	3.3	9.8	7.0	3.8	6.9
Private Sector: Finance & Commerce	1.7	5.2	16.4	14.8	1.8	18.9	9.8
Private Sector: Manufacturing	1.7		3.3	3.3			1.4
Private Sector: Services	10.3	17.2	26.2	18.0	15.8	32.1	19.8
Private Sector: Other	5.2	3.4	1.6		3.5	5.7	3.2
Profession				3.3		1.9	0.9
Self employed	32.8	27.6	32.8	19.7	38.6	15.1	27.9
Other				3.3			0.6
Total n	58.0	58.0	61.0	61.0	57.0	53.0	348.0
Total %	100.0	100.0	100.0	100.0	100.0	100.0	100.0

The sector of employment is related to whether or not respondents belong to a trade union, which, as Table 6.10 shows, indicates a split between Telegraph Hill and London Fields, on the one hand, and the rest. When asked why they belonged, the most common reply was one of belief followed by instrumental reasons (mainly connected with job protection and legal liability). These findings reinforce the idea that what Telegraph Hill and London Fields share is a series of beliefs based around public service and employees' rights compared, at the other extreme, with Battersea and Docklands where there is a much lower membership (although high by some standards) where it is seen as largely irrelevant. There was a high non-response on this question, which must be taken as hostility, so the figures probably overemphasize trade union membership.

One feature of the so-called 'new economy' that is often stressed is that workers are much more mobile, as indicated for example by Sennett (1999). What is perhaps surprising is that over half of respondents had worked for their current employer for more than five years; in Barnsbury 40 per cent had worked for the

Table 6.10 Trade Union membership by area (%)

TU Member	Telegraph Hill	Brixton	Battersea	Barnsbury	London Fields	Dockland Areas	Total
Yes	50.0	36.8	24.1	35.6	54.0	27.9	38.2
No	50.0	63.2	75.9	64.4	46.0	72.1	61.8
Total	100	100	100	100	100	100	100
(n)	(58)	(57)	(58)	(59)	(50)	(43)	(325)

same employer for more than ten years. The only two areas where this fell below 50 per cent were Docklands and Brixton but even here over 40 per cent had worked more than five years with the same employer. Twenty per cent of respondents claimed that they were thinking of changing their job in the foreseeable future, but the way this was often said implies that this was probably more fantasy than a realistic option.

Respondents' Backgrounds

Previous research (Butler 1997) on gentrification in inner London has shown that the middle class who choose to live in its gentrified areas are different from the middle class nationally – in backgrounds and in their attitudes. The same research also showed that those living in different parts of the city also had different characteristics. These findings are confirmed by the present research. Not only were the background differences social but also geographic – they tended to 'recruit' from different 'places' both socially and spatially. Brixton has the highest percentage of respondents who were brought up in London, whilst by contrast Battersea has the highest brought up in the 'Rest of the South East' (ROSE) – or

Table 6.11 Respondents' childhood home by area (%)

	Telegraph Hill	Brixton	Battersea	Barnsbury	London Fields	Dockland Areas	Total (n)
London	22.5	28.2	20.5	23.6	23.5	15.6	22.4
ROSE	33.8	32.4	49.3	26.4	26.5	36.0	34.1
Rest of UK	21.6	21.1	17.8	33.4	35.2	26.7	26.0
Elsewhere	21.0	18.2	12.2	16.8	14.7	21.8	17.4
Total	100	100	100	100	100	100	100
(n)	(71)	(71)	(73)	(72)	(68)	(64)	(419)

Table 6.12 Father's socio-economic group by area (%)

Father's socio-economic group	Telegraph Hill	Brixton	Battersea	Barnsbury	London Fields	Dockland Areas	Total (n)
Higher professional/ Senior manager	38.2	36.6	60.0	63.4	39.7	53.2	48.5
Associate professional/ Junior managerial	8.8	8.5	18.6	5.6	2.9	8.1	8.8
Other administrative & clerical	5.9	2.8	5.7		4.4	4.8	3.9
Own account non-professional	13.2	12.7		11.3	11.8	8.1	9.5
Supervisers, technical & related	8.8	22.5	11.4	5.6	10.3	9.7	11.5
Intermediate	7.4	11.3	2.9	2.8	5.9	6.5	6.1
Other	17.6	5.6	1.4	9.9	23.5	8.1	11.0
Never worked/ other inactive				1.4	1.5	1.6	0.7
Total n	68.0	71.0	70.0	71.0	68.0	62.0	410.0
%	100.0	100.0	100.0	100.0	100.0	100.0	100.0

more colloquially, the 'Home Counties' – by a considerable margin. Barnsbury and London Fields both have a relatively disproportionate percentage of residents drawn from the rest of the United Kingdom.

Respondents' parents' occupations were classified according to their socio-economic group (SEG); the main finding is that in *all* areas the most common SEG for respondents' fathers was 'higher professional/senior manager' (Table 6.12). In the case of Battersea and Barnsbury this was over 60 per cent and for Docklands 53 per cent but even in Brixton, which was the lowest, it was over one-third of respondents. In the case of Battersea a further 19 per cent came from second highest SEG, thus approximately 80 per cent come from indisputably middle-class backgrounds; this compares to approximately 45 per cent in the case of Telegraph Hill, Brixton and London Fields – Docklands occupying a middle position. London Fields was interestingly split between fathers in the highest SEG and the lowest. The studied ambivalence that we have observed in the occupational position of London Field's respondents is perhaps a reflection of their own backgrounds.

This social division (largely middle class but differentiated by area) is further reinforced in terms of the kind of school respondents attended. The percentage attending a private fee-paying school in Barnsbury (40 per cent) was more than double the next highest (Battersea, London Fields and Docklands at 19 per cent). London Fields had the highest proportion of respondents who had been to 'direct grant schools'.[2] Telegraph Hill can be characterized by the proportion (nearly half) who had been to selective grammar schools and Brixton where nearly a third went to non-selective comprehensive schools. This may of course be partly a function of the relative age of respondents in different areas; those in Brixton tending to be younger than those in Telegraph Hill and having gone through the secondary school system after the abolition of grammar schools, which took place earlier and more systematically in London than elsewhere. Approximately 80 per cent of respondents in Barnsbury attended selective or fee-paying schools and a quarter went on to Oxbridge.[3] Crudely, it would appear that London Fields was characterized by the greatest degree of upward/downward social mobility whereas the others reflected, to a greater or lesser extent, their respondents' socio-economic origins – albeit in different ways.

In thinking about the concept of a metropolitan habitus, we have argued that this should be conceived of as a set of feelings, attitudes and behaviours that are likely to be influential on decisions about such 'structural' behaviours as occupation (and therefore social class) and lifestyle more generally. In previous work (Butler 1997) one of us has demonstrated the importance of education and particularly the experience of higher education in the formation of this complex of attitudes (see also Bagguley 1995). The importance of higher education – not just in terms of the reproduction of class privilege but also in the formation of social, cultural and symbolic capital – cannot be overestimated. We show later that nearly every respondent includes at least one person from this stage of life amongst their three closest friends. There are however consistent area patterns in terms of both where and what respondents studied at university – in particular that nearly one-third of respondents in Barnsbury had gone to 'Oxbridge'. If London University, its colleges and the 'Redbrick'[4] universities are included, this accounts for nearly 80 per cent of respondents in Barnsbury and over half of respondents elsewhere.

Approximately two-thirds studied arts and humanities (40 per cent) and social sciences (26 per cent) whilst at university. Fifteen per cent studied science, technology and engineering subjects – the remainder were distributed across a range of vocational or professional subjects such as education, health and accountancy. In Brixton over half studied arts and humanities, but the highest proportion studying social sciences was in Barnsbury – this included those who studied law. The areas with the largest proportion of respondents with degrees in science, technology and engineering subjects were Battersea (22 per cent), London Fields (18 per cent) and Docklands (15 per cent), which perhaps 'fits' with our previous characterization, but nevertheless the dominant educational ethos was in line with the other areas. It is the overwhelming tendency to focus on arts, humanities and

Table 6.13 Higher education institution by area (%)

Institution	Telegraph Hill	Brixton	Battersea	Barnsbury	London Fields	Dockland Areas	Total (n)
Oxbridge	9.7	6.5	9.5	32.4	6.3	2.6	12.3
Redbrick	24.2	32.3	34.9	36.6	31.7	36.8	32.6
Plateglass	6.5	19.4	19.0	7.0	14.3	13.2	13.1
Polytechnic	12.9	6.5	11.1	2.8	6.3	7.9	7.8
University of London	16.1	11.3	11.1	9.9	11.1	10.5	11.7
College of Higher Education	1.6	3.2	3.2		1.6	2.6	1.9
Teacher Training College	9.7	1.6	1.6	1.4		2.6	2.8
Nursing Training						2.6	0.3
Other	19.4	19.4	9.5	9.9	28.6	21.1	17.5
Total n	62.0	62.0	63.0	71.0	63.0	38.0	359.0
%	100.0	100.0	100.0	100.0	100.0	100.0	100.0

social sciences that appears once again to constitute the metropolitan habitus. Overall just over half of the respondents had a post-graduate qualification but there were important area differences here with the highest in Telegraph Hill (69 per cent) and Barnsbury (63 per cent) and the lowest in Battersea (23 per cent) – the high incidence in the former appears to be accounted for by postgraduate professional qualifications (such as the law and teaching).

Wanting 'The Best' for their Children

Children, and in particular their schooling, are a major concern to middle-class people living in inner London – as a conversation around any metropolitan dinner table will confirm. This was no exception in our research where approximately 40 per cent had children living at home. Concerns about schooling however merely represent a far greater anxiety about the responsibilities and uncertainties of parenting in a fast-moving society where 'the running' is no longer made by middle-class norms of deferred gratification and where there is, as Sennett reminded us, no longer a concept of the 'long term'. We have already raised this as a 'defining issue' in the metropolitan habitus and indicated how issues of inter-generational social reproduction are likely to be at the forefront of decision making by those who are working at the 'front end' of the new global economy about where (and how) to live. By this we don't just mean the investment bankers, media executives and consultants but also those members of the 'welfare professions' whose role has, to put it gently, been called into question by two decades of neo-liberal social policy. We believe Richard Sennett's (1999) argument, which was outlined in Chapter 3, that many of the most successful denizens of the new economy, whilst decrying the boring stability of their parents' lives, are now recognizing the downside in their own lives when it comes to their relations with their children. Tellingly, 'the kids' take their parents' current exalted status for granted and don't appreciate their stellar rise from working-class backgrounds. In a recent survey on wealth and inequality, *The Economist* opines

> There are more rich people than ever before, including some 7 million millionaires, and over 400 billionaires. From sipping champagne to taking trips into space, they are getting plenty of pleasure – though, as our survey into the new rich in this issue shows, these sad souls have worries, too, not least about the damaging effect their wealth may have on their children. (*The Economist* 16 June 2001)

Most of the subjects of our research would not be classified as the new rich (although some are), the concerns however are the same. Fears and concerns about schooling are an incomplete, partial and in many ways misleading way to instance this but they do form part of a recognized discourse that relates to policy and family strategies. In previous work on Hackney, Butler (1997) discovered that *not a single family* in one of the areas under investigation was educating its children at schools in Hackney. Education is also – at least in its state-provided ('bog standard')[5] comprehensive guise – one of the major mechanisms for cross-class interaction/socialization. One of our objectives in this research was to investigate the extent to which this was happening in inner London (in other words, what the relationship was between social and spatial distance in gentrified areas). Education is therefore a major concern for those respondents with school age children and, to a lesser extent, those contemplating parenthood or with pre-school children. Thirty-nine per cent of households had children living at home; of these 39 per cent had one child, 44 per cent had two whilst 17 per cent had more than two. The distribution of children between the areas was very uneven: at one extreme, two thirds of respondents in Telegraph Hill were in households with children whereas at the other end in Docklands it was about one in eight. This is not explained by the age distribution which, as Table 6.1 demonstrated, is not very different across the areas – middle age predominates.

The discussion on children is taken up in the context of schooling in the next chapter in which we show that however initially blasé parents are – or by their own accounts were – when choosing to move to inner London, this now dominates a considerable part of their consciousness.

Table 6.14 Distribution of households with children by area

Area	Households with children at home %
Telegraph Hill	63.8
Brixton	36.8
Battersea	41.2
Barnsbury	47.0
London Fields	37.1
Docklands	13.8
Total (n)	100 (159)

Forms of Association

A key objective for the research was to investigate how respondents interacted socially; in particular, whether there was evidence that the social distance between gentrifiers and other inhabitants – identified in previous research (Moore 1982; Butler 1997) – was breaking down or at least varied between areas. Was it the case that some forms of gentrification were more 'benign' than others and that any displacement was compensated for by a 'halo' effect? For instance, it was hypothesized that the presence of incoming middle-class residents might lead to environmental enhancements and improvements in local school performance (which are discussed at length in the following chapter) from which all might benefit. The alternative hypotheses were that either the improvements would be of disproportionate benefit to middle-class residents or they would worsen the situation by excluding the non-middle class.

Our data point to different forms of middle-class exclusiveness and suggest that the middle class tend to associate with other middle-class people – primarily through their children. We have already commented on the ethnic homogeneity of this essentially white group and this exclusivity is certainly pointed to in terms of who they associate with. This works out differently between areas but schooling appears to be the crucial determinant of whom their best friends are and where they live.[6] There is little evidence of numbers of cross-class friendships.

We felt that one way to look at inter-class relations would be by investigating patterns of association of respondents' children, which might indicate the extent of neighbourhood integration. This proved a complicated issue to untangle, partly because patterns of friendship change with age and partly because of the fact that, as the children grew older, they tended, as we have seen, to disperse geographically often travelling great distances to their secondary schools. Not surprisingly, the overwhelming percentage of children made their friends through school (87.4 per

cent) compared to rather fewer than half who made their friends living in the area
(46.7 per cent). Clearly there is an interaction effect here, children at primary
school tended to have school friends who lived in the area. This was particularly
the case in Telegraph Hill where the percentage that was allowed to play and
socialize without direct supervision outside the home was the highest (57.1 per
cent) which coincided with the highest who reported their children making friends
through school (97.1 per cent). In Battersea nearly as many reported school as
being the focus for their children's friendships (94.4 per cent) but the lowest who
were allowed to play or socialize unsupervised in the streets (27.8 per cent).
Although this is affected by the age of the children concerned, this alone does not
account for the difference. Indeed, our perceptions (supported by respondents'
comments) were that Battersea was the 'safest' of all six areas yet these respondents were the most reluctant to allow their children to play outside. We believe
that this reflects respondents' relationship to their area. In Telegraph Hill there were
strong social networks based around friendships formed at the primary school gate
that carried over into the neighbourhood. There was no evidence that the children
played outside these middle-class networks and our fieldwork strongly suggests
that the middle-class pre-school clubs were, and remain, highly exclusionary of
non middle-class children. In Telegraph Hill there is a strong overlap between
(primary) school and neighbourhood that carries over into secondary schooling.
This is not the case elsewhere as indicated in Table 6.15.

We asked respondents where their children's best friends lived. Barnsbury is the
most local with just over 70 per cent of the eldest child's friends living in the same
locality (Barnsbury), followed by London Fields (66.7 per cent) and Telegraph Hill
(63.6 per cent). The lowest is Brixton at 50 per cent – Battersea and Docklands
being 60 per cent. At first sight, the Barnsbury figure is surprising, given the
number of children being educated outside the borough especially at secondary
level. On the other hand it confirms the pattern of a tight middle-class settlement

Table 6.15 Children's friendship/socialization patterns (%)

	Playing/ socializing outside the home	Friends made through school	Friends made through the locality
Telegraph Hill	57.1	97.1	75.0
Brixton	33.3	70.6	47.1
Battersea	27.8	94.4	16.7
Barnsbury	45.8	80.0	54.5
London Fields	27.8	84.2	42.1
Docklands	50.0	100.0	100.0

with many of the children having gone to the same nursery and primary schools and then to the same selective or private secondary schools elsewhere in North London. The figures for London Fields are more surprising but perhaps point to the sense of 'people like us' in what is a much less benignly middle-class area. In Brixton, which is the lowest, there is little sense of community and a much greater individualism, or what we have termed elsewhere the 'flight from social obligation' (Butler and Robson forthcoming 2003a).

This is borne out by our investigation of the friendship and leisure patterns of respondents. We asked a series of questions about where their three best friends lived and also about the context in which they met those friends. With the exception of Docklands and – to a lesser extent – Battersea, at least 40 per cent of respondents claimed that her/his best friend lived in the same borough. In Barnsbury over 40 per cent of those best friends lived in the locality (the area understood as Barnsbury). Even in Docklands and Battersea just under a quarter (23 per cent) had their best friend in the same locality. The figures are given in Tables 6.16 and 6.17. Crudely, the figures support the claim that gentrification is undertaken by 'people like us', who often got together at university, shortly afterwards or even at school. They live in the same areas as people they have known for a long time or work with. Respondents were asked to give this data for their three best friends, here we give the responses for the first named but they are

Table 6.16 Where does your best friend now live by area (%)

	Telegraph Hill	Brixton	Battersea	Barnsbury	London Fields	Dockland Areas	Total (n)
Same locality	34.8	35.8	24.3	42.3	23.5	24.6	31.0 (126)
Same borough	7.2	9.0	14.3	14.1	20.6	4.9	11.8 (48)
Same quarter of London	30.4	35.8	24.3	22.5	22.1	16.4	25.4 (103)
Elsewhere in London	21.7	11.9	21.4	11.3	22.1	34.4	20.2 (82)
Elsewhere in the UK	5.8	7.5	14.3	8.5	10.3	19.7	10.8 (44)
Abroad			1.4	1.4	1.5		0.7 (3)
Total	100 (69)	100 (67)	100 (70)	100 (71)	100 (68)	100 (61)	100 (406)

remarkably consistent for all three – usually one at least from university and one from work.

Respondents were asked to describe where their three best friends lived and the context in which they had got to know them. Table 6.17 summarizes the results for the first-named friend.

There are four main conclusions to be drawn from this, which all support the notion of a metropolitan habitus of feelings, attitudes and beliefs. Firstly, there are clearly a range of situations in which people form friendships, particularly arising out of situations that might be described as depending on 'elective affinity' – hobbies, interests, organizations based around beliefs politics, religion and so forth. These constitute the 'other' category. Secondly, work is an important factor for most respondents; in all areas approximately one in four had met their best friend through work. When we examine all three friends, normally at least one of them was initially met through work. Perhaps not surprisingly, it was highest in Docklands given that many people live there simply as a work-based pied-à-terre. However, it is the salience of long-standing friendships based around university, school and family of origin that is striking. In between 20 per cent (Brixton and Telegraph Hill) and 36 per cent of cases (Battersea) the respondent's best friend originated from when they were living at home or during university. It is also striking that so many of these friends lived in the same area of London or inner London more generally. This reinforces the understanding of gentrification as being based around networks of university graduates who do not leave London and

Table 6.17 Origin of friendship by area (%)

	Telegraph Hill	Brixton	Battersea	Barnsbury	London Fields	Dockland Areas	Total (n)
Family, school or university	20.0	20.0	36.2	27.1	25.4	23.3	25.4 (102)
Work	27.1	27.7	24.6	24.3	22.4	33.3	26.4 (106)
Through the locality	24.3	16.9	11.6	12.9	16.4	15.0	16.2 (66)
Through the children	10.0		8.7	10.0	7.5	1.7	6.5 (26)
Other	18.6	35.4	18.8	25.7	28.4	25.0	25.2 (101)
Total (n)	100.0 (70)	100.0 (65)	100.0 (69)	100.0 (70)	100.0 (67)	100.0 (60)	100.0 (401)

the idea of the 'metropolitan habitus'. Fourthly, although the category 'through the children' obviously only applies to those respondents with children, it is interesting to note that the locality also becomes more important as a source for friendship when there are children concerned. Where there are no children in the household, then the 'other' category becomes more important – hobbies, interests and so forth. This suggests that these are what disappear out of people's lives when they have children and their friendships are based around their history, their locality or their work – in other words, the basic building blocks of their social existence. Only in Telegraph Hill does work become a far less important source of friendship for those with children and this fits with the notion of Telegraph Hill based around a self-conscious sense of community.

We also investigated the nature of respondents' non-work associations and leisure time activities. Respondents were not large users of local authority provided services; just over a quarter (26.5 per cent) used their local library and a third (32 per cent) sports centres although nearly two-thirds (64 per cent) used (and valued) their local park. Eighty per cent had never been anywhere near a local community centre! Even in Telegraph Hill where the community centre was a focal point for the middle-class community, 57 per cent claimed they never used it. In terms of how they spent their leisure time, 60 per cent claimed to do some kind of keep fit or sporting activity. Table 6.18 indicates the proportion engaging in mainstream cultural and leisure activities.

The area variations in these figures are broadly in line with those already identified. Generally speaking, Telegraph Hill respondents are more home centred and less likely to go out. For instance 88 per cent of those in Brixton went to the cinema once a month compared to 47 per cent in Telegraph Hill; 47 per cent in Barnsbury went to the theatre compared to 19 per cent in Telegraph Hill. Nearly 60 per cent of respondents in Barnsbury and London Fields went to galleries/ exhibitions at least once a month, with the lowest here being Docklands (36 per cent). On the other hand Docklands respondents were most likely to go to a

Table 6.18 Leisure

Activity	% engaging at least monthly	Location
Cinema	62	Mainly local
Theatre	28	Central
Art Galleries	46	Central
Musical Events	31	Central
Pub	58	Central/local
Winebar	44	Central/local
Clubs	11	Central

musical event (39 per cent), with the lowest again in Telegraph Hill (25 per cent). When it came to drinking and going out to clubs, the highest proportions were in Docklands and (for clubs) Brixton and the lowest in Telegraph Hill. This corresponds to the idea of those in Docklands having few family responsibilities and often being there during the week with little else to do whereas those in Telegraph Hill had a large commitment to home and family.

Eighty per cent of all respondents 'went out' at least once a week for some leisure/cultural activity and 40 per cent ate out in a restaurant at least once a week. By comparison, 16 per cent invited others to their home for a meal once a week, although 70 per cent entertained like this at least once a month – this was least frequent in Docklands and Battersea and most frequent in Barnsbury and Brixton. When asked about how frequently they went out during the week for leisure purposes over a third of those in Telegraph Hill replied 'less than once a week', and a similar proportion in London Fields and Battersea (and, in the case of Docklands, 39 per cent) replied 'more than twice'. A third of those in Telegraph Hill ate out rarely and the same proportion in Docklands and Battersea ate out more than twice a week. Those in Barnsbury and Battersea were most likely to see a family member once a week – over half of all respondents, whereas in other areas the same proportion answered less than once a month. These findings are complex but suggest that those in Telegraph Hill were very much focused around the immediate family and household, whereas those in Battersea were most focused on the extended family and 'hedonism'. There appeared to be some similarities between Barnsbury and London Fields in a commitment to 'high culture'.

Finally we asked people a set of questions about their leisure time activities and other non-work time associations. These responses are given in Tables 6.19 and 6.20, which indicate some support for initial hypothesis drawn from Savage et al. (1992) about the leisure pursuits of the different sections of the middle class. For example, the role played by sport in Battersea and Docklands fits with the notion of 'undistinctives' outlined by Savage. The proportion of 'hedonists' in Brixton is compatible with the area's promotion as the centre of a new 'hedonism' in London and a post-modern lifestyle. The focus on cultural activities in Barnsbury is compatible with the high-scoring aspects of cultural capital associated with the 'new professionals' but also a relatively high score is placed on sport which again fits with the Savage 'model'. The high proportion of domestic activity in Telegraph Hill is also compatible with the sense of home-centredness already identified. Once again, London Fields remains the most enigmatic, and is perhaps illustrative of its mixed social-class background. Nevertheless, the findings underscore an emerging typology of difference that we discuss in our conclusions below.

Table 6.20 highlights a number of very interesting traits that reinforce not only those identified above in relationship to leisure time activities but also the Savage model of 'ascetics' and 'undistinctives' (Savage, Barlow et al. 1992). Just over half

Table 6.19 Respondent leisure activities by area (%)

	Telegraph Hill	Brixton	Battersea	Barnsbury	London Fields	Dockland Areas	Total (n)
Sport/outdoor activity	14.5	14.5	29.0	20.8	10.3	28.6	19.5 (80)
Cultural	33.3	43.5	30.4	45.8	23.5	33.3	35.1 (144)
Domestic	24.6	11.6	11.6	2.8	13.2	7.9	12.0 (49)
Hedonistic	13.0	20.3	11.6	9.7	16.2	12.7	13.9 (57)
Other	2.9	2.9	2.9	4.2		6.3	3.2 (13)
Combination of above	11.6	7.2	14.5	16.7	36.8	11.1	16.3 (67)
Total (n)	100.0 (69)	100.0 (69)	100.0 (69)	100.0 (72)	100.0 (68)	100.0 (63)	100.0 (410)

the respondents *belonged* to some form of non work-related voluntary association, which many described as their 'commitment', of 'putting something back in'; the point however is that these were rarely in forms of *local* involvement as, for example, school governors, magistrates or councillors. The focus on charity work in Telegraph Hill, Brixton and London Fields is largely concentrated in 'activist' charities concerning issues of social justice and environment (for example, Greenpeace, Friends of the Earth and Amnesty) and is indicative of the conscience-driven, ascetic, welfare professional approach identified by Savage et al. In Barnsbury and London Fields, in particular, this often took the form of cultural activity such as belonging to a choir or playing in an orchestra.

The role played by sport in Battersea and Docklands is noteworthy and once again provides support for the Savage approach – if active leisure activities such as walking are stripped out, then 40 per cent of respondents in Docklands claim to be actively engaged in sporting activities, the highest single category across the survey. The relatively high figure in Barnsbury (26 per cent) engaged in sport is also interesting amongst this most professional of groupings, which once again supports the Savage thesis that the 'new professionals' tend to go in for California sports (Savage et al, 1992: 108–9). The diversity of interests in London Fields is once again notable; they perhaps reflect the most traditional middle-class approach to leisure with an involvement in good works and cultural activity. The table

Table 6.20 Non work association memberships by area (%)

	Telegraph Hill	Brixton	Battersea	Barnsbury	London Fields	Dockland Areas	Total (n)
Charitable	34.3	25.9	22.0	14.0	25.0	11.5	21.6 (51)
Consumption and hobby activities	18.4	33.3	20.0	20.0	11.2	20.0	20.0 (47)
Sport and active leisure	18.4	14.8	36.0	26.0	22.2	42.9	27.5 (62)
Cultural	5.3	7.4	10.0	18.0	27.8	11.5	13.5 (32)
Social, political & religious activity	23.8	18.5	12.0	22.0	13.9	14.4	17.4 (41)
Total	100.0	100.0	100.0	100.0	100.0	100.0	100.0
(n)	(38)	(27)	(50)	(50)	(36)	(35)	(236)

necessarily conflates a number of categories but the relative importance of religion, particularly in Barnsbury where 12 per cent put it as their prime leisure time activity, was surprising. Overall, it constituted 8 per cent. Only 3 per cent cited politics as their main activity – this was highest in Brixton (7.4 per cent) and Telegraph Hill (5.3 per cent). We return to the issue of political and civic activity next.

Overall, 13.2 per cent belonged to a political party, but this overall figure disguised wide local variation from 30 per cent in Barnsbury to fewer than 5 per cent in Docklands with the remainder around 10 per cent. Taken in conjunction with the previous discussion, in which political activity was shown to be a low-scoring prime activity, party political membership is largely passive. Two-thirds of those who belonged to a political party were Labour Party members; only in Battersea did this fall to 50 per cent. Just over half of all respondents claimed that, if there were to be a general election the next day, they would vote for the Labour Party; this rose to nearly 70 per cent in London Fields and Brixton and fell to 20 per cent in Docklands. Overall, the Conservatives were supported by 9.6 per cent, rising to 15 per cent in Battersea and approximately a quarter in Docklands. For all respondents, they came in fourth behind 'other' parties (19 per cent) and the Liberal Democrats (13.7 per cent). Twenty per cent changed their vote in 1997 mostly in favour of the Labour Party; this was highest in Battersea where 25 per cent changed their vote – mainly from Conservative to Labour but also from Alliance to Labour. A similar trend took place in Docklands where 20 per cent changed their vote compared to the previous general election. In other words, in the two areas with the highest non-Labour vote there was a turn to Labour – these followed the national trend. It is also indicative of a general antipathy towards the Conservative Party within sections of the urban middle class that might otherwise be expected to be solid supporters – well-paid private sector workers who often paid for their education and health in the private sector. These were the two areas with the highest proportion (55 per cent) of respondents with private health insurance. This profile supports the idea of some form of metropolitan habitus in which behaviour displays traits not normally found elsewhere: private consumption of social benefits yet strong support for political parties committed to public services even in areas (notably Wandsworth) with a local government that is strongly committed to the privatization of many services. Forty-three per cent of respondents would vote differently at a local election from the way in which they would vote at a general election. Most of these would either vote for the Liberal Democrats or small parties such as the Greens or Independents.

This predisposition towards public services is reinforced by our findings in relation to attitudes towards local services. Respondents were asked to prioritize local services and service provision and, although they were not 'rationed' in their choices, over three-quarters (77 per cent) including those without children, felt that education was the top priority. A quarter of all respondents were prepared to pay

Table 6.21 National party political support (%)

	Telegraph Hill	Brixton	Battersea	Barnsbury	London Fields	Dockland Areas	Total (n)
Labour	60.0	68.1	48.6	52.8	68.1	22.7	53.7 (227)
Conservative	2.9	2.8	14.9	8.3	2.9	25.8	9.5 (40)
Liberal Democrats	15.7	8.3	13.5	15.3	15.9	15.2	13.9 (59)
Other	17.1	18.1	20.3	18.1	11.6	27.3	18.7 (79)
don't know	2.9	1.4	0.0	2.8	1.4	4.5	2.1 (9)
wouldn't vote	1.4	1.4	2.7	2.8	0.0	4.5	2.1 (9)
Total (n)	100.0 (70)	100.0 (72)	100.0 (74)	100.0 (72)	100.0 (69)	100.0 (66)	100.0 (423)

more council tax to improve services. A further 50 per cent would pay more if there was some guarantee it would lead to improved services – put another way, only a quarter were not prepared to pay more tax locally. There is a good measure of altruism here because they were poor users of local services – apart from local parks (64 per cent), leisure centres (32 per cent) and libraries (27 per cent) – they did not make much direct use of them. Most respondents felt that local services were important, it was important that they were properly funded and they were prepared to pay for them even acknowledging they made little use of them. There was widespread dissatisfaction with service provision (particularly education, which is the focus of discussion in the next chapter) and hospital provision, which probably accounts for the 36 per cent with private health insurance with a further third actively considering taking it out. Even this needs to be put in context: less than 10 per cent felt that they received poor service or worse from their general practitioner with nearly two-thirds saying it was good; there was only slightly more dissatisfaction with hospital services – although over 40 per cent said that they had no recent experience and could make no judgements. This suggests a relatively healthy and satisfied population that is concerned about issues that directly affect it and is often prepared to pay or devote considerable energy to devising strategies to reach satisfactory outcomes. Otherwise it is prepared to contribute to general public services through central and local taxation and regard it as part of the 'urban settlement'.

In view of this, it is not perhaps surprising that nearly 40 per cent of those we interviewed read the *Guardian* regularly followed by *The Times* (13 per cent) although 20 per cent do not read a daily paper. This supports the general claims made in the ACORN indices on consumption types quoted in Chapter 3. The *Sunday Times* and *Observer* are both read by 22.5 per cent; 10 per cent regularly read *The Economist* and *Private Eye*. Television is not a major activity, the most popular programmes being news and current affairs (20 per cent) followed by documentaries and soaps (10 per cent) and then films and sport (less than 10 per cent). Respondents are consistent radio listeners with the commonest combinations being Radios 4 (29 per cent) and/or Radio 3 (14 per cent) or Classic FM (13 per cent). A quarter of respondents had either satellite or cable. This provides broad confirmation for the sorts of profiles provided by the ACORN clusters quoted in Chapter 3, which, despite their differences, pointed to similar broad trends. These are further supported when we look at some other areas of consumption: nearly everybody had a car, but in most households there was only one, and a third of respondents used public transport every day. On the other hand, despite working largely in the city, nearly a third never used public transport. One-third of respondents had at least four holidays a year, many of which included at least one long-haul destination. Just under a quarter had a second or holiday home, with twice as many in the United Kingdom as abroad. Ninety per cent shopped at least once a week at one of the major supermarkets (Sainsbury, Tesco or Waitrose mainly) whilst less than 20 per cent used local shops or markets.

Whilst 20 per cent smoked tobacco, most drank alcohol with just under half claiming they drank less than the recommended guidelines. The proportion smoking was consistent across the areas with the exception of Brixton (30 per cent) and Barnsbury (15 per cent) which perhaps reflects on the one hand the concern with a healthy fit lifestyle ('ostentatious thrift' as Nicholas Tomalin described Barnsbury) and the somewhat alternative/oppositional lifestyle of Brixton, which still seems associated, in some of its versions, with smoking. Just under 60 per cent of respondents did some form of regular keep-fit activity, with the highest in Barnsbury and Docklands (probably accounted for by the amount of sport played) and lowest in Telegraph Hill (46 per cent) and Brixton (54 per cent). This is a very high percentage comparatively and is associated with the general focus on lifestyle and health that we believe is part of the general metropolitan habitus.

Only in Docklands did less than ninety per cent drink alcohol but the level and type of alcohol drunk varied interestingly. Over a third of respondents in Battersea drank more than the recommended guidelines whereas in Telegraph Hill, London Fields and Docklands this was less than 20 per cent. What is more interesting is what they tended to drink, which cross refers to the ACORN clusters for the areas discussed in Chapter 3 and the lifestyle profiles drawn up by Savage, Barlow et al. (1992). In fact there was a universal preference for wine drinking (two-thirds gave this as their favourite drink, a quarter mentioned beers and lagers and 10 per cent spirits); only in Battersea and Docklands did less than 50 per cent drink wine most frequently compared to three quarters in Telegraph Hill, Barnsbury and London Fields. Respondents were most likely to drink spirits in Docklands. Nowhere, was cocktail drinking widespread!

In the next chapter, we follow up the same data in relation to schooling and education, which is the major issue for those with children, and examine their attempts to devise coping strategies reconcile the major downside of living in inner London (educational provision) with the preconceptions of the metropolitan habitus. In the last two chapters we start to draw out the commonalities and differences between our areas.

Notes

1. This compares to Gary Bridge's observations about gentrification in Sydney where, given the benign climate, living space was often moved to the back of

the house and the garden space: Bridge, G. (2001b) 'Estate agents as interpreters of economic and cultural capital: the gentrification premium in the
Sydney housing market' *International Journal of Urban and Regional
Research* 25(1): 87–101.
2. Direct Grant Schools were nominally fee paying schools but received a direct
grant from the Department of Education in return for which they took a proportion of children for free or reduced fees depending on parental circumstances.
3. 'Oxbridge' is a concatenation of Oxford and Cambridge – the United Kingdoms's
two elite universities.
4. 'Redbrick' is used to refer to the main urban universities and is distinguished
from the 'Robbins' or 'plateglass' universities mostly built in the 1960s following the expansion of the universities as a result of the 1963 Robbins Report:
Robbins, L. (1963) *Higher Education*, London, HMSO.
5. This term was used by the Prime Minister's Press Spokesman Alistair Campbell
on 12 February 2001 to describe the no-frills mainstream offering of secondary
schooling in the United Kingdom. (http://news.bbc.co.uk/hi/english/audiovideo/
programmes/world_at_one/programme_highlights/newsid_1166000/1166580.
stm)
6. A very similar point was made in Nick Davies' series of articles about Education in Sheffield in the *Guardian* in September 1999: middle class kids tend to
stick together in non-selective schools.

–7–

Children, Schooling and Social Reproduction[1]

Introduction

The relative neglect of households containing dependent children in analyses of gentrification has represented a missed opportunity in the attempt to develop a detailed picture of the practices and strategies through which distinctive middle-class groups are being formed and maintained in different parts of the city. Following on from this, the chapter argues that two important concepts – those of locality and educational provision which themselves are likely to be linked, need to be taken into account when 'mapping the habituses' of middle-class life in inner London. We suggest, however, that the geography of educational provision is bounded by different localities at different stages in the education career. We believe that what is important is how the immediate locality of residence enables access to a wider locality of educational provision, especially at secondary school level. We are able to show how this operates very differently across the areas in which we have undertaken our fieldwork. These clearly have implications for housing choices and, at a micro level, can have quite dramatic effects on housing prices.

'Circuits of schooling' and Cultural Reproduction

Egerton and Savage's (1997) work on class background and educational achievement demonstrates the continuing existence of significant differentials, even when the progress of 'bright' or 'gifted' working-class children is controlled for (see also Goldthorpe 1996; Devine 1998). The authors argue that middle-class groups, and especially professionals, are finding ways to buffer themselves against the possible effects of meritocratic challenge from lower-status high-achievers. This would appear to confirm the ongoing salience of cultural reproduction approaches to the analysis of class formation and, in particular, on the ways in which middle-class groups may skilfully, assiduously and strategically use the sphere of education to their advantage in processes of class formation and maintenance. The notion that children from middle-class backgrounds enjoy a comparative advantage in the education system is, of course, well established. Bernstein's (1975; 1990) work, in particular, demonstrates the nature and effects of this advantage – primarily in matters of cognition, personality and language – in theoretically sophisticated and useful ways. But the argument that middle-class advantage is built into the system itself needs to be evaluated – and perhaps updated – in the context of a growing rhetoric of meritocratic equalization and achievement for all.

This was demonstrated in many different ways during the 1960s and 1970s, largely in the context of a debate about a selective versus a 'comprehensive' system of secondary education (see, for example, Halsey and Karabel 1977; Banks 1968; Benn and Simon 1970; Silver 1973). Essentially, it was shown that middle-class children lived in middle-class areas that had 'better' primary schools with moti- vated teachers, which in turn enabled them to pass selection tests and so move on to selective grammar schools (Jackson and Marsden 1972). Not much changed with the transition to comprehensive schooling (quite apart from the fact that many areas maintained some version of selection and elite schools). Middle-class children did well in comprehensive schools when they formed a critical mass and there was internal selection ('streaming') as Nick Davies showed in his devastating critique of the collapse of secondary education in Sheffield over the last two decades ('Crisis, crisis, crisis: the state of our schools', *Guardian*, 14 September 1999). It was, he argues, the removal of streaming that finally created the system of postcode apartheid in non-selective secondary education. The middle class congregated in areas where there were 'good' schools or, if they were unable or unwilling to live in their 'catchment' areas or pay, then they used their well-honed social and organizational skills to get their children into what they regarded as the better schools elsewhere. It has been shown that good schools cause house prices to rise in their 'catchment areas' by between 15 per cent and 19 per cent (research cited in *The Economist*, 12 April 2001).

Whilst there has always been a market of some form in education (if only between state and private provision), the 1988 Education Act formalized this in two ways – by creating a greater diversity of school types and by increasing the element of *parental choice*. The effects of parental choice in large, dense urban areas have been greatest simply because of the limitations of distance elsewhere. In large cities, such as London, where social and spatial distance are not syn- onymous, parental choice has been the means by which middle-class parents have managed to maintain their relative privilege in terms of access to high-quality education. Gentrification as a process marks a major break with other recent forms of middle-class settlement in that, although gentrified areas are dominated by their middle-class inhabitants, they are rarely in a numerical majority even in well- established areas. It is therefore less likely that they will be able to pursue the strategy of moving into the catchment areas of 'good' schools. In many areas of inner London, there are simply no 'acceptable' secondary schools. The situation is different at primary level – partly because the scale of the school is smaller and it requires a smaller 'mass' of children to transform it and partly because some primary schools, particularly faith schools, have maintained what is seen as an acceptable normative atmosphere in relation to learning and behaviour.

In this situation, middle-class parents have adopted different approaches – particularly around the ways in which 'choices' are constructed. This process, in London, has been extensively studied notably by Stephen Ball and his co-researchers in a series of research projects (Ball, Bowe et al. 1995; Gewirtz, Ball et al. 1995; Reay and Ball 1998). This approach involves looking at education not as discrete institutions but as parts of more extended networks of culturally specific knowledge and practice. Byrne and Rogers (1996) and Conway (1997) using Bourdieu's ideas, have also examined some of the class-specific resources – and strategies derived from them – in the attempt to form and maintain coherent and successful groupings.

A particularly interesting piece of work in this connection is Ball et al.'s (1995) study of how class-specific 'circuits of schooling' operate in London. These circuits, which preceded but were sharpened by the consequences of, the 1988 Education Act, are overwhelmingly the product of local and specific school market-systems. Any given area of the city will of course have its own characteristics, most significantly in its balance of: i) 'comprehensive', ii) grant maintained and iii) independent schools. Although the boundary between the three types of school is not impermeable and there are a small number of exceptions, traditional demarcations continue to hold up strongly. Ball et al. demonstrate the fact that it is middle-class 'cosmopolitans' (rather broadly conceived, and internally undifferentiated in this paper), as opposed to working-class 'locals', who are by far the most active 'choosers' of their children's schools in the education marketplace (confirming studies by Boudon 1974; Blank 1990; Echols, McPherson et al. 1990; Moore 1990; Gorard 1997; Ball and Vincent 1998). This activity has some important and distinctive characteristics; although familiar, it is worth our while to think them through in detail.

The first and most obvious point to make is that middle-class parents tend to be far less constrained (both spatially and experientially) in their choice of schools. This is not simply a matter of geographical mobility, although relative differences in this are of course important: 'For many middle-class parents travel and distance emerge as contingent factors, not priority or determinate ones' (Ball et al. 1995: 62). It is also a question of cultural orientation, experience and *horizon*: middle-class parents are much more likely to be able to envisage their children in 'yet-to-be-realized' contexts. This is a distinctive horizon with spatial, cultural and temporal dimensions, and it significantly frames parental activity in the education marketplace. These choices made by middle-class parents broadly display two major characteristics: they tend to be both more educationally specific, and more long term, than those made by their working-class counterparts.

Ball et al. suggest that this process begins early, with the choice of primary school, and posit a 'preparatory school system related to the secondary circuits . . . for cosmopolitan parents the choice of primary school is often the first of several strategic decisions involved in the *careful construction of their child's school career'* [our italics] (Ball et al. 1995: 68). This seems to be an important point: if such a pattern of long-term instrumentalism is generalizable, then important spatial consequences might follow.

Choice in general – particularly where the 'reputations' of secondary schools are concerned – is usually informed by first hand reports: middle-class parents tend to draw much more on multiple sources of information. This also has an important 'primary' component, as head teachers often play a crucial role in 'influencing or deflecting parental choices and providing crucial "access" and application information'. Not everybody, of course, is in possession of the kinds of cultural capital required to communicate as an equal with head teachers, 'employ forms of direct contact and negotiation, know how to approach, present, mount a case, maintain pressure, make an impact and be remembered' (Ball et al. 1995: 68). The inter-personal and cognitive skills required to do these things successfully express, in themselves, the cultural backdrop against which school choices are being made.

The perpetuation of such backdrops and their social locations form an over-arching category of experience within which straightforward educational-credentialism may be relatively under-emphasized. Many middle-class parents (although this, again, is perhaps more characteristic of 'professional' than 'managerial' families), according to Ball et al., are less concerned with qualifications *per se* than with mapping out and tailoring specific academic careers for their children. Choosing a school is part of the 'matching of the specific qualities or needs of children to the specific programmes or qualities of schools. This was of great importance to the middle-class choosers but rarely mentioned by working-class ones' (1995: 67). Whereas working-class schooling decisions are, in the main, accommodative of education to the household and general social context, the middle-class 'cosmopolitans' in this study tend to go much further in structuring household organization around children and their needs.

Choice of school at this level, then, is influenced by a combination of factors that together make up a package, the most important of which, alongside examination scores, is the 'expressive order' of the school (Bernstein 1975) or the complex activities in the school that are to do with conduct, character and manner. Ball et al. go as far as to suggest (following Slaughter-Defoe and Schneider 1986; Maddaus 1990) that the ethos and climate of a school are of *greatest* importance for parents from particular groups. The social cohesion aspect of this is brought into focus when we consider that one of the fundamental markers of identity in the ethos/package view of the school is the *kind of children who go there*.

Ball et al. conclude their analysis by identifying two distinct 'discourses' of choice; a working-class one dominated by the practical and the immediate, and a middle-class one dominated by the ideal and the advantageous. In the case of the latter, reputation and desirability are traded off against others, as we have seen, like distance and specific matching. Their London-based analysis is thought by Ball et al. to conform closely to Bourdieu's general argument about the 'jockeying' for position central to middle-class cultural reproduction. An increased emphasis on strategic choice is seen as having been triggered, in recent times, by three main factors:

1. 'Credential inflation' and its correlative of qualification devaluation.
2. A related, and increased, democratization of schooling. These two, taken together, pose threats to the maintenance of class advantage by reducing educational differentiation and changing patterns of access to higher education and the labour market.
3. The new possibilities offered in and by the policies of school specialization, increasing selection and choice within a market framework, generating a significant increase in *choice*, an increase that particular groups are well placed to exploit.

However, it is important to note that the kinds of cultural capital that make this possible are embedded in more extended patterns of organization. The fact that material advantages and social networks back such capital up is demonstrated by Egerton and Savage's (1997) analysis of National Child Development Survey data. Here the authors also complicate the issue of cultural capital by observing that Boudon (1974, and endorsed by Goldthorpe 1996) draws a distinction between 'primary' and 'secondary' class effects in the rearing of children. Here, the early advantages accrued by children in terms of cultural capital are extended into a secondary and arguably more important sphere, operating at later stages in the educational process. This points to the fact that middle-class children not only score well in things such as ability tests as a result of their accumulations of cultural capital, but also that there are other mechanisms at work in the continuing repro-duction of educational advantage later in their careers. This should caution us, perhaps, against isolating out and reifying something called 'cultural capital' as the only determinant of success (Sullivan 2001). Egerton and Savage suggest that this success may be as much to do with 'material advantages, social networks, etc. of professionals as with cultural capital. There is a clear indication here that the social advantages of professionals may rely as much on their material resources as their much-vaunted "cultural capital"' (Egerton and Savage 1997: 667).

Circuits of Schooling and Variations in Gentrification

In this section we identify the spatial components of these processes and the range of education strategies used by middle-class parents in our six study areas, and we detail the ways in which these parents are able to exploit their competitive edge in this new marketplace. Education, thought of in these terms, becomes a central mechanism of class formation, played out on local ground as a range of conscious, active and instrumental practices aimed at securing the reproduction of specific varieties of class advantage and experience. We have seen the ways in which middle-class migration into particular areas throughout the 1980s have been connected to the generation of distinctive urban milieus.

Our findings[2] on education would appear to bear out strongly Ball et al.'s (1995) study of how 'circuits of schooling' operate in London which are the product of local and specific school market systems. It therefore follows that what we find varies across the study areas; indeed it would not be an over-exaggeration to state that education is a key source of mediation in those variations. This is partly because there are different educational circuits in each area, which have been 'laid down' in the areas' previous social and economic incarnations. The variation is also partly a function of the social attitudes and economic capabilities of the middle-class residents in each area – in other words an outcome of the metropolitan habitus.

With the exception of Barnsbury and Docklands, parents appear to be happy to send their children to state primary schools that, in almost all cases, are in the area in which they live – although not necessarily the nearest school. In Barnsbury however, almost half of the respondents with primary age children had already taken the decision to educate them in the private sector. In Docklands the numbers are too small to generalize but the private trend would be largely congruent with their expressed values and feelings about the (lack) of local public infrastructure (which they do not necessarily see as a problem). At secondary level, the picture changes quite dramatically – in all areas private education is regarded as an option and, with the exception of Telegraph Hill and Brixton, it is the preferred option for over half the parents and, in the case of Barnsbury and Docklands, of over three-quarters. We return to these area differences below, nevertheless it is worth

Table 7.1 School destinations of respondents' children by area

Area	Telegraph Hill	Brixton	Battersea	Barnsbury	London Fields
State Primary	16	9	14	9	13
Private Primary	2	0	3	7	0
State Secondary	16	8	5	3	5
State Selective	11	0	1	1	0
Docklands	1	2	0	0	2
Private	11	4	15	15	6

Table 7.2 Number of children being schooled outside the borough

Area	Outside Area	Within Area	Total	% out of area
Tel Hill	11	29	40	27.5
Brixton	10	12	22	45.5
Battersea	11	13	24	45.8
Barnsbury	15	14	29	51.7
London Fields	8	12	20	40.0
Docklands	4	1	5	80.0

reflecting on two aspects at this stage: why is there this turn to the private sector at secondary level and whether those using the state sector are using *local* schools? Tables 7.2 and 7.3 address both of these questions:

Only in Battersea is there any sense that respondents actually *prefer* private education – elsewhere the decision to 'go private' is driven by the perceived lack of acceptable state secondary schools. This comes across in the interview data where, time after time, respondents say, with differing degrees of apology, that their preference would be to educate their children both locally and in the state sector.[3] If we strip primary education out of the figures in Table 7.2, not one child in Barnsbury and Brixton is being educated at a state secondary school in the borough. The highest levels of dissatisfaction with education were to be found in Brixton and London Fields where 73 per cent and 57 per cent respectively had considered moving, or were actively doing so, for the sake of their children's education. By comparison the least dissatisfaction was found in Battersea (20 per cent) with Telegraph Hill (33 per cent) and Barnsbury (37 per cent) somewhere in between. In both of the latter this often meant long journeys – the commute by the Blair children to the Oratory School in West London is not atypical.

We asked those respondents either with children at primary school or of pre-school age, about their favoured option for secondary schooling, the results are presented in Table 7.4:

Table 7.3 Reason given for schooling outside the borough of residence

Area	Pro Private	Dissatisfied with LEA provision	More suitable school elsewhere	Other	Total
Tel Hill	2	1	4	4	11
Brixton		10			10
Battersea	4	1	1	2	8
Barnsbury	3	13	1	2	17
London Fields	1	3	1	2	7
Docklands	1	1	1	1	4

Table 7.4 Preferred secondary school options of respondents with primary or pre-school children

Area	State in Borough non selective	State elsewhere non selective	State Selective in Borough	State Selective elsewhere	Private	Other	Don't know	Total
Tel Hill	3	2	9	1	5	3		23
Brixton	1	6	2	2	1		3	13
Battersea	3	1	4	1	6	1	4	20
Barnsbury	2	1	2		9		4	18
London Fields	2	5	1	1	3	1	4	17
Docklands		2			2		1	5

Only in Telegraph Hill and Battersea do respondents envisage, with any real sense of confidence, being able to educate their children locally at secondary level. What constitutes a 'good' or even 'acceptable' school is however highly contested; for the most part, what are traded are perceptions, which then become 'factualized' particularly as respondents get nearer to the primary-secondary transition. In the rest of this chapter, we look first at what respondents told us and second, drawing on official performance statistics and OFSTED[4] reports, we attempt to understand why education has assumed such importance to middle-class life in inner London.[5]

Education, Education, Education: Location, Location, Location

Education was a particularly fraught issue for respondents with children in Telegraph Hill, Brixton and London Fields. In Battersea, as we have indicated, there was 'choice' of accessible private and state selective schools that most respondents felt met their present or future needs. In Barnsbury, despite any professed preference for local state education, respondents felt that secondary state schooling in Islington did not even begin to be 'contemplate-able' which, given their material resources, made 'going private' largely a 'no brainer'. In many ways, education helped to structure the normative order in each area and so mould the nature of the gentrification process. To some extent, this merely reflected existing values and beliefs but it did so in ways that confirmed and made them, as it were, concrete.

Barnsbury

The school is situated in a leafy and popular residential area close to Canonbury and Highbury and Islington Stations. It is in a part of London with high levels of social deprivation, unemployment and social housing, which lie cheek by jowl with some very expensive private housing which surrounds the school. The majority of pupils come from rented accommodation and some come from refuges . . .

One third of the pupils come from neighbouring Hackney, which has one of the highest level [sic] of social deprivation in the country. Children from the high socio-economic districts of Canonbury and Barnsbury do not generally come to this school. A relatively small proportion of the pupils come from homes with professional backgrounds. A high proportion come [sic] from homes with no adult in employment . . . (Office for Standards in Education 1998)

Highbury Grove School has 'form'; twenty years ago it was regarded as a problem because its headmaster, Dr Rhodes Boyson, stood against some of the educational shibboleths of the day, caught the eye of Mrs Thatcher, became a right-wing MP and subsequently a junior minister. What was once one of Islington's most successful secondary schools is now one of the worst-performing in a borough where only 45 per cent of those in its primary schools progress to secondary school in the borough.

Another icon of the educational battles of the 1970s/1980s was William Tyndale, a primary school just off Upper Street on the edge of our research area. It was excoriated at the time for trendy small-group teaching where pupils learned as opposed to being taught by 'chalk and talk' whole class teachers. William Tyndale is now an average-performing primary, which is popular with some of the middle classes of Barnsbury and Canonbury. It comes nineteenth out of forty-eight in the 2001 league table but it has doubled its numbers in the past few years. It is a mixed school in which 'pupils come from a culturally rich, socially diverse, and aspiring community' (Ofsted).

I like the school; it has a good atmosphere with a good mix of social classes and people, quite artistic people around. (BY50)

This however is not the norm for the middle class, as Table 7.1 demonstrates, for it is here more than anywhere else that respondents resorted to private primary education:

the schools are appalling, you're forced into private education from the word go. (BY62)

There is some evidence that a polarized primary school system is now developing in the more gentrified areas, particularly Barnsbury:

The area as a whole has bifurcated – there has been little improvement in provision at the Caledonian Road end of things, while Upper Street has gone mad. It may be my perception but primary schools either seem to be going up or down. (BY62)

This process does not necessarily flow easily for the children who have to bridge at least two cultures:

Education is a negative. Although our daughter is only in primary, she pleads with us not to tell her friends that she plays the clarinet. (BY18)

I was amazed at how polarized it was when we first came. There's people like us and then the people on the council estates – they are very different from us, they don't seem to have resources, personal resources . . . I went to a children's fancy dress party last week with my daughter. I made her a fairy costume, but most of the other kids had things that had just been bought from the shops – they only seem to have what's beamed into them or what they can buy. As my husband says, they seem inert, there's no leaven in the mix, nothing to help them improve, there seems to be nothing to draw on – these are the ones who have been left behind while others – like our builder – have moved out. They won't mix with us, not because of our money, but because they live in their own world, which is very different from ours. (BY43)

Few of the primary schools have anything approaching a majority of middle-class children. For instance, Canonbury (APS average of 30.6 per cent at Key Stage 2)[6] has a proportion of its children receiving free school meals that is 'significantly above the national average' (approximately a quarter). There is huge pressure on the primary schools to 'perform', much of which is driven by Islington's gentrification, which has led to some huge improvements over recent years but at the cost of exclusion, which then becomes spectacularly apparent at secondary level. Hanover, with almost no pupils receiving free school meals, had its Key Stage two results annulled in 2001 because of alleged 'improprieties', which were seen as a consequence of this pressure to achieve. These results would appear to show that, in principle, mixed-class schools can perform well above the national norms despite the socially-deprived nature of much of their intake.

Not one of our respondents has a child at secondary school in the borough of Islington. At some stage or other most of its secondary schools have been in 'special measures' or have otherwise been deemed to be failing. Only 28.7 per cent of pupils across the borough now get five (or more) good GCSE's (grades A*–C) compared to 50 per cent nationally; only two other authorities in the country have worse results (*Guardian* 27 July 2001). In a damning analysis, the company that is now running education in Islington (CEA–Islington) pointed to the dimensions of this failure in which the middle class have largely abandoned the borough at secondary level and in which black boys seriously underperform white boys who in turn underperform white girls and other minority groups (CEA–Islington).

Islington schools are not an option. It would have been nice if they'd been viable, and if we had not had to pay through the nose. (BY60)

Thus what we have in Islington is a 'hollowed out' society where none of the middle class are sending their children to state secondary schools in the area. Some are going to state selective schools in neighbouring boroughs such as Camden and many, as we have seen, are going to elite private schools. The competition to get in is such that many parents are now sending their children to the private feeder preparatory schools.

Battersea

'Between the Commons' has its 'own' school and this probably helps the area's reputational image as a 'friendly' place for families with children to live:

> it has a very neighbourly atmosphere – one of the few remaining, I should say, in London – there are lots of families and people one knows. There are great support networks for the young families, and the whole area is rich in the services required to bring up young children. (BA42)

Generally in London, local authorities have been neutral to gentrification and often hostile (as for example in Lambeth); by contrast, in Wandsworth the council has explicitly facilitated it which has led to the building of a number of private schools. Despite the area's transformation, there are still considerable numbers of non-middle class people living in it. There is a primary school (Honeywell) in the middle of the research area, which has an average point score of 29.7 at Key Stage 2 – above the local and national average (27.3) but some way off the LEA best of a nearby Roman Catholic school (31.1) – it is however the 'school of choice' used by the area's middle-class families whose children often proceed to private secondary schools. They do some preparation for the Common Entrance examination. Unlike many London schools 'only' 15 per cent of its roll are eligible for free school meals.

Ball (1995) makes reference to the 'expressive order' of the school and how strategies are designed for individual children; performance tables are not the sole arbiter and indeed this is well-illustrated by this primary school whose results are only slightly above average. It is the 'ethos' of the school that matters.

> Ethos is the climate for learning: attitudes to work, relationships and the commitment to high standards. (Ofsted – generic definition)

What comes across from the inspectors' report is the 'expressive order' of the Honeywell; children are not only well behaved but work purposively and high-achieving children are 'stretched'.

The area is becoming much more selective and non-middle class children are slowly becoming displaced

> in terms of education, there is a danger of having selective primary schools within the state system, based on people having the means to buy houses in the desired school catchment areas . . . another problem is the 'siblings first' rule – people who no longer live in the area around Honeywell, for example, get their kids in on this basis, and an increasing proportion of children are now driven to the school from outside the catchment area . . . the school will no longer serve the local community. (BA42)

The houses are mid-range (for Battersea!) and people often move on to larger houses in the Wandsworth area but wish to maintain the contact with the school. Thus a situation is developing in which the school will serve its immediate middle-class gentrified catchment area as well as those who qualify through the sibling rule but have moved on elsewhere in the not-so-immediate area. The 'losers' will be those living in public housing on the fringes of its catchment area. The downsides of this are not entirely lost on some of our respondents:

> The schools are good but, as I say, staggeringly homogeneous. My wife and I cannot stand it – we will be moving away soon . . . we don't conform to type here. (BA63)

> It's very monocultural, not at all racially mixed. The primary schools reflect this – Honeywell is all white . . . (BA59)

The focus here has been on primary schools that prepare children for the local and highly acceptable secondary circuits of education in the state and private sectors. There is a range and choice of schools in both sectors that have good performance outcomes in terms of GCSE and A-level scores but are also regarded as 'good' schools in terms of their social composition and 'normative' order. Far from there being pressures to move away from Battersea when children reach the secondary transition, the problems elsewhere encourage many parents to stay who might have otherwise been contemplating a move. Some of these, who can afford it, then make the move, previously referred to, within Wandsworth to larger housing. Reay and Ball (1998) have indicated how the process of school choice operates on a class basis in a borough such as Wandsworth where there are circuits of both private and state secondary schools. They describe how middle-class parents essentially present children with an option list from which a decision 'emerges', usually in favour of schools that are not necessarily the geographically nearest. Head teachers at primary schools also guide parents and children towards certain schools and give valuable hints on how to complete the complex secondary school choice forms.

Brixton

In Brixton the situation is very different; the middle classes have not been success-ful in establishing hegemony over any particular primary school and there is none that forms the focus for the community in the same way.

> there's no norm here which you can see reflected in the primary school. (BN8)

There are, however, some successful schools; one particular primary school that is the top of the performance tables for the local education authority (LEA) is adjacent to the Tulse Hill area and is heavily oversubscribed. It shares a similar 'expressive order' to the primary schools in Battersea and Telegraph Hill and some of those in Barnsbury but the middle class has not been able to dominate it in the same way. Much of the attraction of Brixton to many middle-class people is the 'flight from social obligation' (see Robson and Butler 2001) but this also represents the downside for those with school-age children:

> Education is the big issue around here – the middle-class crisis of conscience is absolu-tely primary . . . especially with Sudbourne now massively oversubscribed. (BN17)

> the primary situation is ridiculous – Sudbourne is our closest but we couldn't get in. You've got to live within three inches of the school and even then they don't guarantee you a place. House prices in the Sudbourne area have just exploded in the last couple of years – it's ridiculous. I want to pull my kids out of the system altogether, get out of London. (BN40)

Many parents have been unable to secure a place at the school of choice, which has led them to try and find alternatives

> It's difficult to know what to do. Sudbourne is our nearest school, but I couldn't get my daughter in there. A few of us in this street had the same problem, so we decided together to send our kids to 'Finniston' [not its real name], try to bring it up that way . . . it hasn't really worked, that group of kids have just sort of become an isolated clique in the school in general. It's not ideal . . . (BN21)

In Brixton there are no 'acceptable' secondary schools in the local authority area of Lambeth – like Barnsbury, not a single child of any of our respondents was attending a secondary school in the borough. It is a strong reason for the demo-graphic instability and the outward movement from the borough. Those who stay educate their children in Westminster or Wandsworth.

> Secondary education is a real problem here. The local school (Stockwell Park) has a very bad reputation. The primaries are OK, but it's very hard to find secondaries. This is part

of the reason why we have decided to move, which we are doing in six months or so . . . My husband has been offered a job in [elsewhere in the UK], which is a relief in a way, because that gives us the motivation to move *and* solve the school problem. If not for that, we would have had to go through the struggle of conscience over education that many of our friends have. The new job has got us out of trouble, really. (BN1)

In similar vein

We'll be moving in about eighteen months because the local authority cannot provide me with a decent school for my son. He'll be going to a county school [in the South West of England] . . . Schools have gone downhill. Apart from this, the area is thriving. There's less of a population turnover than there was. If kids can be got into decent secondary school, then people stay. (BN8)

The lack of 'suitable' secondary schooling couple with rising housing values is, as another respondent observed, likely to make this area more like Islington

House prices seem to be getting out of control – we certainly couldn't afford to buy here now. This might change Brixton, it might become like Islington, hollow in the middle . . . Brixton is already becoming more Islingtonised, with kids being schooled outside the area etc. Rich people buying £200k houses. (BN15)

We have argued in previous chapters and elsewhere (Butler and Robson 2001; forthcoming 2003a; 2003b) that currently Brixton represents a different model of gentrification to that observed elsewhere. It is a model where there is accommodation to different groups, which is markedly different from the 'revanchism' (see Smith 1996 for a discussion) in which the middle class takes over the area or the 'enclavism' where it withdraws from it. We do not wish to argue too strongly that this accommodation equates with social cohesion or integration but it does embrace a wish to live in a multicultural environment even if relations with other groups are 'tectonic' (Robson and Butler 2001: 78). The failure to resolve the issue of social reproduction because of the school system could threaten this and indeed lead to exit or an Islington-style 'hollowing out' process. It is not that the schools are particularly bad; some of them individually are not and, as the Ofsted reports indicate, they are grappling with real deprivation. For example, this is how the Ofsted inspectors introduce their report on one local secondary school

Nearly two-thirds of pupils are from minority ethnic groups . . . Fifteen per cent of pupils are of white UK heritage. Nearly half of the pupils have English as an additional language and 10 per cent are at an early stage of learning English . . . There are 28 refugees, most of whom have come from Somalia. Twenty-five per cent of pupils are on

the special educational needs register and nearly four per cent have statements . . .
Twelve per cent of pupils are on the child protection register and a significant proportion
are or have been in the care of the local authority. The mobility of pupils is an issue . . .
for example, in Year 10, only 43 out of 84 pupils started in Year 7. A high proportion of
the pupils who join the school after Year 7 have been excluded from schools elsewhere.
(Office for Standards in Education 2001: 8)

Perhaps not surprisingly only 18 per cent of pupils get 5A*-C grades but the
inspectors are very upbeat about what the school is achieving; the point, however,
is that it is not just the poor performance of the school but its 'expressive order' that
ensures that it is on all our parents' 'must avoid' list. What seems to be happening
is that the few relatively well-performing schools, those at or about the national
average, are attracting upwardly mobile ethnic minority children, mainly girls, and
that the poor performance is concentrated amongst boys – particularly those from
African and Caribbean heritage backgrounds. The issue is contextualized in
Brixton's emergence as a centre for a hedonistic youth culture, which has become
subtly ethnicized. Some respondents find this hard to come to terms with but it
nevertheless structures their thinking about where their children should go to
secondary school:

The last round of changes seems to have had more effect. It's much more culty now, a
Mecca for young people. But this is causing tensions, the area being taken over by a
white-led youth culture. I think relations between black and white people are becoming
more strained . . . there's a lot of aggressive racism on both sides. My son and his friends
– black and white – are very vulnerable. He's been badly beaten up twice by black boys.
(BN5)

Telegraph Hill

In Telegraph Hill, like Battersea, there is a primary school in the research area to
which nearly all the local middle class sends its children

The area is mixed socially – there is a real sense of community around the school, the
park, the community centre. The great thing is the extent of people's support for one
another. (TH13)

From there, they then move into well-rehearsed local circuits of secondary
education some of which are in the borough and others lie outside – a City Technology College is located immediately adjacent to the research area and it has *de
facto* become the school of choice for many parents. Not all respondents, however,
were uncritical:

> Askes becoming a CTC [City Technology College] has not been good: we didn't really want the kids to go there, as we didn't really like the change over – it took away the fact Haberdashers [Aske] was a local school. (TH45)

This last comment, although 'off-message' in one sense, is very typical of the area in another; it represents the 'script of inclusiveness' of those who might be considered to be already on the inside (Butler and Robson forthcoming 2003a). She already has her children safely in the school of choice, but others have had to access the local private secondary education circuit that contains many high-achieving schools (for example, Dulwich, Alleyns, St Dunstans and Sydenham GDST):

> Education provision in Lewisham is not the best – we don't like having to pay for the kids' school, but we do. (TH33)

In Telegraph Hill there is every indication that the middle class can envisage its children in yet-to-be-realized contexts and that parents are making educationally-specific and long-term decisions with regard to their children. Our argument is that strategic engagement with these 'education markets' is a critical aspect of recent patterns of middle-class settlement in inner London. The role of the primary school is crucial here – it is, as the first respondent (TH13) indicated, at the centre of the community socially as well as geographically. It has in many ways been 'made' by the middle class and transformed but is not in most senses of the word a 'middle-class' school: its Key Stage Two results (see note 6) are just above the national norm and its most recent Ofsted report shows that its overall profile is that of a socially mixed school:

> There is wide social mix at the school. Twenty seven point five percent of pupils are entitled to free school meals, which is above the national average. One hundred and fifty pupils (40 per cent) are on the school's register of special educational needs (SEN), of which 33 (9 per cent) are at stages 3 to 5. This is well above the national average. Forty one per cent of pupils are from ethnic backgrounds other than white. Fifteen per cent of pupils come from homes where English is not the first language . . . (Office for Standards in Education 1998: 10)

The school performs a crucial set of functions for the middle class of Telegraph Hill. First and foremost, it is the basis of the extensive social networks that follow their children through the education system and, in many cases, sustain the area long after the children leave school. It is also a source of information about, and support for, constructing an appropriate 'strategy' for the individual child and mapping that on to one or more circuits of education, in the differentiated post-1988 Education Act market. The head teacher is a source of information and advice about implementing the strategy and how to play the various circuits: for instance, interviews at some selective schools, examinations at others and crucially how to order preferences on the complex forms so that fall-back positions are safeguarded. In its report on this school, the Ofsted inspector notes:

> Pupils have good attitudes to their work and this helps to create a positive learning ethos. They follow established classroom routines and settle to work quickly, which ensures a prompt start to lessons and the efficient use of time. In most lessons pupils listen attentively to the teacher and to each other, for example, when showing sensitivity to the opinions of others during class discussions. In group activities pupils work well together and cooperate with each other. In most lessons they concentrate on their work and sustain interest and involvement in the activities . . .

> . . . The school's ethos is good and appropriately reflects its commitment to equal opportunities and the valuing of all members of the school community. It's [sic] broad aims are successfully realized in practice, particularly in the positive way that pupils' behaviour is managed. (Office for Standards in Education 1998: 21)

It is this that separates this particular primary school from others in the surrounding area, some of which have better attainment rates. What this particular school does, however, is enable middle-class parents to create the social networks that allow them to support their children through the transition to secondary education and often then to negotiate car-shares and other ways of getting the children to the school of choice and home again, often at the end of a long day involving extra-curricular activity.

Unlike in Battersea, secondary education is a major issue in Telegraph Hill. It is located in a borough (Lewisham) which, whilst, unlike Wandsworth, is doing nothing to encourage gentrification does not provide a middle-class infrastructure for either private or state services. Whereas Wandsworth is well provided for in private and high-performing state schools, this is not the case in Telegraph Hill. However, it is not like Brixton either. As we have already mentioned, the local area has a City Technology College at Haberdashers Aske, which is a very old school and, until it became a CTC, took almost as many local middle-class children as chose to enter. Since becoming a CTC its entry criteria have changed so that it has to select from a wider geographic and ability range which has left many 'local' middle-class children with no acceptable local school to proceed to when they leave the primary. The wider area, mainly in neighbouring Southwark, is well-provided for, as we have indicated, with a number of very high-achieving private schools to which many parents have reluctantly sent their children.

Others cannot afford this and there is currently a campaign to build a new Telegraph Hill School which would be a 'local' comprehensive on the model of a similar new school being opened in Southwark. This was the result of pressure from local middle-class parents backed at a crucial juncture by their MP (now Cabinet Minister) Tessa Jowell. The campaign for a local school in Telegraph Hill has been waged by many of the parents at the local primary, whose Chair of Governors is a leading light in the campaign. Lewisham Council has not been supportive and Joan Ruddock (the local MP) has been, at best, ambivalent. This lack of co-operation is leading to a breakdown in relations between residents, the local Labour Party and Lewisham Council. At the time of writing, in summer 2002, the issue is still undecided. The school would undoubtedly be 'successful', given its strong local backing by the middle class and it is envisaged that it would soon build a 'good ethos'. The problem for the local council is that this would put huge pressure on the other existing schools. Whether the school is eventually built will be an indicator of the ability of the middle class to change the ethos of an area over the longer term and so establish its authenticity in an area where the social balances are fragile.

London Fields

London Fields is a relatively recent newcomer to London's gentrification and, like Telegraph Hill, is an enclave. A 'shy' area without a brash infrastructure of consumption, it is also a much more heterogeneous and socially mixed area than any of the others, including Brixton. Nevertheless, for many of our respondents, Hackney's continual state of social disorganization remains a positive aspect of living there:

> It has a terrific diversity and social mix and its own character . . . we have a bond with the community through the children, a real connection, it's a fantastic place to bring up kids . . . It's a brilliant place compared to Islington, which is too self-consciously itself. (LF43)

> [the cultural mix] is more than just tolerance; it's an appreciation of other people's lifestyles . . . The schools do their best to do this well and they support young people's choices and advocacy. (LF45)

These sentiments appear to be sincerely held by many and are being lived through despite the difficulties, although the data show that many parents – in contradistinction to Brixton – do end up educating their children at private secondary schools. Despite the difficulties, many of the primary schools have been 'improving' both their performance and their 'ethos' as a result of the recent determination to drive up standards and behaviour. Much of this can be seen as a consequence of having a greater social mix, which means parents who are more demanding of what the school offers. However, there is no doubt that life for middle-class children can be difficult:

I was let down badly by my son's secondary school, he's having a terrible deal (from bullying not being sorted out) . . . I think it's crucial that kids *walk* to school, *grow up in a neighbourhood*, but they don't make it easy for people. (LF16)

Some, like this parent, have stuck with it, but others are looking at alternatives outside London:

. . . schools are terrible, and under-funded – we will be looking at local schools and schools in Hertfordshire for the oldest boy, keeping an eye on the progress of friends' children locally. (LF25)

She goes on to say that she felt that what was happening in Hackney was that it was losing its 'middle', what she termed the 'efficient' working class:

London is losing its middle: you've either got people like us or refugee families in the local primary school . . . School is where you really see it. (LF25)

No respondents had any illusions about the quality of educational performance but it was usually set in a social context, for example:

Educational provision is appalling . . . It's a tricky one really, with our kids being mixed race – we'll want to move out of the area for better schools, but round here they don't really stand out . . . on the other hand we don't really want them to become part of the local black gang culture, becoming the kind of kids you see patrolling London Fields, so it's difficult to know what to do. All we can do is try and equip them with a strong sense of personal identity and self-worth. (LF41)

Respondents were aware of the consequences for their children but, as this last respondent intimates, they were balancing a series of values and not just prioritizing performance averages. It should be remembered that averages are just that, and some children achieve very good results enabling them to continue into higher education of their choice. What probably matters most is that parents have to invest huge amounts of time in supporting their children through this environment.

Conclusion

Education markets are now rivalling those in housing and employment as determinants of the nature, extent and stability of middle-class gentrification of inner city localities. The reported instability of Brixton is not because of its status as a centre for international hedonistic youth but because it doesn't provide the infrastructure for middle-class family life. For those without children the buzz of the cultural life and the quietness of the street are a desirable combination. This is not the case for those who have children. Although there is a high-performing primary school, it has not become the middle-class school and does not provide either the basis of long-lasting social networks or the necessary route map to plan appropriate secondary education pathways. The stability of Telegraph Hill by contrast is the outcome of a strategic manipulation of the housing and education markets within the context of a global metropolis, which has been achieved through enclavism. In both areas middle-class incomers have managed the classic manoeuvre of gen-trification: coupling a necessary spatial proximity to other urban groups while strategically maintaining and protecting their material and cultural distance from them. However in Brixton, this manoeuvre has not managed to incorporate the education system, which remains relatively autonomous from it.

Battersea and Barnsbury have both managed this manoeuvre and have achieved settled stability in quite different ways despite their relatively similar economic status. Both are based around a highly developed local consumption infrastructure in which 'eating out' is valued over 'joining in'. Whereas for respondents in Battersea this is a large part of what living there is about, for those in Barnsbury it is more complex. For many, the 'idea' of Barnsbury was attractive precisely because of its 'social capital-rich' past, in which earlier rounds of gentrification had involved a commitment by the incomers to the area and its social institutions – becoming school governors, educating their children at local schools (Butler and Robson forthcoming 2003a). Ironically, more respondents in Conservative-voting Battersea educated their children locally and in state schools than those in Labour-supporting Barnsbury who, despite a rhetoric that genuflected to the importance of social capital, eschewed local state schools not just at secondary but, in many cases, at primary level too.

Thus in all four cases, the juxtaposition of the 'ideal' and the 'real' in relation to education markets was creating quite different narratives of the areas that were distinct from each other and provide, we would suggest, quite distinct 'takes' on the gentrification process. In London Fields, the outcomes have been less clear. The area shares some similarities to both Brixton (an attraction to an idealized notion of the 'local'). The lack of a distinct circuit of education is also similar to Brixton, although in London Fields nearly half the parents of secondary school children have resorted to the private sector unlike in Brixton. What it shares with Telegraph Hill is that it is an enclave; respondents found the lack of a consumption infrastructure a positive aspect of the area. There was some evidence that some respondents were prepared to accept many of the negatives – the social dis-organization and deprivation – as positives and wished to support their children through this. There was much less vehemence about leaving London compared to Brixton. They appeared to be much more willing to rely on their own household resources to find individual solutions in the absence of a coherent circuit of education. The gentrification of London Fields, whilst distinctive in cultural terms and based around quite strong social networks, is unlike the other areas we have discussed in that there is neither a 'coherent' housing or education market.

In Brixton, the middle-class housing market has cohered but it lacks a coherent circuit of education, which, as one respondent pointed out, is threatening to 'hollow' out the area as one of middle-class residence as has happened in Islington. In both Telegraph Hill and Battersea there are well-developed, coherent but different housing and education markets based around clearly identifiable state and private circuits of education. In both cases there is a single primary school that largely serves the middle class of the area. The difference being that in Battersea this is becoming increasingly exclusive of other social groups thus reinforcing the 'revanchist' tendency in the housing market that is also reinforced by the structure of consumption.

In Telegraph Hill, the education system at primary level remains socially mixed although the 'ethos' has been transformed into a middle-class one – with a socially inclusive rhetoric. If the current campaign to build a new Telegraph Hill secondary school on the lines of the one recently established in Southwark is successful then this distinctive juxtaposition of housing and education will have come full circle. At present, the cohesiveness of the middle-class community largely relies on the social networks established during the primary school years, which then are sustained by managing these complex educational strategies amongst a number of distinct and dispersed secondary circuits of education.

We have identified the role that education imposes on housing choice often as determinate at the level of the micro-neighbourhood of the primary school catchment area. At secondary school level, it is the wider geographical sub-area of London that matters, but it can only be accessed through the knowledge acquired through a close spatial engagement with the primary school. Middle-class groups therefore continue to exhibit their capacities for adroit engagement within the possibilities of the new, increasingly competitive schooling markets. Education, as Bourdieu argued, continues to play a fundamental role in processes of cultural and social-class reproduction.

Notes

1. A version of this chapter was published by *Housing Studies* 18(1) as 'Plotting the middle-classes: gentrification and circuits of education in London' pp. 5–28. We would like to acknowledge the permission of the editors with thanks.

2. Given the tiny numbers of respondents with children in Docklands, we have excluded the area from our discussion, although they have been included in the tables for completeness.
3. This contention is supported by the finding that, with the exception of Battersea and Docklands, a majority of respondents in all areas identified themselves as most likely to vote for the Labour Party.
4. Office for Standards in Education (OFSTED) who inspect schools; individual inspection reports are available by school on the OFSTED Web site www.dfes.gov.uk/performancetables and www.ofsted.gov.uk
5. This is now recognized at governmental level with the appointment in 2001 of a Minister with specific responsibility for education in London and the appointment in 2002 of Tim Brighouse as 'tsar' charged with improving the performance of London schools. The fact that twice as many parents (10 per cent) are sending their children to private schools in London than elsewhere is taken as indicative of the nature and scale of the problem.
6. The APS refers to the Average Point Score for tests taken at Key Stage Two in children's final year at primary school (aged approximately 11). The APS is an averaging of their scores for the three subjects tested (English, Mathematics and Science). The national average was 27.3 in 2001 against which individual and local authority scores are measured. It has been shown that amongst the factors affecting school performance is the percentage having free school meals, which is one of the best proxies for social and economic deprivation.

–8–

Twenty-first Century Gentrification

Introduction

We have argued that the gentrification of London in the twenty-first century is not just more of the same, a process of upward and onward, but reflects dominant shifts in the *global* organization of social and economic life. What started off as something exceptional has in many ways become something normal (Bridge 2001a; 2001b). The 'original' gentrification of London was by oddballs who eschewed the middle-class suburbs to live in the working-class city – or at least those parts of it which were, until recently, working class. London in the 1960s was split as a city between an upper (or upper middle) class and a working class – the former living in the West End and surrounding areas whilst the working class inhabited most of the rest in areas increasingly consolidated by the spread of council housing in its various forms (Dunleavy 1981; Coleman 1985; Harloe 1995). Today it is something different: to call it a middle-class city would be wrong but neither is it working or upper class. Some academic commentators (for example, Mollenkopf and Castells 1991 but for an alternative view see Marcuse 1989) have noted how the 'working class' element is what has disappeared:

> there are more people like us moving in now, and this is reflected in house prices. When we first came there were hardly any lawyers, accountants, city people, but there are plenty of them now . . . there's no middle round here now, no what I call 'efficient' working class . . . As far as council tenants are concerned, I'd have thought that, if you had anything about you, you'd try and get to where the housing is better, you'd be trying to move out to Walthamstow, or somewhere like that . . . London is losing its middle: you've either got people like us or refugee families in the local primary school . . . school is where you really see it. (LF25)

Although it might be argued that these are definitional changes, this does not deny their importance. They involve the associated changes that have taken place in the role played by class in society, the ways in which we see class and the changes that have taken place in the economy (discussed in chapter one but also see Savage 2000). All of these factors are immersed in a changed spatial environment: cities (and particularly cities like London and Paris) were an important subset of the nation state in a world made up of nation states. By the twenty-first century it does seem that nation states and *their* cities have given way to a global economy in which cities have become 'stepping stones'. They act not only as 'command and control centres' but also their industries increasingly 'drive' the economy as financial and other services have become commoditized and linked together in 'real time' networks that truly transcend time and space (Sassen 1991). These cities are also very 'real' places in contrast perhaps to the ways in which cities were perceived by many in much of the post-war period – as places that were largely avoided by the middle classes. 'Father' may have gone 'up to town' to work but 'mother' and the children would only go on special occasions: to go to a 'show' or for some special shopping or other event. During many of the long years of the post-Second World War boom, cities were not exciting places – or if they were it was the wrong kind of excitement. The suburbs were the natural habitat of the middle class – although, as Silverstone (1996) shows, they were more as well.

The suburbs were based on a strictly gendered division of labour: father went out to work and mother stayed at home and raised the children. This division was reinforced by a number of factors: car ownership, psycho-social theories of maternal deprivation and the decline in domestic service. Women were more or less forced to be stuck in the home because, even where they had training and qualifications, there were few jobs realistically available to them. Most families only had the 'family car', which, in effect, was the man's; there were inadequate forms of public transport and, most importantly, even if jobs were available and accessible, most women were not in a position to take them. A strong element of the 'post-war settlement' had been the concept of the family wage, which was earned by the male breadwinner. This was first reflected in the Beveridge Report with its assumptions about women not contributing equal value and so not needing to pay the same contributions as men because their needs would either be met through his wage or through his 'benefit' (Wilson 1977). In part, no doubt, the Beveridge Report, which was written during some of the darkest days of the Second World War, reflected a wish not to make the same mistakes that had happened during the First World War when 'homes fit for heroes' turned out in the subsequent crises of the 1920s and 1930s to be anything but. This was however reinforced in the post-Second World War era by a raft of studies of family behaviour that emphasized the need for, and importance of, 'nurture' in raising the next generation. This was encapsulated in the role of the mother. Women may have 'manned' (sic) the home front during the war but afterwards the home front was to be literally that: writers such as John Bowlby warned that juvenile delinquency could be blamed directly on so-called 'latchkey kids' and their experience of 'maternal deprivation'. Having been introduced to Spock and his emphasis on the child's needs, it was a brave mother who then went off to work and abandoned the children to 'child care'. The latter, of course, didn't exist as a concept outside the nurseries of the upper class. The reality was that there was nothing of the sort particularly in the growing suburban belt around London. Domestic service had more or less disappeared in the egalitarian and growth economies of the period. A combination of factors therefore ensured that middle-class women in the post-war period, many of whom had served in vital functions during the Second World War, understood that their role was to nurture the new generation.

The suburbs, with their emphasis on space and fresh air, were where the middle class lived. The men worked their way up the ladder – a process which Watson (1964) characterized as 'spiralism'. In effect, men either worked their way up within one organization or they moved strategically up through a number of cognate organizations. Professional managers, in large companies (ICI, GKN and Shell for example), would often move around the country and the globe to different 'postings' on their way up the management ladder whereas professionals, in say medicine or higher education, would move from one institution to another as they gained promotion. In both cases, the family accompanied them and this was not a problematic process. There was no second breadwinner's job to think about and the network of private 'boarding' schools was largely national and often paid for by the employer anyway. If they were unable to afford this, or chose not to, then they could send them to high-achieving 'grammar' or 'direct grant' schools.

It was in this environment that many of today's gentrifiers were brought up and was one from which they only moved away for the first time when they went to university (Williams 1986). The importance of the expansion of the university system in the 1960s for the gentrification of London can hardly be exaggerated. It was, however, largely an endogenous middle-class affair, widening only slightly the class boundaries of recruitment. Its main effect was to include middle-class girls who had increasingly been 'staying on' at school to take A-levels, which were the *de facto* currency for university entrance. Unlike their mothers, they did not wish to be forced into a choice between 'home' (or rearing a family) and a career. Gentrification was a response to this because it enabled women to take advantage of the increasingly open professional labour market that London offered but it also enabled dual career families to be occupationally mobile without the residential changes experienced on a regular basis by middle-class families in the post-war decades. The mixed class nature of most 'gentrified' areas enabled such families to recruit childminders and other domestic workers to care for their children whilst minimizing the time spent travelling to work (Butler and Hamnett 1994). Finally, the inner city provided the excitement and cultural buzz that had been so lacking in many of their childhoods and had been awakened by the experience of being at university.

Gentrification perhaps adequately describes how the restructuring of urban space in cities like London started but does it describe its ongoing nature forty years or so later? We began this chapter by claiming that what has been taking place in London in the 1990s marks a break from what went on previously. Does it still make sense to refer to each bit of transformation as further evidence of the gentrification of the city? Since the term comes with an associated agenda of social displacement, there is a danger that what is essentially a symptom of the wider social and economic changes that are taking place at a global level are used to explain them. What we have showed in this book is that, in many ways, the middle classes feel that they have a fragile grip on the city but they manifest this in very different ways. We would however discount much of the self-confidence and braying noted in areas like Battersea just as much as the denial of relative privilege in Telegraph Hill. Across London the new urban middle classes are essentially anxious, not necessarily about their own social and economic stability and prospects, but for those of their children. In other words, we return to the claims made at the beginning of the book in support of Richard Sennett's articulation of the essential instability experienced by many of those working in the new economy.

What we have argued in this book is that London has become an increasingly middle-class city in a process that has witnessed huge changes both for London and for the middle class(es). We have seen our respondents describe the areas in which they live with large measures of critical acclaim. They, for the most part, like living there but they do not feel secure. It may of course be that the insecurity adds a sense of frisson to their lives that distinguishes them from the 'risk averse' nature of the post-war suburban middle classes. There are four major dimensions to this insecurity:

1. Most significantly – and this is only an issue for those respondents with children – they become increasingly concerned about the issue of social reproduction. They no longer feel confident about passing their relative advantage on to their children. What was once a matter of quiet self-confidence to the middle class is now a source of continual anxiety.
2. The socially mixed nature of the areas in which they live is something that many find disturbing but in quite complex ways. Very few respondents wished to live in a one-class ghetto which is how they saw the traditional suburbs. On the other hand, as we have seen in the quotation above from a respondent in London Fields, the social structure of the areas in which they now live is often perceived as unfamiliar. It was not a traditional working class playing to their middle class.
3. Although there was discussion, particularly in Brixton and London Fields, of the positive aspects of living in areas in which 'race', ethnicity, diversity and multi-culturalism were dominant themes, what was clear from the research was the cultural, 'racial' and ethnic homogeneity of those we interviewed. As we have seen, it was almost entirely white British. This was in direct contrast to the social structure of the city around them and also, particularly in Brixton, and to

a lesser extent London Fields, of the expressed desire to live in mixed and diverse areas. We have described social behaviour in Brixton as 'tectonic' and suggest that this may apply to the social *structure* of inner London more generally.

4. Associated with this, there was a high level of individualism and privatization of the household. There was little evidence of the middle class deploying its resources for the benefits of the wider community. Our evidence shows that they associated almost exclusively with 'people like us' and that much of their time is devoted to the needs of the immediate household. Their children asso-ciated almost exclusively with other middle-class children and many of their friends went back to school and university days.

Although we discovered a considerable diversity amongst the inner London middle class this manifested itself mainly through the choice about where to live. They also had many dispositions in common, which we have identified in terms of a 'metropolitan habitus'. Whilst not wishing to get into a major 'habitus mapping' exercise, the nature of the metropolitan habitus is such as to draw contrasts with both a non-metropolitan middle class (such as the one inhabited by many respon-dents in their childhood) and with other social groups in the metropolis (Butler 1997). This comes across strongly in the data which we have presented in the book and partly explains why the nature of 'gentrification' as a concept is so focused on London – which we have typified in terms of a cosmopolitan-local dichotomy.

The distinction between 'cosmopolitans' and 'locals' was developed by the North American sociologist Robert K. Merton (1948) in a study of interpersonal influence in the town of Rovere in the United States to distinguish between different social groups in a metropolitan environment. 'Locals' were in essence parochial, confining their interest to the community which was their world, and the cosmopolitans, whilst having some interest in Rovere, were also oriented to the outside world – they lived in what Merton termed the 'Great Society' (Hamnett 1973: 98). The concept was further developed by Herbert Gans (1968) in his famous paper 'Urbanism and Suburbanism as a Way of Life'.

The inner London middle classes are essentially cosmopolitan in their outlook – in contrast not just to the non middle-class in London but also to those in other UK cities including their middle classes.[1] Our assertion then is that the middle classes living in London at the beginning of the twenty-first century are living in the 'great society' which has now moved beyond urban and national boundaries to the global stage. Being 'cosmopolitan', however, means very different things even within an overarching 'metropolitan habitus' as we have seen in the different areas that we studied. It might be suggested that our concept of 'enclavism' is antipathetic to the notion of the cosmopolitan but we believe that it represents a different way of relating households' resources to a changed social and historical environment. In the next section, we attempt to focus on these different approaches and particularly on the ways in which individuals and areas socialize each other across the various fields which we have outlined.

Global Nodes and the Remaking of Inner London Neighbourhoods

Three of the areas in our study (Barnsbury, Battersea and Brixton) are not simply inner city areas that have been improved through gentrification but rather, in their different ways, have become key nodal points on the new map of the global metropolis. They function in different ways, and present different aspects of the impact of globalization on urban space. All abut – less so in Battersea – very sharply with very different areas which remain deeply rooted in 'local economies of social exclusion'.

Barnsbury

Upper Street, Islington, which is Barnsbury's 'stomping ground', is a cosmopolitan and commercial space servicing London's affluent middle classes drawn from a wide north London catchment area. It is also a new space, a glamorous and exciting inner urban space in some senses equivalent to the West End without its 'tackiness'. This new space has an international repute and comes with an appeal that is in no sense local. People come from all over the world not to visit Islington because it is Islington (unlike Brixton) but because of what the area's commercial infrastructure offers. This has, however, in the eyes of many of our respondents, had its costs – a perceived homogeneity; the global reputation has been achieved at the cost of local distinctiveness:

> More and more colonization by the upwardly mobile, even in the three years that I've been here . . . There's been a big increase in foreign accents around, more upwardly mobile foreigners, and this is accelerating. This is the globalization of the workforce and Islington has changed, being so central, because of this. (BY4)

> Shops are either really expensive, for example the trendy bakeries and chi-chi deli-catessens, or very poor quality, as in the Cally. There is not much in between, and this is an imbalance . . . restaurants are taking over Upper St. This is a bad idea, as local shops and businesses are dying off . . . the antiques market just doesn't integrate with all the chain restaurants . . . I would prefer a mix of more small, personalized businesses alongside the chains . . . the area, on the whole, is both improving and becoming less interesting. I don't like the new higgledy-piggledy building development – not everything is an improvement. (BY65)

The same could be argued for Battersea where there is another 'non-central' metropolitan centre in Northcote Road. They are however different, in that Battersea is part of Wandsworth and as such is a place that is constructed by, and run according to, the market whereas in Islington, Barnsbury still has a strong social capital cachet.

> The good thing here is the presence of a strong peer group community, a strong but varied professional group, which forms a relatively permanent, stable population (though this is not the case with the increasing numbers of transient foreigners) . . . the architecture, the centrality, local theatres and restaurants are all terrific . . . the general amenities, like restaurants and shops, have been massively upgraded since we came here in '71 – as has the housing stock. This has changed out of all recognition. (BY56)

> It really has a very attractive atmosphere, very pleasant to walk around. The architecture is great, and it has a villagey, friendly atmosphere – you feel a little bit special. There are enough local facilities not to have to go into the centre of town – though if you have to go in you can walk. (BY57)

> It's a nice, relaxed place, with a genuine mix of people. It's an interesting, rather than a boring, place – very varied. There's loads to do with young kids. We have really nice neighbours. (BY62)

Life in Barnsbury has become problematized by its 'success', in contrast to Brixton and Battersea which could be considered as successes in their own terms – in terms of relations between individual and place where, to an extent at least, 'what you see is what you get'. Barnsbury however has a 'social capital-rich' discourse, which is becoming increasingly difficult to fulfil in the new circumstances, and longer standing middle-class residents are becomingly increasingly alienated by the commodification of their area:

> The area has improved over the last 15 years, restaurants etc. But now there is renewed hostility towards the middle class, which happened when we first came here. Now there's a second wave – which you can track in the local papers – with the 'Islington born and bred' people becoming ruder, and even ignoring you in their shops, and bumping up prices for us . . . In the last two years the red Porsches have arrived, new people have been coming in. They want to change things straight away regardless of what's already there. Very arrogant. Not friendly or community minded – they put nothing into the fabric of the community, only money into the commercial infrastructure rather than their personalities or talents . . . they are making a new economy, but are absent from the community . . . I am benignedly tolerated by the 'born and breds' (having been here for so long), but there is real tension, real hostility and a local gang culture. Gangs of kids throw stones at new businesses; they're very hostile to incoming enterprise. My kids won't go out for fear of the local gangs; we have to collect our son from wherever he is.

There's a real division of kids. Ours are housebound during holidays, so it's a poorer quality of life than they could have . . . (BY26)

We speculate that there might be a relationship between this and particular forms of middle-class nostalgia, as commodification inevitably displaces affective localism.

The change in the area has been phenomenal. I was the first gentrified house in the street, I was too naïve to realize just how dangerous it was then (there was a brothel opposite, everything was tumble down and ruined). Gradually people came in and turned these wrecks into very nice houses, though we have lost some characters (not all of whom I miss). (BY45)

I am saddened by the disappearance of local shops – we had a very good dairy produce shop, and the newsagent has gone. There is nothing like this now. It changes the atmosphere of a place – there is no local focus, no meeting point. It's the *rates* that have done this . . . Caledonian Rd has gone downhill astronomically. It's now the opposite of Upper St . . . this end of the street was much more colourful and mixed when I first came – we even had a brothel! The council, under Margaret Hodge, pursued a very wrongheaded policy – they saw the area as a middle-class enclave, and so put in a number of problem families, who were out of their element, it wasn't their place . . . (BY66)

The most striking thing about the area recently has been the dramatic increase in house prices. The people now coming in are very different from those who could afford it when we came – gentrification is not new, but it is now much more wealthy people coming in – though there is still a social mix, some non-rich people in the street. (BY11)

Many middle-class people see residence and community in terms of a kind of ontologically grounded sense of appropriate and necessary behaviour and participation, but are now in danger of being left without the ability to act on this. This sense of 'oughtness' and the area as it now is do not mesh, and there are few avenues whereby it can be realized.

There is now an absence of communal mateyness of the old working class type . . . this was replaced by a more middle class kind of social life, based on meetings and so on, and for a long time this was good. But even this is changing now – the people coming in now are not joiners, so we don't know who they are. Many of them seem to be lawyers, barristers. I'd like to know who can afford the prices!

I don't like Islington Council – now there's a real Pandora's box of naff bourgeois expectations. (BY1)

This leads to a particular kind of middle-class critique of, and unease about, globalization, of which we found echoes of in Brixton and Battersea.

Battersea

Battersea is something different. Although smaller than Barnsbury in scale, it has been the site of a no-less dramatic reinvention through the market.

> It's very green, with access to wonderful, wide open spaces. Wandsworth's planning strategy has been great, for eating in the Northcote Road, shopping in Clapham . . . it's been very well developed. It's now a focal point, attracting plenty of incomers. (BA13)

> It's a good, well run borough, which is still improving. The facilities – libraries, parks, dumps – are good and efficiently run. It is becoming richer, smarter, the shops and restaurants have all improved. It's a good, efficient borough. (BA15)

As with Barnsbury, the area also forms a centre for eating and drinking out which serves a much wider clientèle in south London. Its shops cater for the needs of those heavily into the gentrification aesthetic:

> We bought just before the yuppies started pouring in. The fruit market – a proper south London street market – was thriving. Now it's ASDA and all the normal high street things . . . and it's all young people's bars, trendiness, a honey pot for young people from all over . . . instead of nice, honest grocers being the norm it's coriander, olives, sun-dried tomatoes, flowers at £1.50 a stem – pretentious. It's becoming more uniform, younger and has much less character than it did before . . . the area has two faces. During the evening and weekend it's younger, more middle class and lively. But if you look around during a normal week day you see older, poorer people. (BA1)

> . . . it has little village-type shops, and it is still possible to get all the little things done (no longer possible in Chelsea) . . . though this is starting to change – there are more and more of what I call 'non-normal' shops coming in. (BA31)

> There were really useful shops . . . now the people have changed, and so have their requirements. It used to be a normal high street – now its a yuppie paradise. I've counted *twenty five* bars and restaurants along the Northcote Road alone, and there are more in Battersea Rise. This is why the market has declined. (BA4)

It caters for a more homogenous social group than any other area, but these are, in the main, key personnel in the London economy. Like Barnsbury, it is a place which has changed largely as a consequence of the deregulation of the City and London's recent success.

It's very monocultural, not at all racially mixed. The primary schools reflect this – Honeywell is all white . . . It's enormously expensive, some of our friends have had to move, they couldn't afford to stay . . . there are a lot of very rich people around. You sometimes think 'do we fit in here?' – lots of stripey shirts, city types. (BA59)

The servicers of the global node must themselves be serviced – whether by a night time leisure economy or by a safe and bounded residential area with access to a strong circuit of schooling in which to raise their children. It is part of the logic of London's renaissance that such areas as this had to be brought into existence.

We are perfectly placed here . . . it's quite high up, so it has better air, it's easier to breathe . . . Victoria from Clapham Junction in 8 minutes is great . . . it has a very neighbourly atmosphere – one of the few remaining, I should say, in London – there are lots of families and people one knows. There are great support networks for the young families, and the whole area is rich in the services required to bring up children . . . It's a very lively area, with a lot of young people. It's also hardly English anymore, more continental in atmosphere, which I like a lot . . . this is a wonderful area to eat out in if you're affluent. (BA42)

Thus Battersea is a global space in two senses. First, because it has now become part of the nexus of areas in south-west London with a transnational profile. Second, because it is a newly created residential and leisure haven for many of the people who staff and help make possible the financial services economy; it has become a 'part of the City', as one respondent said. The consequences for changing cognitive or social maps of the city are interesting, with a formerly local south London space ('Up the Junction') now connected to the City, West End and Fulham/Chelsea.

Boys still played football in the street when we moved in, there were hardly any cars. There were many more West Indians – these have completely gone, the last ones have now moved out. The council has sold all the houses. People used to talk about 'going up to town', but now that local population has gone. It's the green wellie brigade now . . . The shops have changed a lot. All of the food shops – with the exception of two butchers – have been turned into wine bars. The local butcher describes it as the 'Croissant belt' . . . So even though a more prosperous middle-class population has moved in, the market is struggling (except for the stalls selling organic produce and olives!) . . . the writers/actors/interesting people who have been here for years are being replaced, on the whole, by city types, you know, the Northern Line straight to Bank . . . people with £45k sports cars. (BA5)

Brixton

Brixton is quite different, although like Barnsbury and Battersea, it is based around an infrastructure of consumption.

The blend of quiet with excitement is just right here . . . since the '85 riots, there is a little less antagonism between black and white people here. It used to be less mixed and friendly, there's definitely less racial antagonism now . . . there is more stability and economic opportunity. There is still a lot of begging and scamming, but this comes and goes, it's a challenge. But it's already much safer . . . the attitude of people from outside can be irritating, but that's also part of the attraction of the area for me. (BN22)

The market has been at work here too, and Brixton is now, probably, one of the main leisure areas of Europe's young. It has also been subject to the same processes of change that have affected Barnsbury and Battersea

Brixton is not as pleasant as it was. The population has changed. The kind of people who lived here before were more interdependent, more of a community. As it gets more upwardly mobile and middle class, the less accessible people become. Community spirit is affected. Also, the crime rate goes up as it becomes more middle class . . . Brixton has a particular problem: it's still full of different groups, with more coming all the time, and these are becoming more suspicious of each other. It's less open . . . there are less street cleaners and rubbish collection is not good . . . the local hospital closed, so there are greater distances to travel all the time. All of these kinds of things undermine neighbourhood. (BN34)

It's become very trendy and less friendly. My neighbour lives in New York half the time. The newer people don't say good morning which is very disturbing. There are still a few of the older West Indians families around, they're good neighbours, but generally it's up and coming, trendy. (BN12)

Nevertheless, the area has been connected to globalization in perhaps different ways, and remains – unlike both Upper Street/Barnsbury and Northcote Road/ Battersea – somehow 'local' – which not all people find attractive:

Central Brixton still bears the scars of recession – it's shabby and dirty, and there are still a lot of the casualties of 'care in the community' around. There are a hell of a lot of people begging in Brixton, which is a sign of poverty. Although the amenities have improved, these are not having any direct impact on the majority of the population, who are excluded – this creates an undercurrent of tension, which means that this is not a pleasant place to live. It's a not uncommon occurrence to experience one kind of social aggression or other; a beggar who is angry, a young person will push you off the pavement into the road. There is a constant buzz of aggression. I don't use Brixton so much now. Maybe the Ritzy or something to eat, but I don't use the market etc . . . I get in my car and drive to Sainsbury's in Clapham, and if I can avoid the station, I do. It was absolute misery when I had to use it on a daily basis . . . This street was, almost without exception, African-Caribbean or white working class when I came here, and virtually all these people have now gone. A lot of the African-Caribbeans have sold up and gone back, or died, and the white working class people have moved further out . . . the main thing has been the embourgoisement of the whole area. Some of it is very baffling, like the new shop fronts on Railton Road – I mean, why, who is it all for, who will occupy or buy them? I have a sense that these changes are not impacting positively on the less well off, particularly African-Caribbean, communities . . . But I do like being here, I feel committed to multiculturalism – though I don't know how much a part of it all I am. (BN10)

'Local' in Brixton, as in other gentrified areas of inner London, is a social as much as a spatial concept. As a totality it is more contested, the Upper Street/ 'Cally' contrast of Islington is a spatial contrast which does not exist here. As we have already seen, 'local' in Brixton translates into 'ethnicity' very quickly, which, for many, is part of the attraction of living here:

The diversity here is the thing. Time spent with people not like you is always quality time, meeting something different from you, someone from a different plane of existence. That's the great pleasure of living in Brixton. If gentrification is going to undermine this kind of diversity, then it is not to be welcomed. (BN22)

Perhaps more than any other area the downsides of both are foremost in respondents' minds. Brixton is not an easy place to live, or as we saw in the previous chapter, to bring up young children but the level of personal threat seems to be relatively low:

Last week some neighbours had a party, with a huge sound system, that lasted until 7am. With this kind of thing, nobody can sleep until it's finished – this makes me think it would be nice to move out of London. The lack of seclusion, of peace and quiet, can be difficult . . . Though my car was broken into recently, I think that the perception of crime is greatly inflated. I have no doubt that there is a very vigorous drug market, but we are not directly affected by it. There is no feeling of danger in the area, of my personal safety being under threat – though I tend to avoid potentially threatening situations. But I've never been threatened in 13 years . . . We are currently in an unsteady sort of situation. Brixton is always susceptible to cycles of boom and bust . . . things appear to be on the upturn, most of the money seems to be going into the cultural infrastructure – implying high levels of disposable income – this might be a significant change . . . But I think the perception of the area has improved more than the actual area itself, as was the case with Glasgow . . . so Brixton has been talked up, but it seems quite fragile to me – we would be the first to feel the effects of any downturn in the economy. (BN33)

Many of the older residents feel that the more recent incomers don't know how to manage this situation, as one of the very few African-Caribbean middle-class respondents put it:

The influx of new people coming in is causing problems, it's changing the vibe of the place. They're very quick to call the police if the slightest thing happens. This (their overreaction) causes animosity . . . The ownership of the new commercial enterprises in Brixton wants to attract new crowds, and the door policies of the new places are keeping Black people out . . . Some of my friends are joking, saying 'let's have another riot, scare them away'! (BN11)

There is a recognition that gentrification is changing the area in ways that make it increasingly hostile to the 'diversity' that is so valued as one of its attractions.

We are not well served by the amenities, but apart from that there are no negatives. There's not much evidence of crime. It has a good cultural mix centred on long-settled families – it has good networks for young families, and we're close to [Sudbourne] the local school . . . it's a pleasant, closeted enclave, being increasingly invaded by trendy white people, an overspill from Clapham and Dulwich . . . culturally, Brixton has an identity which it's pleasant to belong to, a trendy atmosphere. It's a mix between residents and those attracted by its cultural features. (BN17)

It is the attractiveness however to these 'trendy white people' which are on the one hand 'improving' it but, on the other hand, leading to displacement and exclusion

I love it here very much. We're high up on top of the hill, so its airy, with fantastic views, and the best park in London is just around the corner. Its very neighbourly and safe, very warm and villagey – people here look out for one another . . . The developments in central Brixton have been a very good thing, the Ritzy and so on. Taxi drivers don't groan now, people don't raise their hands with as much abandon as they used to when you tell them where you live – although it's not entirely obvious where the 80 million pounds has gone . . . but it's obviously becoming more gentrified. I was on the crest of the first 'yuppie' wave here, and the old Baijan geezer was still selling paraffin from downstairs then. This large ramshackle old house has been converted into three dwellings – it's a clichéd boom area. A former squat across the road is now on the market for £250k, even really squalid old places are now fetching high prices. There's been a hell of a lot of sharp practice in all of this, you know, 70 year old ladies in rented flats being offered £30k to get out and so on. (BN37)

It is not easy to characterize how or why this sense of locality has survived – when one considers, for example, Brixton is visited by far greater numbers of people from overseas than Battersea, and is much more responsive to demographic globalization. We believe that it is a consequence of its settlement by the African-Caribbean community, which intervened between it having been a white working-class slum and a gentrified area. This is what distinguishes it, at least in part, from Battersea and Barnsbury; although the former had a large Afro-Caribbean population it was apparently displaced much more easily. Again, unlike Battersea and Barnsbury, Brixton has now become a very particular kind of nodal point, attracting the newer migrants from all over as people increasingly go on the move.

> It's an endlessly fascinating and changing neighbourhood, I'm always amazed at how the population changes. There are always different waves of people coming, most recently South Americans. (BN42)

> I really like living here; it's such an accepting place. It's a melting pot, but tolerant, half black and half white. Also loads of gays and foreigners. (BN38)

So Brixton is a little more slippery than the others, but nevertheless a genuinely 'global' phenomenon for different reasons. It has a chaotic vibrancy and unpredictable immediacy of its own, which can be summarized as global in two ways.

It is a key site of the new youth/hedonistic/leisure economy, which is without question an important aspect of the new global economy. This is an expression of London as capital of 'cool Britannia' and its increasing attractiveness to the huge international youth trend towards drug- and club-based fun. London, for a complex of reasons, has become the European capital of this kind of hedonism and Brixton is firmly established as a brand leader at the 'funkier' and 'multicultural' end of the market. The area's symbolic status in the history of black, and particularly African-Caribbean Britain is of significance given this group's ascendancy in many popular cultural forms and symbolic desirability to people from countries that have no such population. Many of our respondents chose to locate in the area for reasons not unconnected to this fact.

The area is a nodal point on the European circuits developed by refugees and economic migrants – itself an important aspect of globalization, but one which registers far less in Islington and not at all in Wandsworth. All of this is, of course, bound up with the (above) speculation about Brixton being some sort of new global space, in which the middle classes play their part in the uncertain, unpredictable but socially necessary experiment of coming to terms with the kinds of novel social structures and interactions being thrown up by globalization in general, and more specifically by the fact that the world is on the move – an irreversible component of the new reality. Brixton is one of the key places in which we can glimpse what this might actually mean in an area that is not merely an 'underclass' ghetto. Might therefore Brixton be seen as a model for the future?

Telegraph Hill

Telegraph Hill – as we have already indicated – together with London Fields represents a very different 'take' on the gentrification/globalization theme. We have typified Telegraph Hill as an 'enclave' in which a sense of middle-class community is assiduously being built on the basis of extensive networking and in which there are high levels of satisfaction with the result but which also disguise high levels of anxiety. The sense of satisfaction weaves together the social and spatial set up of the area:

> It's well laid out, with broad streets. The road is like a river, very nice houses, lovely trees. Environmentally very pleasant . . . the area has come up a bit because of the desirability of the houses . . . the Jubilee Line and DLR [Docklands Light Railway] extensions have improved the ease of communication between people. (TH9)

> The immediate physical location – the park, wide leafy streets – is great. I like the community spirit and fluidity of interaction and organization. It's a friendly place with plenty of like-thinking people . . . I have the impression that it has become more 'middle class professional', and that newcomers are always welcome as long as they are of the 'right minded' type. (TH6)

There is an element of smugness that is somewhat off-putting, which is summed up by the above comments and comes across again and again – 'the best thing about this place is the people' (TH23) – they have sought and found the holy grail of friendship and community in the big, alien and ultimately unfriendly city. It has however been at the cost of its 'others'. More than anywhere else there is a sense of 'struggling' – which is partly about time-management and partly about an insufficiency of economic resources:

> This is a very strong community – there are a lot of us who bought at the same time, struggled with mortgages, kids all went to the same school. A lot of the people we met in the first six months of moving here are still friends. (TH26)

There is a strong contrast here with Brixton in which 'otherness' is highly valued as an abstract value, as an aspiration that, in reality, passes most people by in their daily interactions but that is also very real as a motivating factor for coming and continuing to live in the area. In Telegraph Hill there is a lot of 'genuflection' to diversity and difference but it is much more of a kind of checklist of 'political correctness' that, although present in the area in no way intrudes on respondents' lives, even in the tectonic form we discovered in Brixton:

> I really like it here. It's a friendly area, we know our neighbours – we have one another's keys. It's ethnically diverse and there's a good spread of ages. Also a lot of gay people, a pink zone . . . crime is rare, though a neighbour has been mugged. (TH27)

This description reflects a very widespread set of beliefs about the area but it is only a partial reflection of the interactions of respondents on a day-to-day basis. There is a high degree of support amongst the middle class, who do indeed have each other's keys, but the social mixing with the 'ethnically diverse' and gay people is not borne out by our investigations. Many of his neighbours would not agree about crime, about which there is a high degree of anxiety that came across often despite the expressions of satisfaction with the area. The overwhelming sense was of an urban village in which the dark side was often hidden – the following comment was highly representative:

> It's a superb place, very friendly and mixed . . . it has socially strong networks, like a rural community. (TH28)

The urban village is a recurring theme in the sociology of the city (Gans 1982) and reflects a strong sense of 'belonging' amongst residents:

> I love it here. I had a rootless childhood, and I love the very strong sense of community that the children have. It's like a village in the centre of London, it has that kind of support system. And the kids feel they belong here. I love the idea of their friendships carrying on over time . . . I wouldn't move away from here to anywhere else in England. (TH41)

The narrative of belonging is probably stronger here than in any other area and it is also probably coupled more often with how much they value diversity. Nevertheless there is also recognition that the two are not always compatible

> I like the size of the place (the house) and our huge garden . . . the people are friendly, there is some community spirit . . . location-centrality-convenience . . . The area has really gone up since we came here. A lot of the houses were squatted and we lobbied for them to be sold, to get the squatters out . . . We feel that we've contributed to the improvement of the area. It reflects on us, our values. That's why we tried to start the neighbourhood watch . . . It's New Cross: it's mixed and it's a bit too dangerous. Too much street crime. Too many yellow police boards asking for information about people being murdered . . . there is a bit too much of this sort of thing to make you feel comfortable. I always pick my wife up from New Cross station now . . . it's the social housing element, the care-in-the-community side of things – a variety of people wandering around shouting to themselves. It's not *too* disturbing, but it is a cause for concern . . . but it's interesting, it's mixed – I always say I live in New Cross, not Telegraph Hill, which I find embarrassing . . . aircraft noise is atrocious. (TH16)

There is a sense that there is gulf between how respondents would like to think of the area and how it has perhaps become. There is, in other words, a good measure of 'reflexivity' involved here and there is a tendency amongst respondents to construct reality around how it 'ought' to be. This perhaps is only possible because, for a large number of them, it has at times been able to deliver on at least part of this, of like mindedness:

> There are nice houses, spacious and with large gardens. I like the sociability, the friendliness here. We socialize in the street . . . I like the social mix, but that is beginning to disappear. It has a slightly lefty, socially conscious, anti-racist ethos – people 'like yourself'. (TH25)

Most are aware in some way or other of the contradictions here at the heart of their lives and that the 'enclavism' is a way of holding both onto New Cross (in the way one respondent just referred to) but also to the so-called 'upside' of the globalized city.

> It's a friendly, stable area with lots of families. People are really settled here in houses with long gardens, surrounded by green spaces . . . the area has a character of its own it's not at all anonymous like so much of London . . . and it has a nice social mix, it's not a ghetto in any way . . . property values are rising fast, which is a shame as it will become more and more gentrified . . . there are worries about the globalization of the city, it all becoming the same. I think it's good that there's no good tube here, it keeps the property speculators from coming into the area. (TH52)

London Fields

London Fields is, in some respects, a hybrid of Telegraph Hill and Brixton, it shares the enclavism of the former with the diversity of the latter. Like Telegraph Hill it is lacking in a developed consumption infrastructure but, unlike Telegraph Hill its attraction is its location in the local economy – that of Hackney. With the exception of the one respondent whom we have quoted above, respondents in Telegraph Hill were in denial of the wider area (New Cross) in which Telegraph Hill is located. New Cross is not pretty and has a reputation as a rough and dangerous part of a more or less unreconstructed South London. Its white working class has – as we previously noted – largely fled to the outer reaches of London and North Kent although often to return as jobbing builders for the gentrifiers and to support Millwall (Robson 2000). By contrast, one of the attractions of London Fields for many respondents was its location in Hackney – what we term 'Hackney in the mind'. Hackney, whilst excoriated for its corruption and inefficiency by many respondents, also represented a radical and working-class tradition with which they identified. The basis of this identification was a combination of personal and political.

Being a middle-class person taking advantage of an old working-class area, I have guilt from feeling like I'm exploiting this and don't mind paying higher taxes – the quality of life of non middle-class people here is very poor, this is an overall negative . . . it's an incredibly deprived area, and you don't feel as if anyone is doing anything to improve it . . . services, education, street cleaning, medical services are all appalling . . . the poverty that the 'working classes' – I don't suppose that's the right sociological term now – live in around here is appalling, and you can feel it all the time, the guilt about that . . . I choose not to do anything about alleviating the situation so that's all it is, guilt. You see it most starkly at the health clinic, where people are obviously in need of help but the system just continues to let them down and fall apart . . . the nature of Broadway market is starting to change, there's the kind of chi-chi health shop – all done out in metal – which wouldn't look out of place in Soho but is completely out of place there . . . this is very interesting, as the area hadn't changed at all for twenty years . . . I mean, an art gallery in Broadway market, as well – *really* bizarre. (LF39)

Respondents living in London Fields were, as we have seen, often atypical; for example, there were more people who had been upwardly socially mobile into the professional middle classes than in other areas (often from working-class back-grounds) but there were also more who were downwardly mobile from professional and upper-middle class backgrounds. Either way, there was an identification with a working-class past for which, however distortedly, Hackney remained strongly representative; this was usually expressed in terms of 'social mix' that was much less idealized than in Telegraph Hill

We like the social and ethnic mix, everything from guttersnipes to barristers . . . We know an awful lot of people locally because we taught in local schools; we're very well connected in the area. (LF3)

The social mix is the ultimate thing with Hackney, there's a total mix in terms of mentality . . . You can see it in the pubs – there's middle class pubs, working class pubs, 'artistic' pubs, gay pubs, everything. I use all of them . . . it has a kind of mix that I haven't found anywhere else in London . . . the different pubs all have different kinds of people. I went out the other night, and one minute I was drinking with an old Irish bloke, the next with the guy who produced the second Stone Roses album . . . it depends on your mood, but you'll find all levels here. (LF19)

However, these positives were often balanced by a very realistic assessment of the downside of the area

Dalston Junction is a high crime area, there are some very nasty areas around now, you have to be very wary . . . this doesn't effect me so much, but a lot of my younger lodgers have had problems, the girls have been hassled, the boys mugged . . . the area has a certain edge, you have to be very aware of personal security. (LF24)

It's very dirty, and can have a very migratory feel . . . people don't seem to have an idea about civic or social responsibility. (LF27)

Dalston is pretty nasty, drug dealing, prostitution, stuff like that. And it's very, very dirty. But this does not really impinge on this immediate area. (LF28)

There is an appreciation of some of the benefits of gentrification, which is felt to be less likely to completely transform the area – the social structure appears to be more 'negotiated' than elsewhere:

It always seems to be two steps forward, one step back for Hackney: a few times it's promised to take off but never quite come to fruition. We'll see if this housing boom sticks. It may, as people who want to live in Islington, or Shoreditch or whatever, but can't afford it, can come here . . . The population changes very fast. The middle classes move out as soon as kids come to secondary school age, and there's a lot of refugees and a generally shifting population. This can be a good thing, but it does undermine substantial and permanent change. (LF30).

I like the realism, nothing too fancy or posh, just people doing their jobs . . . Ridley Road market *reeks* of reality, where somewhere like Hampstead is so contrived, which I can't stand . . . We're into a second cycle of improvement now, after the slump – the streets are getting cleaner, Broadway market is beginning to move, there's a little art gallery there now, there are these kinds of small signs of movement, of gradual improvement . . . people themselves (as opposed to council) are more aware of the mess and are wanting to make it better. (LF5)

They keep trying to change things for the better round here but this seems doomed to failure. (LF31)

Though it's still pretty run down, there are more fashionable looking people hanging around . . . Holly Street has been well regenerated, but otherwise I feel there's more upgrading *said* to be happening than there actually is, apart from all this silly hype about house prices. (LF29)

Hackney is definitely on its way up, it *is* happening this time, on a wave of regeneration finance (like Brixton a few years ago). The first wave of Islington-fleeing gentrifiers didn't stick, but the current wave definitely will, and it will be much better for the area as a whole, produce a much better feeling in general. (LF18)

There was more awareness of the ethnic implications of this regeneration in London Fields than elsewhere and some sense that divisions of class were now giving way to those based around 'race'

> There's quite a lot of movement in the area as a whole, with people with a lot more money coming in . . . a definite split between people like us in these houses (very middle class) and the council houses – no black people in home ownership, but lots in the flats. The incomers are all white middle class with newer cars than ours. (LF28)

Although London Fields' lack of infrastructure is something it shares with Telegraph Hill, this was changing. Respondents did not regard the lack of watering holes as a way of maintaining a sense of community in quite the same way as in Telegraph Hill. London Fields has, for some time, been developing as an 'artists quarter' and this has recently received a boost from Hackney's attempt to encourage the 'cultural industries' through the 'creative Hackney' strategy (Attfield 1997; Foord 1999; Green 1999). The rapid development of Hoxton and Shoreditch as homes to the creative industries with their 'live-work' spaces complemented the developments in South Hackney around London Fields. A number of cafés have sprung up together with a few alternative shops; this is regarded as much more acceptable by respondents than the branded bars of Barnsbury and Battersea and likely to provide local employment. This remains to be seen. The role that artists have played (unwittingly) in gentrification elsewhere suggests that they are more subtle shock troops than the *Slug and Lettuce* but in other respects are more effective and formidable in marking change. Already it is said that many artists are moving out of London Fields as they are unable to afford the rents when leases come up for renewal (Green 1999):

> Hackney always feels as if it's poised to do something, but no one is ever sure if it will happen . . . the Hackney Arts movement has come along recently – I think it's part of the Hoxton drift, with Hackney now morphing into Hoxton, Shoreditch, a phalanx of areas as opposed to being out on its own as it was before. (LF64)

> . . . Having so many artists in the area is fun . . . lots of new little bars and things . . . and what's happening in Hoxton and Shoreditch is interesting. (LF45)

Not all respondents were hostile to the arts-led regeneration in terms of what it might do to the area and their investment in housing:

> All the really trendy areas are just too expensive . . . this is a kind of compromise solution . . . I see that they're planning an Arts Development at London Fields, which will leave us in a prime position . . . waiting for the transport to join up . . . I'll develop this place and sit out the 'Social change in Hackney', see what happens. (LF8)

Much of the negativity was focused on the performance of Hackney Council which in terms of the quantity and quality of vitriol was far greater than elsewhere. In Battersea respondents had generally supported the council's pro-gentrification stance and in Telegraph Hill had found that they could work with it on a day-to-day basis. In Barnsbury and Brixton, the reputation of the local council for inefficiency and incompetence was widely felt particularly in relation to educational provision. Nevertheless the scorn felt for Hackney Council was unmatched, mainly for the ways in which it had let down the very people who needed its help most. Many of the ills of the area were displaced on to the council.

Hackney council is beyond a joke, it's . . . internally riven by Labour party feuding . . . to see a borough so poor and yet so badly run is tragic. (LF1)

The mismanagement of the council is appalling, so that the poverty which is the area's main characteristic remains in place . . . I loathe the council, they are just pathetic, the staff in all departments seem uniformly awful and incompetent . . . though the improvement in the social housing here is one of Tony's show-offs, the drug situation has got worse – it moves about but it's always there, you can't miss it . . . the general situation in the area seems to be both improving *and* worsening. (LF36)

The sense that, out of this chaos there is improvement, is widespread and the rebuilding of the infamous Holly Street estate with central government money is reiterated many times.

. . . The redevelopment of Holly St is a great thing. Thank God! That ridiculous waste of money in the 1960s, now all being destroyed . . . there is a small impression growing that Hackney *may* be taking more notice, doing more – at least they're packaging it better! . . . they seem to be asking people's opinions, although most local people are not used to this and so don't give their opinion, don't go to meetings. (LF67)

There was a feeling that the lack of a middle-class population allowed the Labour Party to take advantage of local people, because nobody really had the skill to check them:

The council is unprofessional and totally incompetent, and there is a very big population of unemployed and lowly paid people, its not as socially mixed, in this sense, as some other parts of London . . . we need more professional people in the area . . . (LF5)

However it is not clear that this would necessarily solve the problem in the direction that many respondents claimed they wanted to see the area moving:

There is a lack of community. There is a need for people to get off their butts here, because the council won't do it . . . there's a lot of anti-social behaviour, people from the estate climbing into one another's gardens etc. and a bad drug problem, disaffection of youth. Good kids getting frustrated, their parents not doing enough – they always want other people to do things for them . . . the anti-social behaviour really is becoming too much, people treating the street as if it was their own, the estate spreading along the thoroughfare . . . a lack of respect for property and privacy . . . e.g. we've been trying, through the Tenants Association, to re-educate the locals in the use of public space – they're used to just roaming all over the place whenever they feel like it. They don't always respect or recognize the boundaries of private property. This is a problem now that there are more private owners in the street, and a private company has tried to create a communal garden for their development and there have been a lot of trespassers . . . life round here very much takes place out in the open, in public space . . . Another thing is that you've got to keep up the *front* all the time. This is very tiring, this having to always be alert, always keeping it up. I think this is why a lot of people leave London . . . you have to train yourself to survive in London, develop those skills. (LF18)

So, even in London Fields despite the 'diversity' rhetoric, the cultural divide is expressed as strongly as it is in Barnsbury or Telegraph Hill.

Docklands

The five areas that we have focused on here have all been gentrified by 'collective social action'; we would therefore perhaps expect a rather different approach to the issues in Docklands, which, as we have seen, is characterized by a very different set of values, attitudes and feelings. In other words, we would not see this as part of the 'metropolitan habitus' – the rationales for living there are likely to be entirely different as well as the expectations and experiences of residents. Janet Foster's (1999) study already hints at this – socially there are three major groups here: the old white working class, the new middle class and – at least in the Isle of Dogs – the Bangladeshis moved from the north of the borough by the council. The politics of 'race' and complaint are likely to be operating at a much more explicit level here (Cohen 1996). However, as Foster indicates, the new middle class is likely to position itself outside this. This is confirmed by our respondents who for the most parts, in so far as they talk about other social groups at all, either see the 'social mix' working well or else see the old and resentful working class as the problem.

A good area to live, so quiet and peaceful, no trouble . . . even though it's more developed now, it still feels cut off . . . there are more and more people like me coming in, and this is helping the development, because there are more people who know how to get things done, things get done. The locals never did anything about things. People like us have transformed the whole area for everybody, everybody's benefited . . . there are two very distinct communities here – council people and people like us – and though the two don't meet, there's not a lot of contention . . . (ID26)

On the whole what is valued is what is marketed – water and convenience for the city with not too much social obligation:

The water is lovely and its close to work, which is convenient of course, but I also really like the people – they are genuine, the kind of people I'm used to (I grew up in southern Italy). I'm comfortable with white trash! . . . I'm very happy here, but may move if too many more professionals move in – I work with them, I don't want to live near them as well . . . (SQ28)

This is city living as the marketing people might have wished it

The light, the air, the variety of life on the river and the changing landscape on it; these are all marvellous. This sense of space is a powerful influence – on our terrace you wouldn't know that you weren't back in Dorset, from whence we came. This is very different from the other side of the river, where you have a sense of being closed in . . . there are more people like me moving into the area now – my neighbours include a Banker, a Theatre Administrator, a Sotheby's valuer, A Church verger, an Estate Agent, an Economist . . . also a good number of my (journalistic) colleagues live here. (ID21)

We always thought that Docklands would be different from the other areas and this is entirely borne out by the findings reported in the last four chapters. What perhaps is surprising is that they are *so* different, the flight from social obligation in most cases appears to be utter. It is apparently a way of living in the city without having to negotiate aspects of urban life. In this sense, Docklands is entirely unlike the other new build and 'rehabs' of industrial buildings undertaken in the centres other English cities: Leeds, Manchester, Newcastle for example. In these cities, the attraction to living in the centre is the 24/7 'full on' lifestyle which could not be further from that of those living in Docklands. They approximate more to Savage's concept of 'undistinctive' corporate types than anywhere else in our study. In large part this is a function of their work lives and household histories – for example, empty nesters returning to the city or those whose primary residence is in the country and the flat in Docklands is a pied-à-terre from which they return at weekends. There has been an increase in warehouse and factory conversions in central London recently which have been attractive to the hedonistic 24/7 lifestyle seekers but these tend to have been concentrated to the north and east of the City in Clerkenwell, Hoxton and Shoreditch and many are live/work spaces. We did not include any of this group in our study but we speculate that they would approximate more to the non-metropolitan city-centre livers and to Savage's post-moderns.

In the final and concluding chapter we pull together this experience of living in contemporary gentrified London – with its diversities and its commonalities spread across a series of mini-habituses that contribute to the overall sense of a metro-politan habitus.

Note

1. I am grateful here to a number of colleagues (notably Rowland Atkinson, Martin Boddy, Liz Bondi, Gary Bridge, Loretta Lees, Michal Lyons) who have shared with me their knowledge of what sparse research has been undertaken on cities other than London and Edinburgh. In particular, I would like to thank Mike Savage who has showed me the findings of his research in the Chorlton area of Manchester, where his respondents draw clear distinctions between themselves and those who live in gentrified areas of London such as those investigated in this study. Many of them had considered the possibility of living in London and make very explicit comparisons to particular areas of London but part of the attraction of living where they do is that it is not London and that they are not part of the cosmopolitan cognoscenti. In other words perhaps, although neither Savage nor his subjects use the term, they are not part of a 'metropolitan habitus'. A conference on gentrification 'Upward neighbourhood trajectories' was organized by Rowland Atkinson in late September 2002 as this book was being completed and a number of the papers there began to address the issue of non-metropolitan gentrification. Many of the papers are available at http://www.gla.ac.uk/departments/urbanstudies/gentpaps/gentpap.html.

–9–

Conclusions

Mapping the Habituses

In this final chapter, having constructed the social typologies of the fields and identified, or at least hinted at, the strategies pursued by the actors in some of those fields, we now turn to an analysis of them by way of conclusion. We begin by drawing up the trajectories and strategies produced in the interaction between habitus and the constraints/opportunities that are determined by the structure of the field(s) under consideration. We do this by comparing the habitus, the constraints, and opportunities and, finally, the strategies adopted. We then consider whether or not gentrification constitutes a distinct 'field' in relation to the 'metropolitan' habitus.

There is a temptation to use the habitus as a mapping device to bring out differences and so construct some theoretical insights, but we support the view taken by Longhurst and Savage (1996) that we should also look for commonalities across the habitus. Although there are important area differences across the metropolitan habitus, there are probably greater commonalities: a relatively coherent set of common attitudes, beliefs, feelings and perspectives. The goals are broadly similar; however the means for achieving them vary, mainly in terms of the relative possession, and subsequent deployment, of stocks of economic, cultural, symbolic and social capital. We have shown, for example, how in Docklands economic capital is largely used to purchase outright the kinds of social and symbolic capital that are carefully and systematically marshalled in Barnsbury and Telegraph Hill. If gentrification is concerned with the creation of a particular aesthetic in, for example, the exterior presentation and interior display of carefully restored Victorian property, which demonstrates the possession of considerable cultural capital and sensitivity by the occupant (Jager 1986), then by this definition Docklands is not gentrification. This would however be wrong, not only from a position of common sense but more seriously because, in fact, the designs are carefully crafted to refer to particular vernacular styles, which are, at least formalistically, connected with the area's immediate and more distant past as a working-class production area with a history that has now been utterly subsumed by the forces of global capital (Wright 1985b).

In the remaining five areas cultural and symbolic capital are critical to an appreciation of why the area is a desirable place to live: in some areas this is blatant (notably Telegraph Hill), in some it is latent (Battersea) and in others (notably Barnsbury) it is important but mediated through the possession of economic capital. The same arguments can be advanced for social capital, which unlike the other forms can only be realized in social relationships which again are the basis of the middle-class habitus in Telegraph Hill and in recent history in Barnsbury. In Brixton, there is generally a flight from the obligations of social capital in the manner pointed to by traditional urban theorists such as Simmel (1950) and Wirth (1938) who saw the city as offering a freedom from the cloying constraints of 'gemeinschaft'-type societies.

There are different narratives by which the habitus is articulated to its own social members, outsiders and recruits. We return to these below. The differences, however, are in many ways less significant than the commonalities, which point to an essentially socially liberal group who, to some extent at least, transgress existing social divisions within the middle class as, for example, posited by Savage et al. (1992). Whilst the latter's tripartite division has been a useful heuristic device that we have used throughout the book, it seems clear that only in Docklands is there any real suggestion of the 'undistinctive' type working largely in the private sector in corporate activity. Even here there are few managerial workers, but rather more commonly specialist or technical functionaries responsible for 'engineering' new forms of financial or media products.

In both Barnsbury and Battersea there are many more 'cross-overs', which lends support for the post-modern type, but this is too ill-defined to have sufficient theoretical weight. However, the associations that Savage point to in relation to sporting and leisure activities are supported by these groups and consumption remains an important field. In Telegraph Hill and Herne Hill there is more evidence of the liberal ascetic types working in the welfare professions, but again these 'cross-over' into new occupations in the private, public and voluntary sectors in which financial objectives and criteria have become more dominant than those of service and welfare. The form of post-modernism found in Tulse Hill is rather different from that proposed by Savage; many of these people work in existing industries but in new functions (such as, for example, as Web design). They do not possess sufficient stocks of economic capital to buy their way out of social obligation, as in Barnsbury or Battersea, but neither do they wish to substitute social networking as in Telegraph Hill. Thus, this most urban of groups is in some ways the most fragile and vulnerable, which shows particularly when they come to face issues of social reproduction. They are the most likely to cash in their urban property assets and leave London, whereas elsewhere respondents assiduously created strategies designed to accentuate the opportunities and eliminate the threats.

The constraints everywhere, with the partial and ironic exception of Battersea, revolved around the perceived hostility and inability of local government to resolve issues of social reproduction and collective consumption. In Battersea the local authority was widely praised for its policies encouraging the development of state and private school networks and other environmental enhancements – elsewhere it was excoriated. Only in Telegraph Hill was there a working relationship and that was now in danger of being jeopardized over the proposal for a new secondary school in Telegraph Hill. Everywhere respondents systematically used their stocks of cultural, economic and social capital to construct strategies to cope with the downsides of living in a globalized city where not only were the institutions of social reproduction regarded with suspicion but so was their ethos. In a sense the threats were not the displaced locals with whom relations were managed in a variety of ways but the less tangible pervasiveness of a global 'now' culture, which many respondents saw as threatening to the values of social reproduction. As Sennett (1999) remarked, many of those who spent their working lives rooting out the 'long term' from the economy now realized that it was hard to offer appropriate advice on the virtues of deferred gratification and 'doing a job properly' to their children. Equally there was a concern that the distinctiveness that they built into their domestic and neighbourhood environments might be devalued by the homogenization of global culture – in which Upper Street and Northcote Road, for example, lost the distinctive cachet that made them so valued.

On the other hand, the metropolis was recognized as having a huge potential for inculcating cultural capital in the next generation, not just through the major cultural institutions of London but also precisely because it was at the 'cutting edge' of global culture. An example of this would be the attraction of the night time economy in Brixton or the new 'artistic quarters' in Hackney near to London Fields. Most of the respondents in Barnsbury, whilst expressing concerns about education and danger, recognized that geographically and socially they lived near to almost all that was happening in the city and could introduce it to their children in ways which massively enhanced what they received formally through the education system. Many women had rather surprised themselves by giving up work to ensure that this happened in a systematic and coherent programme of socialization. In different ways, but with equal passion and determination, parents in Telegraph Hill and London Fields used the resources of the household to reproduce their cultural capital and to devise appropriate strategies.

Although these variations are important and represent far more than simply differences in stocks of economic capital, they are dwarfed by what they share, which we have termed the metropolitan habitus. It compares not just with the non-urban middle class but also with those outside London in the large 'metropolitan' conurbations. They are not however 'metropolitan' in the same sense, lacking, as they are, London's global links as a *cosmopolitan* metropolis. What has been described in this book is not just the working out of social class but the realities of living in a global city in which global culture is mediated through relations with other classes, generations and ethnic groups in ways that white middle-class parents fail to understand and about which they have considerable reservations. However, these are also the forces which make London such an attractive place to live. Gentrification here refers to a very specific form of cosmopolitanism in which the 'locals' are more likely to be the non-metropolitan middle classes and the displaced white working class as contrasted to the other social groups that now make up the 'other' of London.

Gentrification as a Field?

Can we regard gentrification itself as a 'field', as a plane of strategic activity? A field can comprise the interaction effects of other free-standing fields. In this case we would understand it as being structured by those of the household, school, leisure/consumption and employment in the context of a metropolitan habitus. These we would suggest are structured in such a way as to provide the fundamental requirements of ordered middle-class life in a metropolitan setting such as that presented by London. As such, this would therefore be very different from those presented in other non-metropolitan cities elsewhere at least in England. In other words, can we regard gentrification as a set of competitive, metropolis-wide structural inter-relationships? We are posing the possibility that there might be such a constellation of social positions, which constitute a field of middle-class inner-city settlement and habitation. Bridge (2000) has argued, in an important contribution, that gentrification can be regarded as a specific form of the habitus:

> . . . gentrification as a form of habitus presents us with a conundrum and one that goes to the heart of Bourdieu's class analysis as well as our explanations of gentrification. Habitus is largely about the structuring structures that make sure classes are reproduced over time. It is about classifiable practices as well as their classification. But gentrification seems to represent new practices and orders of classification. If the different tastes that lead to, say, inner urban loft living, rather than suburban housing, are merely small perturbations within the overall middle-class habitus, then why all the fuss about gentrification? Why is gentrification held up to be symptomatic of the cultural practices of the *new* middle class? If gentrification is a minor variation in the reproduction of the middle class then why did it happen at all, given the fact that in terms of existing tastes of the middle class (i.e. the existing habitus) the inner urban areas to which early gentrifiers might move were seen as inherently risky. The difficulties that these questions raise suggest why most of the discussion of gentrification and habitus tends to relate to areas where gentrification is well advanced or, if it is in the early stages, research is focused on areas that in some senses are soft, or more secure, for habitus adaption (artists' districts in Manhattan is the classic example . . .) (Bridge 2000: 206–7)

In this book, we have stressed the issue of difference within the context of a distinctive metropolitan setting whilst noting a primary contrast between metropolitan versus non-metropolitan settings. To paraphrase, we are proposing that the urban middle class becomes a 'class for itself' rather than merely 'a class in itself' by virtue of its residence in a global metropolis. Following on, we have suggested that it is of some importance how people acquire the attributions of the habitus and how these then become disposed. In this final section, we consider the ways in which individuals become attracted to the particular areas and how these areas 'socialize' them into them.

We noted in Brixton a dialectic that recognizes and draws the local excluded into a 'Brixton of the mind', which is unquestionably 'tectonic' but which insists on the middle-class right to belonging and identification. This is despite what appears to be a significant difference between Tulse and Herne Hills; in the former we discern a flight from, or refusal to engage in, social capital building, in the latter its conscious construction. On both sides of the park, Brixton represents an irreplaceable model of city living.

By contrast in Telegraph Hill there is no 'New Cross of the mind'; rather a middle-class enclave that is rendered distinctive by juxtaposition with what is around it. The area's hegemonic narrative of belonging functions, we thought, like a 'theme' course in creative writing: newcomers are given an outline and invited to get on with it. This appears to make it no less successful an experiment, in its own terms, in building an urban village. Just as in Brixton, there was a gap between rhetoric and reality but a somewhat different one. In Telegraph Hill, respondents were, as it were, invited to participate in creating a community and were provided with some basic tools so to do. They were mainly focused around the household and social reproduction whereas in Brixton they were focused around the idea of Brixton. In both cases, a satisfactory pursuit of the strategy had the (often unintended) consequence of marginalizing 'the other' that, in abstract, was an important element in the discourse. However, there is another important difference between the two areas apart from their approach to their locality, which lies in their approach to 'global culture'. A large element of the attraction of Brixton is its 'night time economy' with its bars, clubs, eating places and cinema, which are at some form of cutting edge. Even if they rarely go and the areas in which they live are to an extent cut off from the entertainment zone around the underground station, our respondents saw this as an enormously important element of living in Brixton, which they did not wish to see blunted by housing market émigrés from Balham and Clapham. This was simply not the case in Telegraph Hill where its isolation was perceived as the best defence against the impact of globalization, which in its turn represents social homogenization and a loss of distinctiveness.

Battersea and Barnsbury are another coupling but one that is achieved by 'riding the wave' of contemporary globalization – in both areas all the symbols of this phenomenon were exhibited but in ways that would seem to display (at least relatively) taste and distinction. This applied not just at the level of the ubiquitous 'themed' drinking places but also the provision of food, decorating materials and 'ideas' for the bathroom and kitchen. As one respondent put it, you could buy many varieties of ciabatta or varieties of olive oil but a wing nut – forget it! Although apparently similar, the routes into these two gentrified 'play zones' for south-west and north London were very different. In Battersea belonging is enabled by a narrative more in the nature of a 'template' for middle-class living, in which residents slot into a set of pre-existing market-based structures – with the conse-quence of much lower levels of reflexivity, these being less appropriate, necessary or possible. Even if it didn't turn out that way, the place was transitory – some-where to stay until you had made your 'pile' in the City with which you could buy one in the country. This is not to comment on the nature of the social relations or the stock of cultural capital held by respondents but to make the point that, for most of them, their considerable assets of both were mediated primarily through the market and via the possession of actual or potential economic capital.

Barnsbury was different in that there was no template as such; the discourse of entry was based much more around a 'narrative of belonging', which, although it was social-capital rich, in fact required high stocks of both economic and cultural capital to access. The contradiction here was that the discourse rested on a prior round of gentrification that was predicated on at least some measure of social integration, which the current residents were, despite protestations to the contrary, unwilling to enter into. The prime example of this was schooling although this was symptomatic of a general ability to 'talk the talk' but an unwillingness to 'walk the walk'. Many of the longer term residents felt that Barnsbury, and Islington more generally, was becoming increasingly like Wandsworth; what perhaps was a critical difference is that they wanted to live in the inner city and had a longer term perspective than respondents in Battersea who treated it either as a temporary stage as part of a longer term move to the country or else as part of a more traditional town *and* country existence. Life in Battersea was made easier by the fact that its gentrification seems to have established the hegemony of the market over the wider area in a much more consistent and upfront way than in Islington where there remains an issue of 'authenticity' amongst the incomers. Its traditional working-class population, although often not visible in its non high-rise tenements, remained a presence which was increasingly perceived as a threatening one.

Amongst the 'collective action' gentrification areas this leaves London Fields, which in some ways is the most difficult to 'read'. It shares an ambiguous relation-ship with Islington with which it has a number of essentially uneasy links. There is a long-standing upgrade trail from London Fields to Barnsbury – the current Prime Minister and his wife are not atypical of this: young, with not much eco-nomic capital or income at the start of their careers but likely to experience a rapid rise in both. There is also a route the other way of single people with a small flat in Islington who want more space for their money. In both cases the migration has not always worked: as a number of respondents told us, there were many cases of people fleeing east to London Fields searching either for more space or more authenticity but who could not 'hack' the latter and moved on. Also, there were a number of households in London Fields who might well have moved on but couldn't stomach the social costs of the move to Islington. What matters a lot to those living in London Fields is the 'idea' of Hackney; this is a version of the same attractions of Brixton but is based around an often idealized notion of Hackney as a radical and working class location – although the idealism quickly disappears when confronted with the 'reality' of Hackney and its local council. In many ways this is the least 'formed' of our areas in that there is no clear process of socialization and the Hackney identity is not as clear as that presented by Brixton, which is able to concretize it in relation to Brixton's developing cultural and consumption infrastructure. On the other hand, although lacking in such infrastructure, it is not eschewed as it is in Telegraph Hill. The development of the arts and cultural quarters in Hackney is welcomed by many respondents – partly in the potentially misguided belief that jobs in this sector are somehow more real than other service jobs and partly for the benefits it brings in terms of shops and cafes, which are more authentic than the branded varieties found elsewhere. London Fields is thus slowly being transformed through what Sharon Zukin has termed an artistic mode of production (Zukin 1988). If the logic of the transformation of SoHo in New York, which Zukin plots, is followed in Hackney, then it may not prove to be such a good long-term strategy in terms of social inclusion.

Finally, we consider Docklands. Here in a sense, we turn all that has been taken before on its head. All the responses we got in Docklands largely related to the 'idea' of the place as it was marketed: easy travel to work and water (which presumably symbolize peace and relaxation). They also confirmed some of the things not in the brochures: social differences that were largely perceived as intractable and lack of social obligation. However, the latter was not entirely consistent particularly in the Isle of Dogs where there were the beginnings of the stirring of middle-class conscience amongst some people who had been there for some time and did not regard it solely as a convenient pied-à-terre in London. Nevertheless, overall, what appears to be lacking here is any conception of what we have termed the 'metropolitan habitus' – indeed as some of our respondents suggested, it was the most surburbanized (in terms of attitudes as well as style) location in inner London. It is driven by work and gender/household divides in similar ways to those characterized in the suburbs in the post-war decades. In this respect, following Smith (1979) and Warde (1991) social life appears to be very much driven by the workings of the urban land market. This is not to say that there are no interesting things to say about Docklands but it is a very different model of urban living from that found in other areas of London where the motivations to settle are essentially habitus driven. In contrast, the social action component of Docklands is provided for in the marketing brochures and is generally reflected back through the mouths of our respondents – water, convenience, style, safety and so forth.

Our overall conclusions are that economic and cultural globalization has been a major influence on the 'sources of variation' in gentrification across inner London. We suggest that this manifests its influences at the level of the household and across the four fields of employment, consumption, education and housing identified by Bourdieu. In addition, we believe that the ways in which the middle classes are making neighbourhoods can be distinguished by the different ways in which they deploy their stocks of cultural, economic and social capital.

In all of these cases, we believe that the 'idea' of the place gives rise to a particular narrative, script or template, which acts to incorporate newcomers and is differentially attractive or repellent to people depending on their background, employment and cultural locations. Of course, the local places are just as much a creation of globalization as the global places but the 'mindset' of the inhabitants is very different. We use the concept of a *template* to discuss the way newcomers are absorbed into Wandsworth as distinct from the *narrative* that characterizes life in Barnsbury, Brixton and London Fields and, somewhat differently, Telegraph Hill. In Telegraph Hill this seems stronger than elsewhere. It forms the basis for a *script* that tends to situate newcomers within a pre-existing narrative of community building, development and belonging.

However, the broad distinction that we tentatively draw is that these gentrification strategies are ways of accommodating to the stresses and strains of globalization. This, after all, is the way in which the world is heading, with Brixton as one of the vanguard sites: towards collapsing boundaries, heterogeneity, movement, hybridized social forms – all the volatility and dynamism of globalization in its social sense. Could it be that the established middle classes of Brixton and those remaining in London Fields have made an attempt to participate in this uncertain future in a much more engaged way than their peers elsewhere in gentrified inner London? Could this be a new but logical outcome of the good faith perhaps implied in the ascetic liberal consciousness – a committed participation in the uncertain but socially necessary project of de-segregating demographically chaotic and potentially disastrous nodal spaces on the map of globalization? Could the work of conscience be evident here? Conscience involved in the experiment of making these new kinds of place livable for everybody? By contrast, might Docklands, complete with gated compounds, replace Thamesmead (as portrayed in Stanley Kubrick's film *Clockwork Orange*) as the potential nightmare scenario for living the inner city?

Conclusions

Can London be thought of as the world's most important site of this kind of experimentation? It is certainly difficult to imagine any equivalent to Brixton in any North American city. London is not only a global node, but also a metropolis arguably less racially segregated than any other city in the industrialized world. Is London now riding the wave of the future, the vanguard city in which the consequences of globalization are being most realistically dealt with? Put another way, there may be places as mixed as Brixton and London Fields in this world, but are there any as (relatively) stable? Have the values and dispositions of the British ascetic middle classes finally found a historical role? Have the new 'corporates' (defined as the functionaries of the financial engineering industry) found their niches in Battersea and Barnsbury? It is the diversity of London that enables such a flexible form of the metropolitan habitus to be constructed.

Bibliography

Abercrombie, N. (1996) *Television and Society*. Cambridge, Polity.

Aldridge, A. (1998) '*Habitus* and cultural capital in the field of personal finance.' *Sociological Review* 46(1): 1–23.

Allan, G. (1989) *Friendship: Developing a Sociological Perspective*. New York, Harvester Wheatsheaf.

Amin, A. and N. Thrift (2002) *Cities: Reimagining the Urban*. Cambridge, Polity.

Argyle, M. (1994) *The Psychology of Social Class*. London, Routledge.

Atkinson, R. (2000) 'Professionalization and displacement in Greater London.' *Area* 32: 287–95.

Atkinson, R. (2001) 'The hidden costs of gentrification Displacement in central London.' *Journal of Housing and the Built Environment* 15: 307–26.

Attfield, A. (1997) 'Bread and Circuses? The making of Hoxton's cultural quarter and its impact on urban regeneration in Hackney.' *Rising East* 1(3): 133–54.

Bagguley, P. (1995) Middle class radicalism revisited. *Social Change and the Middle Classes*. T. Butler and M. Savage. London, UCL Press: 293–309.

Ball, S., R. Bowe, and S. Gewirtz (1995) 'Circuits of schooling a sociological exploration of parental choice of school in social class contexts.' *Sociological Review* 43: 52–78.

Ball, S. and C. Vincent (1998) '"I Heard It On The Grapevine": "Hot" Knowledge and School Choice.' *British Journal of Sociology of Education* 19(3): 377–400.

Banks, O. (1968) *The Sociology of Education*. London, Batsford.

Beck, U. (1992) *Risk Society*. London, Sage.

Benn, C. and B. Simon (1970) *Half Way There: Report on the British Comprehensive School Reform*. London, McGraw Hill.

Bernstein, B. (1975) *Class Codes and Control*. London, Routledge.

Bernstein, B. (1990) *The Structuring of Pedagogic Discourse*. London., Routledge.

Blank, R. (1990) Educational effects of magnet high schools. *Choice and Control in American Education*. W. Clune and J. Witte. Philadelphia, The Falmer Press. 2: 77–109.

Blokland, T. and M. Savage (2001) 'Network Class and Space.' *International Journal of Urban and Regional Research* 25: 221–6.

Bondi, L. (1991) 'Gender divisions and gentrification a critique.' *Transactions of the Institute of British Geographers* NS16: 190–8.

Bondi, L. (1999) 'Gender class and gentrification enriching the debate.' *Environment and Planning D: Society and Space* 17: 261–82.

Boudon, R. (1974) *Education, Opportunity and Social Inequality*. New York, Wiley.

Bourdieu, P. (1984) *Distinction: A Social Critique of the Judgement of Taste*. London, Routledge.

Bourdieu, P. (1986) The Forms of Capital. *Handbook of Theory and Research for the Sociology of Education*. J. Richardson. New York, Greenwood Press: 241–58.

Bourdieu, P. (1987) 'What makes a social class? On the theoretical and practical existence of groups.' *Berkeley Journal of Sociology* 32: 1–18.

Bourdieu, P. (1990) *In Other Words: Essays Towards a Reflexive Sociology*. Cambridge, Polity Press.

Branson, N. (1979) *Poplarism 1919–1925: George Lansbury and the Councillors' Revolt*. London, Lawrence & Wishart.

Breughel, I. (1996) 'Gendering the polarisation debate a comment on Hamnett's "social polarisation economic restructuring and welfare state regimes".' *Urban Studies* 33(8): 1431–9.

Bridge, G. (1994) 'Gentrification, class and residence: a reappraisal.' *Environment and Planning D: Society and Space* 12: 31–51.

Bridge, G. (2000) 'Rationality, ethics and space: on situated universalism and the self-interested acknowledgement of "difference".' *Environment and Planning D: Society and Space* 18: 519–35.

Bridge, G. (2001a) 'Bourdieu rational action and the time-space strategy of gentrification.' *Transactions of the Institute of British Geographers* NS26: 205–16.

Bridge, G. (2001b) 'Estate agents as interpreters of economic and cultural capital: the gentrification premium in the Sydney housing market.' *International Journal of Urban and Regional Research* 25(1): 87–101.

Brownill, S. (1990) *Developing London's Docklands: Another Great Planning Disaster?* London, Paul Chapman Publishing.

Buck, N., I. Gordon, P. Hall, M. Harloe and M. Kleinman (2002) *Working Capital: Life and Labour in Contemporary London*. London, Routledge.

Buck, N., I. Gordon and K. Young (1986) *The London Employment Problem*. Oxford, The Clarendon Press.

Burtenshaw, D., M. Bateman and G. Ashworth (1991) *The European City A Western Perspective*. London, David Fulton Publishers.

Butler, T. (1997) *Gentrification and the Middle Classes*. Aldershot, Ashgate.

Butler, T. and C. Hamnett (1994) 'Gentrification class and gender some comments on Warde's "gentrification of consumption".' *Environment and Planning D: Society and Space* 12: 477–93.

Butler, T. and V. Rix (2000) The Royal Docks: continuity and change. *Eastern Promise: Education and Social Renewal in London's Docklands*. T. Butler. London, Lawrence & Wishart: 59–83.

Butler, T. and G. Robson (2001) 'Social capital, gentrification and neighbourhood change in London: a comparison of three South London neighbourhoods.' *Urban Studies* 38(12): 2145–62.

Butler, T. and G. Robson (forthcoming 2003a) 'Negotiating their way in: the middle classes, gentrification and their deployment of capital in a globalizing metropolis.' *Urban Studies*.

Butler, T. and G. Robson (2003b) 'Plotting the middle classes: gentrification and circuits of education.' *Housing Studies* 18(1): 5–28.

Butler, T. and M. Savage (eds) (1995) *Social Change and the Middle Classes.* London, UCL Press.

Byrne, D. and T. Rogers (1996) 'Divided space-divided school an exploration of the spatial relations of social division.' *Sociological Research Online* 1(2): http://www.socresonline.org.uk/socresonline/1/2/3/.html.

Calhoun, C. (1993) Habitus, field of power and capital: the question of historical specificity. *Bourdieu, Critical Perspectives*. C. Calhoun, E. LiPuma and M. Postone. Cambridge, Polity: 61–88.

Campbell, C. (1995) The Sociology of Consumption. *Acknowledging Consumption*. D. Miller. London, Routledge: 96–126.

Carpenter, J. and L. Lees (1995) 'Gentrification in New York, London and Paris: an international comparison.' *International Journal of Urban and Regional Research* 19: 286–303.

Castells, M. (1996) *The Rise of Network Society.* Oxford, Blackwell.

Champion, A. and T. Ford (1999) *Attempts at isolating the main components of the distinctive social composition of London's migration exchanges.* Department of Geography, University of Newcastle upon Tyne.

Cohen, P. (1996) All White on the Night? Narratives on nativism on the Isle of Dogs. *Rising in the East? The Regeneration of East London*. T. Butler and M. Rustin. London, Lawrence & Wishart: 170–96.

Cohen, P. (1998) 'Urban regeneration and the polyversity: the road to Beckton Pier.' *Rising East: the Journal of East London Studies* 1(3): 24–51.

Coleman, A. (1985) *Utopia on Trial: Vision and Reality in Planned Housing.* London, H. Shipman.

Conway, S. (1997) 'The reproduction of exclusion and disadvantage symbolic violence and social class inequalities in 'parental choice' of secondary education.' *Sociological Research Online* 1(2): http://www.socresonline.org.uk/socresonline/2/4/4/.html.

Cox, R. and P. Watt (2002) 'Globalization, polarization and the informal sector: the case of paid domestic workers in London.' *Area* 34(1): 39–47.

Crilley, D., C. Bryce, R. Hall and P.E. Ogden (1991) *New Migrants in London's Docklands.* London, Department of Geography, Queen Mary and Westfield College.

Crompton, R. (1995) Women's employment and the 'middle class'. *Social Change and the Middle Classes.* T. Butler and M. Savage. London, UCL Press: 58–75.

Devine, F. (1998) 'Class analysis and the stability of class relations.' *Sociology* 32(1): 23–42.

Douglas, M. (1996) *Thought Styles.* London, Sage.

Dunleavy, P. (1981) *The politics of mass housing in Britain, 1945–1975: a study of corporate power and professional influence in the welfare state.* Oxford, Clarendon Press.

Eade, J. and C. Mele (1998) 'Global processes and customised landscapes: the 'Eastern Promise' of New York and London.' *Rising East: the Journal of East London Studies* 1(3): 52–73.

Echols, F., A. McPherson and J. Willms (1990) 'Parental choice in Scotland.' *Journal of Education Policy* 5(3): 207–22.

Egerton, M. and M. Savage (1997) 'Social mobility individual mobility and the inheritance of class inequality.' *Sociology* 31(4): 645–72.

Engels, F. (1971) *The Condition of the Working Class in England.* Oxford, Blackwell.

Esping Anderson, G. (1990) *The Three Worlds of Welfare Capitalism.* Cambridge, Polity.

Fainstein, S., I. Gordon and M. Harloe (eds) (1992) *Divided Cities New York and London in the Contemporary World.* Oxford, Blackwell.

Fainstein, S. (2001) *Competitiveness, Cohesion and Governance: A Review of the Literature.* New Brunswick NJ, Rutgers University.

Fielding, A. (1995) Migration and middle-class formation in England and Wales, 1981–91. *Social Change and the Middle Classes.* T. Butler and M. Savage. London, UCL Press: 169–87.

Foord, J. (1999) 'Creative Hackney: reflections on Hidden Art.' *Rising East: the Journal of East London Studies* 3(2): 38–66.

Ford, T. and T. Champion (2000) 'Who moves into out of and within London? An analysis based on the 1991 Census 2% Sample of Anonymised Records.' *Area* 32: 259–70.

Foster, J. (1999) *Docklands: Cultures in Conflict, Worlds in Collision.* London, UCL Press.

Friedman J. and G. Woolf (1982) 'World City formation: an agenda for research and action' *International Journal of Urban and Regional Research* 6: 309–44.

Gans, H. (1968) Urbanism and suburbanism as ways of life. *Readings in Urban Sociology.* R. Pahl. Oxford, Pergamon.

Gans, H. (1982) *The Urban Villagers : Group and Class in the Life of Italian-Americans.* London, Collier Macmillan.

Gewirtz, S., S. J. Ball and R. Bowe (1995) *Markets Choice and Equity in Education.* Buckingham, Open University Press.

Giddens, A. (1990) *The Consequences of Modernity.* Oxford, Polity.

Glass, R. (1964) *London: Aspects of Change*. London, MacGibbon & Kee/Centre for Environmental Studies.

Goldthorpe, J. (1996) 'Class analysis and the reorientation of class theory: the case of persisting differentials in educational attainment.' *British Journal of Sociology* 47: 481–505.

Goldthorpe, J. and G. Marshall (1992) 'The promising future of class analysis: a response to recent critiques.' *Sociology* 26(3): 381–400.

Goldthorpe, J. H. (1987) *Social Mobility and Class Structure in Modern Britain*. Oxford, Clarendon Press.

Gorard, S. (1997) 'Market Forces, Choice and Diversity in Education: The Early Impact.' *Sociological Research Online* 2(3): http://www.socresonline.org.uk/socresonline/2/3/8.html.

Green, N. (1999) 'The space of change: artists in the East End 1968–1980.' *Rising East* 3(2): 20–37.

Hall, R. and P. Ogden (1992) 'The social structure of new migrants to London Docklands: recent evidence from Wapping.' *London Journal* 17(2): 153–69.

Hall, R., P. Ogden and C. Hill (1997) 'The pattern and structure of one-person households in England and Wales and France.' *International Journal of Population Geography* 3: 161–181.

Halle, D. (1991) Bringing materialism back in: art in the houses of the working and middle classes. *Bringing Class Back In*. S. McNall, R. Levine and R. Fantasia. Boulder, Westview Press: 241–59.

Halsey, A. H. and J. Karabel (eds) (1977) *Power and Ideology in Education*. Oxford, Oxford University Press.

Hamnett, C. (1973) Cosmopolitans and Centralists. *D201*. Milton Keynes, Open University.

Hamnett, C. (1989) The social and spatial segmentation of the London owner-occupied housing market: an analysis of the flat conversion sector. *Growth and Change in a Core Region*. M. Breheny and P. Congden. London, Pion.

Hamnett, C. (1991) 'The blind man and the elephant: the explanation of gentrification.' *Transactions of the Institute of British Geographers* NS16: 173–89.

Hamnett, C. (1994a) 'Socio-economic change in London professionalisation not polarisation.' *Built Environment* 20: 192–203.

Hamnett, C. (1994b) 'Social polarisation in global cities: theory and evidence.' *Urban Studies* 31: 401–24.

Hamnett, C. and D. Cross (1998) 'Social polarisation and inequality in London the earnings evidence 1979–95.' *Environment & Planning C* 16: 659–80.

Hamnett, C. and P. Williams (1980) 'Social change in London: a study of gentrification.' *Urban Affairs Quarterly* 15: 469–87.

Harker, R., C. Mahar and C Wilkes (eds.) (1990) *An Introduction to the Work of Pierre Bourdieu*. London, Macmillan.

Harloe, M. (1995) *The People's Home? Social Rented Housing in Europe and America*. Oxford, Blackwell.

Harrison, P. (1985) *Inside the Inner City: Life under the Cutting Edge.* Harmondsworth, Penguin.

Hirschmann, A. (1970) *Exit Voice and Loyalty.* Harvard, Harvard University Press.

Hutton, W. (1995) *The State We Are In*. London, Jonathan Cape.

Jackson, B. and D. Marsden (1962) *Education and the Working Class; Some General Themes Raised by a Study of 88 Working-class Children in a Northern Industrial City*. London, Routledge & Kegan Paul.

Jager, M. (1986) Class definition and the esthetics of gentrification: Victoriana in Melbourne. *Gentrification of the City*. P. Williams and N. Smith. London, Allen & Unwin: 78–91.

Jenkins, R. (1992) *Pierre Bourdieu*. London, Routledge.

Lane, J. F. (2000) *Pierre Bourdieu: a Critical Introduction*. London, Pluto.

Lash, S. and J. Urry (1994) *The Economies of Signs and Space*. London, Sage.

Lee, D. (1994) 'Class as a social fact.' *Sociology* 28(2): 397–415.

Lees, L. (2000) 'A reappraisal of gentrification towards a "geography of gentrification".' *Progress in Human Geography* 24: 389–408.

Ley, D. (1996) The New Middle Class and the Remaking of the Central City. Oxford, Oxford University Press.

Lockwood, D. (1995) Marking out the middle classes. *Social Change and the Middle Classes*. T. Butler and M. Savage. London, UCL Press: 1–12.

Longhurst, B. and M. Savage (1996) Social class, consumption and the influence of Bourdieu, some critical issues. *Consumption Matters: the Production of Experience and Consumption*. S. Edgell, K. Hetherington and A. Warde. Oxford, Blackwell/Sociological Review.

Lynch, K. (1960) *The Image of the City*. Cambridge MA, MIT Press.

Lyons, M. (1996) 'Employment, feminisation and gentrification in London, 1981–93.' *Environment and Planning A: Government and Planning* 28: 341–56.

Maddaus, J. (1990) 'Parental choice of school: what parents think and do.' *Review of Research in Education* 16: 267–95.

Marcuse, P. (1989) '"Dual City" muddy metaphor for a quartered city.' *International Journal of Urban and Regional Research* 13(4): 697–708.

Marshall, G., H. Newby, D. Rose and C. Vogler (1988) *Social Class in Modern Britain*. London, Hutchinson.

Massey, D. (1995) Reflections on gender and geography. *Social Change and the Middle Classes*. T. Butler and M. Savage. London, UCL Press: 330–44.

May, J. (1996) 'Globalization and the politics of place place and identity in an inner London neighbourhood.' *Transactions of the Institute of British Geographers* NS 21: 194–215.

Merton, R. (1948) Patterns of influence: a study of interpersonal influence and of communications behaviour in a local community. *Man in the City of the Future*. P. Lazarsfeld and F. Stanton. London, Collier-Macmillan.

Mollenkopf, J. H. and M. Castells (1991) *Dual City: Restructuring New York*. New York, Russell Sage Foundation.

Moore, D. (1990) Voice and choice in Chicago. *Choice and Control in American Education*. W. Clune and J. Witte. Philadelphia, The Falmer Press. 2: 153–98.

Moore, P. (1982) Gentrification and the residential geography of the new class. Unpublished paper from Scarborough College, University of Toronto.

Munt, I. (1987) 'Economic restructuring, culture and gentrification: a case study of Battersea, London.' *Environment and Planning A: Government and Planning* 19: 1175–97.

O'Connor, J. and D. Wynne (1995) City Cultures and the New Cultural Inter-mediaries. ESRC Research Report, Manchester, Manchester Institute for Popular Culture.

Office for Standards in Education (1998) Inspection Report: Edmund Waller Primary School.

Office for Standards in Education (1998) Inspection Report: Highbury Grove School.

Office for Standards in Education (2001) Inspection Report: Lillian Bayliss School.

Ogden, P. and R. Hall (1998) 'One person households and migration in France and Britain: some comparative evidence from censuses and longitudinal sources.' *Update: News from the LS User Group* 20: 9–17.

Park, R., E. Burgess and R. Mackenzie (1925) *The City*. Chicago, University of Chicago Press.

Portes, A. (1988) 'Social Capital its origins and applications in modern sociology.' *American Review of Sociology* 24: 1–24.

Raban, J. (1974) *Soft City*. London, Hamish Hamilton.

Reay, D. and S. Ball (1998) '"Making their minds up" family dynamics of school choice.' *British Educational Research Journal* 24(4): 431–48.

Rex, J. and R. Moore (1967) *Race Community and Conflict A Study of Sparkbrook*. Oxford, Oxford/IRR.

Robbins, D. (1991) *The Work of Pierre Bourdieu*. Milton Keynes, Open University Press.

Robbins, L. (1963) *Higher Education*. London, HMSO.

Robson, G. (2000) *'No One Likes Us, We Don't Care': The Myth and Reality of Millwall Fandom*. Oxford, Berg.

Robson, G. and T. Butler (2001) 'Coming to terms with London: middle-class communities in a global city.' *International Journal of Urban and Regional Research* 25(1): 70–86.

Rose, D. (1984) 'Rethinking gentrification: beyond the uneven development of Marxist urban theory.' *Environment and Planning D: Society and Space* 1: 47–74.

Sassen, S. (1991) *The Global City: London New York Tokyo.* Chichester, Princeton University Press.

Savage, M. (2000) *Class Analysis and Social Transformation.* Milton Keynes, Open University Press.

Savage, M., J. Barlow, P. Dickens and A. Fielding (1992) Property Bureaucracy and Culture Middle Class Formation in Contemporary Britain. London, Routledge.

Scarman, G. (1982) *The Brixton Disorders 10–12 April 1981.* Harmondsworth, Penguin.

Sennett, R. (1999) *The Corrosion of Character: The Personal Consequences of Work in the New Capitalism.* London, Norton.

Sennett, R. and J. Cobb (1972) *The Hidden Injuries of Class.* London, Norton.

Silver, H. (ed.) (1973) *Equal Opportunity in Education.* London, Methuen.

Silverstone, R. (ed.) (1996) *Visions of Suburbia.* London, Routledge.

Simmel, G. (1950) The Metropolis and Mental Life. *The Sociology of Georg Simmel.* D. Weinstein. New York, Free Press: 409–24.

Slaughter-Defoe, D. T. and B. Schneider (1986) Newcomers: Blacks in Private Schools. Chicago: Northwestern University, School of Education and Public Policy.

Smith, A. (1989) 'Gentrification and the spatial contribution of the State; the restructuring of London's Docklands.' *Antipode* 21(3): 232–60.

Smith, N. (1979) 'Towards a theory of gentrification: a back to the city movement by capital, not people.' *Journal of the American Planning Association* 45: 538–48.

Smith, N. (1987) 'Of yuppies and housing: gentrification, social restructuring and the urban dream.' *Environment and Planning D: Society and Space* 5: 151–72.

Smith, N. (1996) *The New Urban Frontier: Gentrification and the Revanchist City.* London, Routledge.

Smith, N. and P. Williams (eds) (1986) *Gentrification of the City.* London, Allen & Unwin.

Sullivan, A. (2001) 'Cultural capital and educational attainment.' *Sociology* 35(4): 893–912.

Taylor, C. (2001) 'The geography of choice and diversity in the 'new' secondary education market of England.' *Area* 33(4): 368–81.

Urban Taskforce (1999) *Towards an Urban Renaissance. Final Report of the Urban Task Force Chaired by Lord Rogers of Riverside.* London, Department of Environment Transport and the Regions.

van Krieken, R. (1997) 'Sociology and the reproductive self demographic transitions and modernity.' *Sociology* 31: 445–71.

Wacquant, L. (1989) 'Towards a reflexive sociology: a workshop with Pierre Bourdieu.' *Sociological Theory* 7(1): 26–63.

Wacquant, L. (1991) Making class(es): the middle classes in social theory and social structure. *Bringing Class Back In*. S. McNall, R. Levine and R. Fantasia. Boulder, Westview Press: 39–64.

Warde, A. (1991) 'Gentrification as consumption issues of class and gender.' *Environment and Planning D: Society and Space* 6: 75–95.

Warde, A. (1996) Afterword: the future of the sociology of consumption. *Consumption Matters: The Production and Experience of Consumption*. S. Edgell, K. Hetherington and A. Warde. Oxford, Blackwell: 302–12.

Watson, W. (1964) Social mobility and social class in industrial communities. *Closed Systems and Open Minds*. M. Gluckman and E. Devons. Edinburgh, Oliver & Boyd: 129–57.

Williams, P. (1986) Class constitution through spatial reconstruction? A re-evaluation of gentrification in Australia, Britain and the United States. *Gentrification of the City*. N. Smith and P. Williams. London, Allen & Unwin: 56–77.

Willmott, P. (1987) *Friendship, Networks and Social Support*. London, Policy Studies Institute.

Wilson, E. (1977) *Women and the Welfare State*. London, Tavistock Publications.

Wilson, W. J. (1980) *The Declining Significance of Race: Blacks and Changing American Institutions*. Chicago, University of Chicago Press.

Wirth, L. (1938) 'Urbanism as a way of life.' *American Journal of Sociology* XLIV: 1–24.

Wright, E. O. (ed.) (1985a) *Classes*. London, Verso.

Wright, E. O. (1997) *Class Counts*. London, Verso.

Wright, P. (1985b) *On Living in an Old Country: The National Past in Contemporary Britain*. London, Verso.

Wright, P. (1991) *A Journey through the Ruins: A Keyhole Portrait of British Postwar Life and Culture*. London, Radius.

Young, M. and P. Willmott (1962) *Family and Kinship in East London*. Harmondsworth, Penguin.

Zukin, S. (1988) *Loft Living: Culture and Capital in Urban Change*. London, Radius.

Zukin, S. (1995) *The Cultures of Cities*. Oxford, Blackwell.

Index

Abercrombie, N., 42
Abercrombie report, 21n3
ACORN types, 49–53, 55, 57, 59, 62, 65–7
Acre Lane, Brixton, 57, 90
advantage
  class, 30, 139–40, 143, 164
  long-term, 34
  relative, 21
affluence, 30, 52, 57, 60, 65, 66, 85
African-Caribbean communities, 55, 59, 93,
    173–4
  see also black people; ethnicity;
    multiculturalism
age
  distribution, 126
  of respondents, 111, 124, 126
alcohol consumption, 51, 53, 55, 58, 62, 137
Alliance Party, 134
altruism, 136
'American dream', the, 19
antagonism, 40, 64
anti-urbanism, 86
anxieties, 4, 11, 164, 175
architecture, 81, 87, 114
artistic mode of production, 100, 191
artists and gentrification, 180
arts
  economy, 61–2
  festival, Telegraph Hill, 55, 99
  Hackney and, 191
'ascetic' lifestyle, 27, 36, 41, 132, 192
  see also liberal ascetic types
Asian middle-class settlements, 110
aspirations, 5, 11, 12, 45
asset deployment, 25, 33, 34, 36, 44
  model, 3
Atkinson, R., 27
attitudes, 44, 46, 67, 74, 124, 182
  to local authorities, 84, 87
  social, 112, 144

authenticity, incomers and, 83, 85, 87, 190, 191
authority, 23, 40

Bagguley, P., 45
Balham, 56
Ball, Stephen, 29, 141–4
Bangladeshi community, 63–4, 182
Barcelona, 20
Barnsbury, 51–3, 79–85, 189–90
  education, 71, 72, 144–9, 158
  globalization and, 166–8
  housing, 74–6
Barratt builders, 66
bars, 56, 59, 87, 132, 180, 189
Basildon, 20
Battersea 'Between the Commons', 25, 52,
    58–60, 85–90, 189–90
  education, 71, 144–6, 149–50, 158, 159
  globalization and, 169–70
  housing, 74–6
Beck, U., 16, 17
behaviour, 124, 135, 156, 168
  social, 36, 37, 42
belonging, 83, 87, 176, 189, 190
  see also narrative of belonging
benefits, social, *see* welfare
Berlin, 20
Bermondsey, 66
Bernstein, Basil, 46, 139–40
Beveridge Report, 162
black middle-class settlements, 110
black people, 19, 94, 110, 148, 174
  see also African-Caribbean communities;
    ethnicity; multiculturalism
Blair, Tony, 77n3, 190
  children, 145
Bondi, L., 29
Boudon, R., 143
Bourdieu, P., 2, 11, 16, 27, 29, 67
  field and, 38–41

Index

public, 31
private, 135
the city and, 15
consumption infrastructure, 5, 79–80, 84, 85,
   87, 91, 166, 170, 177
contested space, 99
'control group', 52
Conway, S., 141
'cool Britannia', 174
coping strategies, 2, 24–5, 28–32,187
corporate/undistinctive types, 36, 73
   see also undistinctive lifestyle
cosmopolitanism, 8, 55, 56, 141, 165–6,
   187–8
cosmopolitan-local dichotomy, 165
council housing, *see* housing, social
credential inflation, 143
crime, 98, 102–3, 176
cultural activities, 31, 53, 55, 57, 58, 62, 133
cultural ambience, 7
cultural capital, 2–4, 11, 16, 29–31, 99, 103,
   185–7, 190, 192
   consumption and 46–7
   education and, 12, 47, 69, 71, 72, 73, 143
   employment and 44–5
   housing and, 45–6, 75
   power and 38–40
'cultural industries', 180
cultural theorists, 17
culture, 3, 44, 55, 94, 132, 148
   alternative, 61–2, 137
   class and, 17, 42
   global, 4, 187, 188, 189
   working class, 95

Daily Mirror, the, 55, 62
Davies, Nick, 140
decorative art, 42
deferred gratification, 24, 125, 187
demographic mix, 60
demographics, 33
deprivation, 95, 96, 100, 103
deprived
   boroughs, 8, 13
   populations, 53, 65
dichotomization, 13
difference
   affective, 27

occupational, 11
social, 55, 191
typology of, 132
   see also metropolitan habitus, difference
disadvantage, racialized, 19
displacement, social, 1, 65, 70, 164
   gentrification and, 127
   improvement and, 173, 174
   see also working class, displacement
dispossessed, 60, 66
distinction, cultural, 16
'distinctiveness', 18, 30, 187
diversity, social, 2, 11, 82, 89, 94, 96, 100–1,
   103, 110
   declining, 93, 99
   hostility to, 173
division
   cultural, 182
   occupational, 43
   of labour, gendered, 162
   racial, 179–80
   social, 18, 26, 82, 186
Docklands, 1, 3, 4, 12, 26, 27, 63–7, 103–8,
   191–2
   education, 144–6
   gentrification and, 185
   globalization and, 182–3
   housing, 74–6
   marketing of, 104, 107, 182–3
   see also Britannia Village; Isle of Dogs;
      Surrey Quays
domestic service, 13, 114, 162, 163
downsizing, 10

East London Line, 55
eating out, 53, 55, 58, 62, 132, 169
'economically inactive', *see* unemployment
economic capital, 2–4, 11–12, 29–31, 85, 96,
   185–7, 190, 192
   consumption and, 46–7
   education and, 12, 47, 70, 71, 72, 73
   employment and, 44–5, 76
   housing and, 45–6, 74, 75
   power and, 38–40
Economist, The, 126, 136
economy
   global, 4, 11, 91, 162
   informational, 13

Index

new, 2, 10, 15, 24, 28, 64
  service, 13
Edmund Waller school, 53
education, 2–4, 30–5, 47, 95, 103, 125–6,
    139–46, 187
  by area, 146–57
  colleges, 34
  field of, 68–73
  league tables, 30, 147
  markets, 140, 141, 157–9
  private tuition, 72
  quality of provision, 70
  see also university
Education Act (1988), 70, 140, 141
educational choice, 4, 87–8
  see also 'school of choice'
Egerton, M., 139, 143
'elective affinity', 130
'embodied dispositions', 1, 29
employment, 7, 13–14, 33–5, 41, 76, 121–2,
    180
  field of, 3, 4, 44–5, 68
  instability, 164
  respondents, 118–22
'enclavism', 165, 175, 177, 189
Engels, F., 18
  *The Condition of the Working Class in
    England*, 18
entertainment district, 91
  see also play zones
environment, 11, 95, 96
environmental concerns, 98–9
environmental enhancements, 127, 187
equality of opportunity, 68, 73
ESRC, 1
  Cities Programme, 12
ethnicity, 10, 50, 62, 109–11, 176
  local as, 172
  see also multiculturalism; 'race'
European Union, 8, 13
Europe, urban development in, 19–20
everyday experience, 41–2
ExCel Exhibition Centre, 64, 65
exchange value, 105
exclusivity, 2, 43, 64, 127
exhibitions, 131
exploitation, 17
extended family, 132

facilities, social, 1, 35
Fairview, 66
families, 10–11, 12, 24, 85, 162
  dual career, 163
  work and, 23–4
  see also households
fields, 16, 36–7, 38–41, 42, 67, 188–93
  see also consumption; education;
    employment; gentrification; housing
fieldwork, 26
fieldwork areas, 25, 49–51
  see also Barnsbury; Battersea; Brixton;
    Docklands; London Fields; Telegraph Hill
financial services, 9, 74, 170
First World War, 162
fixing, social, 16
flexibility, 10, 24, 31, 47
Fordism, 20
  'post-Fordist', 28
Foster, Janet, 182
Friedman, J., 13
friendships, 3, 127, 130, 165, 175
Fulham, 59

galleries, 53, 55, 62, 131
Gans, Herbert, 165
  'Urbanism and Suburbanism as a Way of
    Life', 165
gated communities, 64
gay communities, 92, 176
gender, 15, 27, 42
  see also women
general election (1997), 134
general practitioners, 136
gentrification, 1–5, 9, 19, 21, 24, 34, 50, 190
  aesthetic, 185
  artists and, 180
  class and, 162–6
  consumption and, 76–7
  field of, 188–93
  globalization and, 8, 192–3
  of inner London, 7–11
  'race' and, 110
  research, 14–15, 25–8, 31
  strategies, 192
  university graduates and, 130–1, 163
  see also capital, gentrification by; collective
    action gentrification

respondents and, 176
  school-gate, 31
inter-generational time, 33
interviews, 1, 2, 50
  see also respondents
Isle of Dogs, The, Docklands, 26, 63, 64, 65–6,
  104, 191
Islington, 2, 8, 9, 14, 61

Jenkins, R., 36–41
jobs, *see* employment; occupations
juvenile delinquency, 162

keep fit activities, 53, 58, 131, 137
key fields, *see* fields

labour
  market, 7, 68
  theory of value, 17
  unionized, 13
Labour borough, 99
Labour Party, 134–5, 181
land market, 17, 26
landscape, 64
Lansbury, George, 59
Lash, S., 16
'latchkey kids', 162
Lees, L., 9, 110
legislation, 59
leisure
  activities, 3, 30, 31, 35, 36, 129, 131–4, 171,
    186
  economy, 170, 174
liberal ascetic types, 36, 73, 186, 192
  see also ascetic lifestyles
Liberal Democrats, 134, 135
life-cycle, 34
'lifestyles', 25, 27, 36, 41, 50, 137
  identities, 34
  see also ascetic; post-modern; undistinctive
local area
  economy, 82
  involvement in, 3, 31, 133
  markets, 68
  practices, 43
  services, 135–6
'local', as social concept, 171–2, 173
local authorities, 3, 15, 131, 177, 187

Islington, 84
  Lambeth, 90, 94
  Lewisham, 55
  London Fields, 102, 103
  Telegraph Hill, 98–9
  Wandsworth, 59, 87, 88, 90
localities, mapping of 35
'locals', 8, 35, 64, 89
  incomers and, 27, 52, 67
Lockwood, D., 43
London Docklands Development Corporation
  (LDDC), 63
London Fields, 60–2, 190–1
  education, 71, 144–6, 156–7, 158, 159
  globalization and, 177–82
  housing, 74–6
  park, 61, 99
London Transport, 55
lone parents, 65
Longhurst, B., 41–2, 185
'long term'
  concept of, 125
  virtues, 24
Lyons, M., 25, 52, 59

Mackenzie, R., 19
Madrid, 20
Manchester, studies of, 16, 18
Manchester Road, Isle of Dogs, 65
markets, 68, 85, 190
  educational, 34–5, 70
  metropolitan, 35
Marshall, G., 43
Marxist tradition, 17
Marx, Karl, 37
material resources, 143
maternal deprivation, 162
men, employment and, 162, 163
meritocracy, 73
Merton, Robert K., 165
metropolis, global, 34, 166, 189
'metropolitan habitus', 1, 3, 9, 67, 130, 165,
  187
  commonalities, 41–2, 43, 185, 186
  'defining issue', 125
  differences, 82, 89–90, 91, 185, 186, 189
  lacking, 104, 191
middle class, 2, 5, 8, 9, 21, 23–6, 33, 182

Index

white gentrifying, 11–12
working class urban, 13
postcode
  apartheid, 140
  data, 49
post-modern lifestyle, 27, 36, 41, 73, 132, 186
post-war
  family life, 10–11
  reconstruction, 20
'post-war settlement', 162
poverty, 8, 60, 65
power, 7, 38, 40
  of class, 28
  field of (politics), 39
Power, Ann, 21
pre-school clubs, 128
  Under Fives' Club, 54
pride, 94–5
Private Eye, 136
private sector, 27, 76, 120, 135, 144–5, 186
privatization, of services, 135
privilege, denial of, 164
production, mass, 20
professional labour market, 163
professionals, 53, 55, 57
  public sector, 41
  young urban, 64
  new, 132, 133
property
  as investment, 105
  rights, 29
Protestant Ethic, 12
'provinces', 7
public
  institutions, 57
  services, 8, 135, 136
  transport, 30, 59, 64, 136, 162
pubs, 53, 54, 87, 90, 100, 178

qualifications, 55, 125, 142, 162
qualitative data, 79
quantitative data, 79
Queensbridge Road, London Fields, 60, 99

'race', 9, 10, 15, 19, 64
  gentrification and, 110
  politics, 182
radio listeners, 51, 136

Railton Road, Brixton, 57, 90
rational action theory, 16
Reay, D., 29
Redriff Road, Surrey Quays, 66
re-engineering, 10
refugees, 7, 174
reinvention of area, 169
religion, 55, 134
renovations, 45, 114
'rent gap', 26
reproduction
  cultural, 4, 5, 30, 31, 33, 34, 35, 36, 52
    education and, 139–43
  of advantage, 143, 144
  social, 31, 73, 95, 125–6, 164, 186–7, 189
    education and, 69, 70, 71
  theory of, 40
research, 1, 3, 9, 39
  empirical, 37, 41
  questions, 34
resources, 11
  cultural, 30
  economic, 175
  local, 35
  see also capital
respondents, 4, 28
  backgrounds, 122–5
  Barnsbury, 79–85
  Battersea, 85–90
  Brixton, 90–95
  characteristics of, 109–12
  children, 125–7, 127–9, 131
  Docklands, 103–8
  employment, 118–22
  friendships and, 127–31
  housing decisions, 112–14
  incomes, 116–18
  London Fields, 99–103
  reflexive, 83, 97, 98, 176, 190
  Telegraph Hill, 95–9
restaurants, 56, 59, 60, 87, 99
  see also eating out
retirement age population, 55, 58
'revanchism', 19, 60
Rex, John, 20
Robson, G., xi, 29
Rogers Report, 10
Rogers, T., 141

Index

vibrancy, 90
Vienna, 20
voluntary associations, 133

Walthamstow, 9
Wandsworth, 2, 12, 25, 27, 57, 59
Warde, A., 26, 42, 191
water sports, 64
Watson, W., 163
wealth, inequality and, 81, 126
Weber, Max, 12
Weberian tradition, 17, 37
welfare benefits, 13, 14, 135
well-off, *see* affluence
Well Tempered Clavier (music), 42
West Ferry Road, Isle of Dogs, 65
white-collar sector, 17
white settlement, 2
Wimpey builders, 64, 66
Wirth, L., 75, 186
women
  role of, 162, 163

work and, 163, 187
Woolff, G., 13
work, 2, 3, 12, 14
  family and, 23–4
  friendships and, 129–30
  ill-paid, 7, 14
  see also employment; occupations
working class, 17, 33, 63–4, 89, 141, 142, 178, 190
  displacement, 14–15, 27, 161, 177
  gentrification and, 15–16
  white, 66, 95, 182
working lives, 10–11, 12, 183
Wright, E. O., 16, 17

young people, 5
youth monoculture, 4
'yuppie' stereotype, 27

zoning, 18–19
Zukin, Sharon, 46, 191